*Another Season's Promise*

# Another Season's Promise

## Hope and Despair in Canada's Farm Country

## INGEBORG BOYENS

PENGUIN
VIKING

VIKING

Published by the Penguin Group

Penguin Books Canada Ltd, 10 Alcorn Avenue, Toronto, Ontario, Canada M4V 3B2

Penguin Books Ltd, 27 Wrights Lane, London w8 5TZ, England

Penguin Putnam Inc., 375 Hudson Street, New York, New York 10014, U.S.A.

Penguin Books Australia Ltd, Ringwood, Victoria, Australia

Penguin Books (NZ) Ltd, cnr Rosedale and Airborne Roads, Albany, Auckland 1310, New Zealand

Penguin Books Ltd, Registered Offices: Harmondsworth, Middlesex, England

First published 2001

Epigraph © 1981, Stan Rogers. Used by permission of
Ariel Rogers and Fogarty's Cove Music

1 3 5 7 9 10 8 6 4 2

Copyright © Ingeborg Boyens, 2001

Printed and bound in Canada on acid-free paper ∞
Text design and typesetting by Laura Brady

CANADIAN CATALOGUING IN PUBLICATION DATA

Boyens, Ingeborg, 1955–
Another season's promise: hope and despair in Canada's farm country

Includes bibliographic references and index

ISBN 0-670-89386-2

1. Farm income—Canada—Case studies.   2. Farm life—Canada—Case studies.
3. Family farms—Manitoba—Case studies.   4. Wieler family.   I. Title.

S451.5.A1B69 2001      338.1'0951      C2001-900573-3

Visit Penguin Canada's website at **www.penguin.ca**

# Contents

*Acknowledgements* / vii

Introduction / xi

*One* Crisis? What Crisis? / 1

*Two* Lessons of the Past / 19

*Three* Desperately Seeking Readlyn / 40

*Four* The Cost of Doing Business / 63

*Five* Follow the Money / 85

*Six* The Business of Farming / 96

*Seven* Go Global / 131

*Eight* Endangered Species Support / 150

*Nine* House Rules / 155

*Ten* The Missing Political Card / 187

*Eleven* Pick Pork: A Case Study / 214

*Twelve* Back to the Future / 243

*Bibliography* / 267

*Index* / 270

# Acknowledgements

☙ When Michael Schellenberg from Penguin Canada first proposed this book, I have to admit I hesitated. I was afraid of getting caught in a quagmire of Crow rates and whining farmers. However, I am so grateful he persevered. He gave me an excuse to embark on a journey into a world I found to be populated with proud, independent people whose way of life is the very backbone of Canada.

It was those people who made the journey so worthwhile. I am indebted to the dozens of farmers I met along the way for the perspectives, patience and hospitality they so consistently showed me. I must single out Paula and Warren Jolly for the time they took to educate a writer from the city. And of course, special thanks go to Lorna and Gary Wieler and their boys for opening up their lives for me.

Thanks also go to the late Clay Gilson, Daryl Kraft from the University of Manitoba and Brian White from the Canadian Wheat Board. My heartfelt appreciation goes to professors Rene Van Acker and J.E. Rea for reviewing the manuscript and setting me straight.

*Acknowledgements*

Several people helped me piece together the facts: Simon Neufeld, Brenda Suderman and Anette Anton Mueller. I am indebted to my employer of many years, the CBC's *Country Canada*, for first introducing me to the issues of food and farming in this country and to the people who make agriculture work. Thank you.

When I surfaced from my journey through rural Canada, Michael was there with his thoughtful editing skills. Thanks to him and to Dawne Kepron, whose passion on the subject convinced Penguin to go ahead with the project. Thanks also go to all the people at Penguin for their work in making this book a reality.

And special appreciation goes to my husband, Gregg Shilliday, who regularly let me drag my soapbox to the dinner table. You are my inspiration and my guide. This book is for you.

*"For the good times come and go, but at least there's rain*
*So this won't be barren ground when September rolls around*
*So watch the field behind the plow turn to straight dark rows*
*Put another season's promise in the ground."*

—Stan Rogers, "The Field Behind the Plow"

## *Introduction*

❧ Ever since Terry Fox dipped his artificial leg into the Atlantic on April 12, 1980, the driven and the determined have crossed the country by wheel-chair, foot, bicycle or canoe in an effort to draw attention to an assortment of worthy causes. On February 1, 2000, an unassuming, soft-spoken farmer joined that number—on his Massey-Ferguson 860 combine.

The progress of Nick Parsons and his one-man crusade to save Canada's family farms demanded a mixture of scepticism and admiration. There was something almost ridiculous about a fifty-two-year-old farmer inching his old combine at twenty-five kilometres an hour from Victoria to Ottawa. He seemed an anachronism in a time when agriculture was trying to present itself as modern, stylish and progressive—just like any other sector of twenty-first-century life. Yet the little man with the salt-and-pepper beard, thick-rimmed glasses, ball cap and serviceable cover-alls was simply applying a farmer's matter-of-fact approach to fixing a problem. He was not the representative of any agricultural organization. (In fact, many of the country's official farm agencies seemed vaguely embarrassed by the picture of a man piloting a combine to Parliament Hill.) Rather, Nick Parsons was the personification of an economic crisis that had been squeezing Canadian farmers since 1998.

Increasingly, there were disturbing stories of farmers committing suicide, abandoning their farms, filing for bankruptcy. The official statistics grimly noted that the average realized net farm income—that is, the "profit" without any allowance for work by family members—was $12,624 for 1999, the lowest level, adjusted for inflation, since the 1930s. In Saskatchewan, Canada's agricultural heartland and therefore the hardest hit, the 1999 estimate of expected income for the average farmer in 2000 was less than zero. This contrasts with a high in 1976 of more than $60,000, calculated in 2000 dollars. Farm families across the country were forced to take off-farm jobs, rent out their land or sell out altogether. In the fall of 2000, Statistics Canada reported there were 22,100 fewer farmers on the Prairies than there had been the year before. A way of life that had been built on a century of sweat and toil on the farm was disintegrating.

Parsons and his family lived on a 1,250-acre grain farm in Dawson Creek, B.C., that was supposed to be their refuge from a turbulent world. They had emigrated in 1990 from England after tough times pushed them from their farm there. But the good life in Canada began to sour with bad weather in 1996 and only got worse as grain prices plummeted. In the winter of 2000, the Parsonses' savings virtually spent, the down-to-earth farmer resolved to do what he did best. He tuned up the combine, this time not for a set around the fields but for a 4,000-kilometre trip along the Trans-Canada to Ottawa. He had a nebulous plan to ask the prime minister for more funding for farmers. Parsons knew that his was hardly a novel request. "I just want to get on the road to make a statement."

Along the way the shiny red combine, nicknamed "Prairie Belle," attracted the curious and the concerned. It was hard to miss as it lumbered along the shoulder of the highway through the snow-blanketed Prairies, the rough, raw Canadian Shield and the slumbering farms of Ontario into the urban heartland. A big sign in front defiantly proclaimed

to all doubters: FARM CRISIS VERY REAL FOR WESTERN CANADA'S
FAMILY FARMS.

Not surprisingly, Parson's odyssey touched a nerve in the countryside.
It inspired a homegrown song, "Hey Nick, hey Nick, we're really proud
of you." Along his route farmers volunteered generous donations to help
pay for the $10,000 trip, even though Parsons insisted he was not asking
for them. One young boy offered five dollars along with a request: "Hope
you can save Daddy's farm."

Crossing the divide between farm and city, Parsons found himself out
of his element. Passersby gawked and cursed at the strange lumbering
machine that was slowing traffic. In Toronto, police threatened to fine
him $500 if he left the combine downtown overnight. He talked his way
out of the fine but was summarily escorted out of town in the morning.

Nevertheless, by the time he reached Ottawa, the slow-talking Nick
Parsons had scored with an urban media accustomed to the over-polished
images of politicians and media-managed spokespeople. When he
descended from his combine at the foot of Parliament Hill, swarmed by a
scrum of political reporters, he said with disarming simplicity, "I'm afraid
this is not really my thing."

Despite his growing celebrity, Parsons had not been able to win a commitment for a meeting from Prime Minister Jean Chrétien. After doing
the media rounds, however, Parsons was suddenly whisked away to 24
Sussex Drive. Perhaps demonstrating his "common touch," Chrétien
offered Parsons the time to talk about the farm crisis that he had not
granted to the leaders of farm organizations. After forty-five minutes
with the prime minister, a star-struck Parsons could only recollect that he
had had a whiskey—maybe two. But he had not won any particular commitment from Chrétien for additional aid to Canadian farmers. Upon
reflection, without any rancour or regret, Nick Parsons had to admit he
had doubts whether his seven-week trip had really been worth it.

Most political observers would have been surprised if Parsons had got
more than a glass of whiskey. Could one middle-aged farmer on a combine really cause the doors of the federal treasury to spring open? In the

sceptics' opinion the federal government had already done all it intended to do for Canadian farmers. While Parsons was trundling through Winnipeg, Ottawa announced another $400 million in support for producers in Saskatchewan and Manitoba. That was a bonus instalment to a much-touted federal-provincial, $1.7-billion aid package called the Agricultural Income Disaster Assistance (AIDA) program. As far as Ottawa was concerned, the farm crisis was a political problem to be patched up with the promise of emergency support. And as far as the public was concerned, farmers had received what they wanted.

There would be no more money, the government declared. But it was not a case of Ottawa having no more cash: the deficit-fighting days were over. In February federal finance minister Paul Martin had announced he expected the largest federal surplus in history. His problem was figuring out how to spend the revenues. For a while Ottawa mused about offering support to several Canadian National Hockey League teams. Finally, Martin settled on a pre-election blend of tax breaks and targeted spending.

The government seemed to have little interest in offering long-term income support to farmers. In fact, the federal administration did not have any specific agricultural policy to define how family farms fit into the overall agricultural picture. From Confederation to the late 1950s federal agricultural policy was designed to secure Canada's control over the West and to produce food for Canada, its trading partners and its war allies. In the 1970s the government identified its national goals for the farm sector as being economic development, rising and stable incomes, full employment, and harmonious international and federal-provincial relations. In contrast, the government of 2000 had not articulated a policy on the viability of the family farm, on the health of the land or on the issue of rural depopulation. Canada stood in stark contrast to the European Union, which had a policy specifically designed to ensure that farm producers could afford to live on the land and tend it as responsible stewards.

The closest Ottawa came to an agricultural policy was its strategy to promote global free trade—a move that would entrench agriculture's position as a significant contributor to the gross domestic product (GDP) but would unfortunately not protect family farms. The export strategy was part of a fundamental shift to an increasingly industrial agricultural system. Under this system—heavily promoted by government—Canadian farmers would unfortunately be the victims of falling international commodity prices, increased transportation and input costs, a subsidy war with Europe and the United States and the inability to extract a fair share from a market system dominated by multinational corporations.

Chrétien's political bailout package was not nearly enough to relieve the pain dealt by structural changes to the agricultural system. There was something rotten at the very core of modern farming. Canada had somehow taken a wrong turn, no longer viewing agriculture as a way of life that had sustained the country for a century, and instead developing an industrial business that sacrificed those who toiled in the fields on our behalf. Sadly, the prime minister's visit with Nick Parsons was simply an exercise in public relations, not the expression of a long-term, sustainable policy for agriculture.

Parsons was riding a wave of discontent that had begun to swell the previous year in Saskatchewan. A number of farmers had embarked on what might be dismissed by some as publicity stunts, but they expressed a desperation born of misery. In the summer of 1999 the Prairies were alive with farm protest meetings. In Regina, traffic jams became routine as slow-moving tractors and farm rigs crept down the streets in a show of protest. Things became more confrontational in the winter, when farmers chained the doors of the Saskatchewan legislature, symbolically locking Premier Roy Romanow inside. In January in Regina, dozens of farmers infused with a new militancy installed themselves at the Saskatchewan legislature—and refused to move until their demands for provincial aid were met. Their sit-in lasted one week, until police removed them at two o'clock one morning. Lillian Kurtz, a farm wife from Stockholm, Saskatchewan, launched an eleven-day hunger strike. Her self-denial did not lead to a promise of more farm aid.

Then the focus of the protests moved eastward, to the urban heartland and the political decision-making centres. In January in Toronto, supporters set up the Family Farm Tribute concert, featuring Gordon Lightfoot, Burton Cummings, the Toronto Symphony Orchestra and Prairie Oyster. It was an event designed to raise awareness, not money. For the latter, farmers continued their pressure on Ottawa. The Doral Inn in the nation's capital became a "farmers' embassy," a meeting place for farmers intent on pitching their demand for aid to political representatives.

When Jean Chrétien called a general election for November 27, 2000, he granted farmers another chance to make their point. And they did so from the backs of half-ton trucks, along snow-blanketed rail lines, across the highways that are the lifeline for rural Canada. You could taste the despair hanging in the brittle November air on the Prairies. But an election was not about to change the prospects for farming at a time of massive structural upheaval.

In my job as a producer for cbc's *Country Canada*, I had seen many poignant expressions of the economic crisis that farmers were experiencing: a young boy pushed to the front of the audience so his soft boy's voice and sad brown eyes might make the case for help even more compelling; the elderly couple watching numbly as the possessions of a lifetime were auctioned off; the farm woman who listened hour after hour to telephone calls from farmers who could not understand how things had got so bad. The stories were undoubtedly true, but the cynic in me wondered if they were all that new. Talk of a "crisis" in farming seemed to happen with depressing regularity. In the early 1990s the panic message had been the same. In fact, as I remember, the protests then were even bigger and more impressive. Whereas about 3,500 protestors gathered at Saskatchewan Place in January 2000, 13,000 had made the same trip in January 1993. There was always lousy weather somewhere—a flood, a hailstorm, early snow. All provoked cries of "crisis." Yet there was always plenty of food in my neighbourhood grocery store. And although my weekly shopping bill had gone up significantly in the past decade, I could still easily afford the delicacies of sun-kissed summer even in the dead of winter. Hunger was something that I as an urban Canadian never feared. If there was a "crisis," it was happening somewhere else.

Like many urban Canadians, I had only the vaguest impression, like a distant memory, of a farm life where the challenges are physical. Where hands are callused from hard, manual labour. Where back strain comes from heaving straw, not from sitting too much. Where the sure, confident eye of someone who knows his land sees more than just a field of indistinguishable plants. Over years of city living I had become detached from the life of basic values—hard work, co-operation, help and friendliness—that defines the farm. Life in the country, I imagined, was the story of a simpler existence where the morning begins with birdsong, not the white noise of traffic, transformers and humming of machines. So I felt mildly irritated by farmers' persistent pleas for more government handouts. And I knew that my fellow urban dwellers, protected from the country by a ring of concrete thoroughfares and a string of suburban shopping malls, were even more cut off from rural problems than I was.

This disconnection was reflected in a short news item I found on the back pages of my local newspaper. It reported that in a survey of 2,400 European nine- and ten-year-olds, three-quarters believed that cotton grows on sheep. British children believed bananas were homegrown. Dutch youngsters thought their country produced oranges and olives. Surely, I thought, Canadians and their children are no better informed.

This is the psychological landscape that Nick Parsons was driving through—a place where it is possible to survive without knowing a thing about cooking, never mind farming or animal husbandry. Parsons broke through the boundary between the rural and urban solitudes by metaphorically taking the farm to the city. His unadorned, unassuming style spoke of a simpler time, a time of basic core values. Although his combine odyssey may have seemed as silly as Don Quixote tilting at windmills, he maintained a calm dignity, like the Man of La Mancha, that exemplified the plight of today's farmers. It was the poignant picture of Nick Parsons on his combine, crawling across Canada, that propelled me to embark on my own journey to determine if there truly was a farm crisis and, if so, what could be done about it.

By the end of March 2000 the cycle of the seasons was exerting its pull. Nick Parsons was back home, planning what he would seed in the year 2000. He was no longer a protestor, just a farmer; and like farmers everywhere he was optimistically dreaming that this would be the good year. Meanwhile, I was off to see if hope for another season's promise still reigned in the people who populate the Canadian countryside, those who grow our food in the face of near-desperate odds.

# One

## Crisis? What Crisis?

*April 6, 2000*

*On the road out of Winnipeg, as thoroughfare becomes highway, as suburbs lose their energy, the sky spills open. It laps at the flat horizon, outlining a distant church steeple, a grain elevator, a copse of cottonwoods. Unmarred by clouds, it hints at spring. The cycle of the growing season on the Canadian prairies will soon begin.*

*The highway to Kane in southern Manitoba pays passing homage to the small towns along the way by asking motorists to slow down. But there is no need for speed signs on the dirt road off the highway up to Gary and Lorna Wieler's farm. There are no homes on this 5-kilometre stretch of potted gravel. And no cars, though I'm told the school bus rattles by here twice a day.*

*The patchy snow has melted away in the Wielers' yard, early this year by prairie standards. Farm equipment, painted in John Deere green, lies about, seemingly ready to spring into action. The buds are just beginning to swell on the shelter-belt Manitoba maples, still starkly grey against the clear sky. Across the yard, hidden from view behind the high wooden livestock fence, the cows and their new calves bellow in anticipation of the pasture's fresh spring grass.*

*Inside the Wielers' modern, beige split-level, the aroma suggests times past. It is the yeasty smell of baking bread. Lorna Wieler is baking sheets and sheets of buns with assembly-line efficiency for Saturday's church "borscht and pie" dinner. This is her one day at home this week — home from the business she set up this year, offering spring cleaning to other farm women who are too busy working to keep up with the spic-and-span demands of a traditional farming community.*

*Gary Wieler is at the kitchen table, wearing his meet-the-writer clothes. Like many farmers he seems constrained by the forced inactivity of the season — one would think restless for spring, another season's promise. He and Lorna balance each other out. She is talkative, chatty; he considers his thoughts carefully before speaking.*

*She is thirty-six, he forty-one — young by comparison with many Manitoba farmers, 31 percent of whom are fifty-five or older. The hope for the future of Canadian farming rests with people like Gary and Lorna Wieler.*

*Their wedding, seventeen years ago, was a union of urban and rural. When Gary brought Lorna from the city to his third-generation family farm, she was ready to give it a shot. They dreamed not of earning a fortune but of building a way of life. They did so by assembling their own family unit: three boys, aged fourteen, twelve and eight. The influence of the urban is seen today in the wild profusion of silk flowers in a crystal vase on the kitchen table, a stylish flourish amidst the practicality of a busy farm life. And Daphne, the brand-new corgi-cross pup, has the run of the house, contrary to the usual farm rules, which say that critters belong outside.*

*Despite appearances, the Wielers' carefully constructed way of life is under attack. Farming has become more challenging than it ever was for Gary's father or grandfather, even during the Depression. The Wielers* *describe their farm as small, but with 850 seeded acres it is larger than the Manitoba average of 783 acres. They have diversified into cattle, with the hope that when grain prices are down, cattle prices might be up. But grain prices are so low that the value of twenty-five cows and their calves can hardly offset them. Add to that the wild card — Mother Nature. A constant unpredictable rain last year meant they lost money on half of their grain and oilseed crops. At the end of the year they registered earnings of $20,000, most of it from off-farm work. Although it does not sound like much, the Wielers' careful use of every dollar made it stretch far enough. Who knows what this year will bring?*

*Seeding is just a month away, but the Wielers are vague about their plans. No one can say what prices will be like when it is time to harvest. A review of statistics and market trends have offered the Wielers little guidance. Even though prices are painfully low — $5 a bushel for the best grade of wheat, down from $7 a bushel in 1995–96 — Gary says they will plant at least four hundred acres of wheat. It's what Gary calls the "comfort crop" because he knows in his bones how to grow it. "If you figured it out on paper," he says, fingering the tablecloth, "nothing would make us money."*

*Outside, under the warming sky, he still has trouble rallying the optimism farmers are supposed to have at this time of year. It's almost as if a dark cloud only he can see has rolled up overhead. When I ask him if he is looking forward to spring, he shrugs. "Not really. It's rough when you work so hard every year and it never gets any better."*

❧ Farmers are usually optimistic in the face of all odds, reinvigorated each new spring by the beauty and richness of their land. Here in "next-year country," farmers like the Wielers typically put aside the problems of the last year and focus instead on what is ahead. But the new millennium has dawned with an ominous grey sky hanging over the farm economy, eroding the precious sense of hope and anticipation that once characterized farm life. Producers across Canada are facing the first growing season of the twenty-first century caught in an economic squeeze worse than anything seen since the Great Depression of the 1930s.

Never before, especially during times of prosperity like those today, have there been economic pressures on the farm to match those the Wielers face. During the Depression years every sector of the economy was under stress. When the stock market plunged in 1929 to send the world's economy into a decade-long collapse, all parts of Canadian society shared in the misery. However, the Depression's effects were particularly vicious in Western Canada, as farmers attempted to eke out a living in the face of low prices while nature joined in the attack by delivering years of relentless drought. Today, the Canadian economy booms in almost every sector but agriculture. The federal government is enjoying a surplus. The unemployment rate fell in May 2000 to 6.6 percent, the lowest level in twenty-four years. The Royal Bank announced a record $2.2-billion profit in 2000. On the farm, meanwhile, commodity prices remain abysmally low, input costs are staggeringly high, and help from the government—despite the promise of AIDA—has been savagely cut. These three conditions are unique. In combination they add up to a true "farm crisis."

Of course we have heard the talk of crisis before. Farmers have overused the phrase "farm crisis" to the point where it has become a routine refrain, devoid of shock value. There was talk of a farm crisis in the 1970s, the 1980s and the early 1990s. Canadian farmers have managed to become the butt of jokes by complaining about everything. First there's the weather—either too hot, too cold, too wet or too dry. And what about the bugs? Disease? Prices? Much to the frustration of the unassuming Wielers, there is a perception that farmers always have something to gripe about, that they are always looking for handouts. The public in turn has hardened its heart. It has learned that the cycles of agriculture come and go; good years invariably follow the bad.

For the most part that has been true—at least until now. The current reality is less of a cycle and more of a downward spiral. Farmers are in a trough they are unlikely to emerge from anytime soon. And it is starting to anger many of them, especially in the West. For decades they have done exactly what they were told to do. They got bigger; they diversified; they became more efficient. At the turn of the century the produce of a Canadian farm could support about ten people. Today a modern farm sustains as many as one hundred. However, that increased productivity has not improved farmers' lives. Instead, they have become unsuspecting partners in a strategy to industrialize agriculture—to turn a unique biological and social process into an industry like any other. Along the way they have watched their way of life become a business—and, unfortunately, one that does not pay well enough to sustain itself.

Paradoxically, despite dropping incomes for many farmers, increased farm productivity has improved the economic statistics that are trumpeted by government and many agricultural economists. Farmers are supposed to be consoled by the knowledge that they have produced more, making an important contribution to Canada's trade surplus. Since the mid-1970s, Canadian agri-food exports have quadrupled. In 1998 we exported $22.8-billion worth of commodities and food products, including 80 percent of our wheat crop. The federal government hopes we will export much more in the future. Ottawa's goal is to command 4 percent of the world's agricultural trade by 2003.

Equally, in 1998, the agri-food industry accounted for 8.4 percent of Canada's gross domestic product, or GDP. According to government statistics, the so-callled agri-food industry, comprising farmers, along with suppliers, processors, transporters, grocers and restaurant workers, represented the third-largest employer in Canada. Agribusiness generated about $95 billion in sales in 1997. Unfortunately, most of those revenues were earned by multinational corporations that took them out of the country.

The federal government has clearly shaped its views based on those economic indicators. In fact, in October 1999, Prime Minister Jean Chrétien released a set of rosy projections to the Saskatchewan and Manitoba premiers, telling them the farm crisis was overplayed. Federal agriculture minister Lyle Vanclief followed up weeks later by offering a "tough love" message to farmers, essentially telling them that if they found themselves in trouble, they should get out of the business. Our politicians may sometimes acknowledge we have a family-farm crisis, but they insist the agricultural system overall is healthy.

It was to bolster farm incomes that the government came up with the AIDA program in December 1998. Farmers widely criticized the initiative for its onerous eligibility requirements, its huge bureaucracy costs and its inability to get money to farmers. By the end of 2000 only 41 percent of the promised $1.7 billion had been paid out to farmers.

But the program did improve the income statistics. Agriculture and Agri-Food Canada prepares a five-year forecast every summer. In August 2000, the number crunchers predicted that realized net incomes—the amount of farm revenue earned from all sources after the depreciation of equipment and buildings and services-in-kind have been deducted—would be up considerably in 2000, although they would then fall through to 2004. According to the numbers, the prospects for agriculture were good, even on the Prairies. The forecast said total income in 2000 would double in Manitoba and Saskatchewan and triple in Alberta compared with the 1999 levels. This was a noticeable improvement for Saskatchewan, where the average farmer's realized net income in 1999 was just $1,783, significantly less than minimum wage. (The 1999 forecast had predicted the average 2000 earnings would be less than zero for the first time since 1933.)

The 2000 forecast gave credit for the turnaround to improved livestock prices and to government supports for farmers. Unfortunately, as the forecast noted, starting in 2001 farmers would take home less money as government payments dried up—$2.92 billion in 2001 compared with $4.17 billion in 2000. In fact, once the government's disaster support program ended in 2003, incomes would fall dramatically. So even by the government's own statistics, the only thing standing between a farmer and failure was public support.

•   •   •

6

Of course, statistics and economics do not tell the complete story of what is happening in rural Canada. From the perspective of economists or of the business press you might get the idea that the whole point of an economy is simply to produce goods and services. For example the GDP, the value of a country's economic production, gives equal weight to the end results of a natural disaster as it does to signs of economic vitality. The sale of sandbags to fight the Red River flood in 1997 boosted the GDP, but it says nothing about the desperation of the people who used those sandbags to ring their homes against the rising tide of water. Canada's politicians boast of our agri-food exports but say little about the fact that we import nearly as much in processed food as we export.

Farmers are disappearing from the map of Canada. In the fall of 2000, Statistics Canada's Labour Force Survey reported that there were 22,100 fewer farmers on the Prairies than there had been the year before. It was a staggering number, one that had many economists sputtering in confusion. Yet an examination of the month-by-month statistics clearly shows that employment in agriculture has fallen steadily since the fall of 1998. It seems that Canada's agricultural heartland is losing its most precious resource—its people.

There is a value in those people that is, sadly, often dismissed. They are the ones who know how to tend the environment and grow our food. They have production skills and knowledge about maintaining the productivity of an essential resource in an environmentally sustainable way. When Gary Wieler looks out over his farm, he knows where the swells of the rich soil are, whereas the rest of us might describe it only as a flat, unremarkable landscape. Most of us would be at sea if we had to grow the plants and raise the animals that sustain our lives.

Statistics and indicators tell nothing of a farm family's heartbreak as their way of life is destroyed to make way for an industrial system. Many producers, like the Wielers, never expected to make a fortune; but their modest expectations are out of step with an increasingly urbanized society that promotes consumerism and chases the mighty buck. In many ways families like the Wielers are the last keepers of a prairie value system that gave birth to medicare and co-ops, not to mention a simple neighbourly concern for one another.

Throughout our history, farming has been a family enterprise. The farm is a place where hard work is expected of all family members. Children are assigned the task of feeding the pigs. The women cook the meals that fuel the day's work. The men are out in the fields under a hot sun until the fading light signals the end of the workday. Everyone suffers from a creaky back, thickening along well-worn hands and sun-browned skin up to the hat-line. Hard work is an accepted precursor to a bountiful harvest.

Unlike the model we may know from the urban workplace, the "managers" on a farm work directly with the "labourers." Decisions are made jointly by the family unit. If the farm is passed down through the generations, the retirees—the grandparents—continue to play an important role. The family farm represents an ergonomically healthy, flexible way of life, where the rules of the modern office or factory do not apply.

The term "family farm" is associated with treasured values and a rich rewarding way of life. Many Canadians, whether from stories their parents told them or from personal experience, recall the self-reliance that comes from living on a farm. It is borne of a life close to nature, bringing with it an understanding of the seasons and of the wonders of life and death in the wheat field and the cattle yard. Even though they are increasingly devalued in our society, physical strength, ability and determination are skills that matter on the farm. Mucking out a barn is satisfying in those terms. Cultivating a field and watching the furrows stretch behind the tractor is worthwhile. A family farmer who knows his land can tell from a handful of dirt and the scent on a spring day's breeze how the land will fare. That is a skill whose value cannot be easily quantified.

Farming has rarely been lucrative in a dollars-and-cents way, but in the past, farmers were celebrated for their grit in the face of disaster, isolation and economic hardship. They were viewed as a vital part of Canadian society. Agriculture opened up the West and enticed new immigrants to come and develop our heartland. Farmers were our essential workers.

After all, they produced our food and, along with air and water, food is something we cannot do without. Even today a family-based enterprise like a farm produces much more than wheat or corn or beef. It also produces a community. Sadly, this social product is largely invisible to economists and policy-makers, who see only what they can count.

Throughout our history, farming has been a way of life. Industrialization is now encouraging a system where work is done by employed labourers who have no stake in what they do; where the old values do not matter as much as competitiveness and efficiency; where farming is considered the preserve of the dumb; where creativity and innovation are less important than the corporate systems guide. Farming has become a business.


The farming way of life created the landscape that tugs at our emotions. Rolling prairie wheat fields, Alberta ranges dotted with cattle, dairy silos silhouetted against an endless sky—these are the images of farming that anyone who has travelled the Trans-Canada will know. About 65 million acres in the West are planted to crops and another 20 to 30 million are in pasture. Farming takes up about 7 percent of the country's land mass—more than twice the area of our national and provincial parks and wildlife reserves. So although the Canadian Shield and the west coast surf may be the favoured subjects for many visual artists, it is the familiar agricultural landscape that has seeped into the very being of all Canadians.

Hard as it is to believe, all that landscape is controlled, according to Statistics Canada's 1996 census, by just 276,548 farms. Fewer than 3 percent of Canadians live on a farm, and that number has been shrinking as more and more producers and their families have left the land in recent years for a more manageable life in towns or urban centres. Some estimate that one in three of the remaining farmers were forced off the land in 2000. Ours is now an urban country with few connections to the farm short of a school field day to some accommodating tourist farm.

Eastern Canada, where about two-thirds of Canadians live, is the most agriculturally diversified region of the country. Farmers there grow livestock, fruits, vegetables, oilseeds and grains (particularly corn, soybeans and soft white winter wheat for processing or feed). Western Canada produces most of our oilseeds and grains, notably varieties of wheat designed for bread and pasta.

Not all agricultural producers are suffering equally. Canadian farming can be roughly divided into two types, one regulated by supply management systems and the second regulated by the basic rules of the free marketplace.

Supply management is a quintessentially Canadian arrangement. It is a polite and civil system that tells a farmer through a "quota" how many eggs or chickens, or how much milk, he is allowed to produce and sell. Supply management was developed in the 1970s as a means of avoiding the turbulence of the free market. In Canada, the dairy, egg and poultry sectors are cushioned from the open market by supply management marketing boards. These segments of agriculture make up 28 percent of national farm receipts. Because these farmers produce perishable goods, they are usually situated close to urban markets, typically in Central Canada. For example, about 70 percent of Canada's total dairy production takes place in Quebec and Ontario. Supply management does shield many farmers from the ups and downs of the market, removing boom-and-bust cycles and ensuring a fair return on investment.

A comparison with the cutthroat competition that rules just south of the border offers an indication of how cushioned Canadian supply-managed producers are. Dairy farmers in the United States, for example, often compete head-on with one another, developing massive operations with thousands of cows. About 45 percent of American dairy farmers ended up leaving the business in the 1990s in the wake of the brutal competition. Those who are left produce too much milk, which the federal government then buys. In 2000, Washington was expected to dump or give away 9 million pounds of butter and 485 million pounds of milk.

Farmers who grow grains, oilseeds, livestock, and fruit and vegetable commodities are not as protected as their supply-managed counterparts.

They are subject to the raw rules of supply and demand, as well as of the international marketplace, since many of these commodities are traded globally. The basic marketplace rules apply here: if there is lots of supply and little demand, prices go down.

That is exactly what has happened to grain and hog markets since early 1998. Global grain production has increased at a phenomenal rate in the last two decades. The European Union is flooding the international market with 42 percent more wheat than it did in 1980; Australia is producing 44 percent more; Argentina sold 26 percent more. Although our wheat was once described as "king" in agricultural circles, Canada is now a smaller player in the global wheat marketplace. Canada accounts for only about 20 percent of the world's wheat exports. By contrast, for the first two decades of the last century Canada was the world's number-one wheat exporter, with 50 percent of the international market.

Demand, reflecting political events, has shifted at the same time. Exports of wheat to the former U.S.S.R. have shrunk to almost nothing since the breakup of that country. Iran is now the largest importer in the Middle East, replacing Iraq, which has been subjected to trade embargoes since the 1991 Gulf War. We now compete with other exporting countries for sales into China, Bangladesh, Japan, South America and the Middle East.

The net effect of oversupply and reduced demand is critically low commodity prices. Canadian farmers must now hope to produce exceptional yields every year just to recoup their costs. Even canola, once regarded as the Cinderella crop of the Prairies, has lost its lustre in recent years. Production of canola oil's big competitor, palm oil, collapsed in 1997, which led to a brief surge in canola prices, to the point where canola briefly displaced wheat as the crop producing the highest cash receipts. But palm oil soon rebounded, and there are now abundant stocks of soybeans—which also produce a vegetable oil—so the price of canola has fallen again.

Unfortunately, there is little expectation that oilseed and grain prices will rise much in the next few years. In a March 2000 report the World Trade Organization (WTO) predicted commodity prices would stay low for the next ten years. The Canadian Wheat Board's assessment was that world demand for wheat will remain flat for at least the next five years. And the Organization for Economic Co-operation and Development (OECD) also predicted a continuing price collapse.

Agricultural economists say the biggest problem for Canada and other exporting countries is that the grain market is not increasing. The market has not grown significantly since 1980; instead it has held firm at about 100 million tonnes a year. In the 1970s accelerating wealth in developing countries in Latin America and Africa led to increased grain and oilseed imports by those nations. But double-digit inflation beginning in 1981 sapped the advancement of those developing countries, and the import increases stopped.

Daryl Kraft, head of the agricultural economics department at the University of Manitoba, looks out at the world from his utilitarian office on the university campus. The room is big, by virtue of his position in the university hierarchy, but it is filled with old, uncomfortable wooden furniture—the leftovers of some 1970s campus-decorating binge. But Kraft does not seem to notice. He is focused on ideas, not creature comforts.

Kraft is thinking about how to feed the world. It is not as if hunger has been vanquished, even though we hear about a massive oversupply of grains and oilseeds that is depressing prices. Kraft says about 800 million people in the world are now undernourished, but they live in countries that cannot afford to import food. If Canada hopes to have markets in the future, it will essentially have to pay for those markets through foreign aid. Until foreign aid makes it possible for those countries to buy what they cannot now afford, the world's would-be exporters will not have good prospects for trade. Says Kraft, "The pie is not growing. And there are more countries scrambling for a piece of it."

The same logic applies to other agricultural sectors. As countries become more affluent, they begin to consume more meat. That has been of huge benefit to Canadian pork producers, who began selling their product to new global markets. In 1997–98 the hog industry was undergoing rapid expansion, particularly in the Prairie provinces, where governments

vigorously promoted pork production. Unfortunately, while new operators were getting into the business, Asia and Russia—potential markets
for Canadian pork—experienced severe economic crises. With oversupply
and reduced demand, prices fell. By the fall of 1998 producers were losing
$40 per hog, and there were grim reports of producers, unable to feed
their pigs, turning a gun on them.

Livestock and grain farmers tend to be located in Western Canada,
the country's agricultural heartland. About 80 percent of farmland is
found in the West, and that is where the "farm crisis" is most real. That is
also where most of this book is based. The story of Western agriculture
also applies to producers in other areas of the country who are struggling
with higher input costs and reduced support from government. But the
story of Western agriculture goes one step further, in that it deals with
farmers who have to manage in an open-market system that has clearly
failed them.


Thanks to the global marketplace Gary Wieler is in direct competition
with farmers he will never know in Argentina, Australia and the United
States. Many of their pockets are lined with government dollars even
before they step into a tractor to prepare for spring seeding. The European Union and the United States subsidize their farmers to protect them
from chronic market failure. The European Union spent $90 billion in
1999 to assist its farmers. That adds up to $6 of support for each bushel
produced. Although the U.S. government likes to describe itself as a free
trader, the United States offered its farmers $28 billion, or $2.75 a bushel,
in aid in 1999.

In the mid-1980s, Canada's support for wheat producers was the same
as that paid out by the European Union and the U.S. Since then the Canadian government has cut support to farmers as part of its effort to reduce
the deficit. Funding, like the Crow benefit for rail transportation, has
been stripped away. Farmers saw a 50 percent drop in government support between 1993 and 1998. Canadian farmers now get the equivalent of

$600 million a year in government assistance, or just 40 cents per bushel. AIDA has done little to improve the situation.

Canada and the United States managed to balance their budgets at the same time—by 1998. Yet, despite current surpluses, the Canadian government insists it has no money to subsidize farmers. Agriculture Minister Lyle Vanclief simply says of Canada's competitors, "The reality is their pockets are deeper than ours." The federal government's argument is not to increase subsidies for Canadian farmers but to use international trading forums to try to convince the European Union and the U.S. to cut their subsidies. The federal government seems to be arguing that if we just clear away the trade-distorting subsidies, the market will work for our farmers. Unfortunately, by then there may be few farmers left.

Ottawa hopes that it can convince the World Trade Organization to order Europe and the U.S. to cut their supports or that it can negotiate a trade deal in which Europe and the U.S. would voluntarily give up their supports. That seems like wishful thinking at best. Both agricultural powerhouses are already curbing their subsidies to conform with trade agreements like the former General Agreement on Tariffs and Trade (GATT), but they show no inclination to cut much further. Canada may be looking for subsidy reductions, but the question is, what will our adversaries ask in return? Can we expect increased pressure on the Canadian Wheat Board and supply management structures?

The Canadian Federation of Agriculture (CFA), the umbrella group for most farm organizations in the country, is not critical of the federal government's attempts to curb subsidies in other nations; but it says farmers need support *now* to help level the playing field. CFA president Bob Friesen warns we could soon see a rural "meltdown" unless Ottawa and the provinces make a firm commitment of support. An April 2000 report from the federal government's Standing Committee on Industry also made a direct plea for additional support: "It's time now for the government to reinvest in agriculture."

•   •   •

Modern food production happens in a chain that includes oil, fertilizer, seed, chemical and machinery companies on the input side and grain companies, railways, packers, processors, retailers and restaurants on the output side of the business. Almost every link in the chain—except for farmers—is dominated by massive multinational corporations. And it seems everyone in the chain—except for farmers—is making money.

Farmers cannot get their fair share of the market price for food. While a bushel of corn sold in 1998 for less than $4, an equivalent bushel of packaged cornflakes sold for $133. According to a presentation by the National Farmers Union to the Senate Standing Committee on Agriculture and Forestry, cereal companies like Kellogg's, Quaker Oats and General Mills were 186 to 740 times more profitable than farms. If farmers were able to earn returns on equity comparable to those enjoyed by other players in the food chain, there would be no farm income crisis today.

Farmers have no control over the prices they get on the free market, nor do they have any control over the prices they have to pay for doing business. The cost of the fuel, chemicals, seeds and other necessities of the farming enterprise have increased in cost four and a half times since 1974. A decreasing level of competition runs parallel to the staggering price increases. For example, three companies dominate the farm machinery market and dictate the prices for essential equipment. Three companies control oil, gas and diesel fuels. Farmers have to spend money on seeds, fertilizers and pesticides for crop production. They have few choices as to where and how they are going to spend their money.

Today in North America we have become almost cavalier about food and the people who produce it. After all, we have been spared wars or natural disasters that might strangle the supply of food. For most of us, food is just a short shopping trip away, and it is there at a reasonable price. Canadians spend only 9.8 percent of their disposable income on food. That is the lowest rate in the world. And it has fallen dramatically over the years: in the 1950s, Canadians spent 22 percent of their income on food.

Consumers in other industrialized countries are not so lucky. According to the OECD, Americans spend 10.9 percent of their incomes on food, the British 11.5 percent, the Japanese 17.8 percent, and Mexicans 33.2 percent. When it comes to cheap food, Canada is clearly the leader. This good news for consumers unfortunately contributes to the crisis facing farmers.

Most consumers do not often think about the fate of our farms. They live in cities, far from the smells and sights of the countryside. All they know about the family farm is what they have heard in stories of times past. Where food comes from is a puzzle that is perpetuated by our modern agri-food system. The typical grocery superstore offers as many as 30,000 products. In the local 7-Eleven "food" from vending machines, coffee makers and snack-food aisles competes for your dollar with video games. Nothing bears much relationship to what people imagine farmers are growing in the fields they pass on the way to the cottage.

Urban Canadians have read the stories about Nick Parsons or seen election protests by despairing farmers on the nightly news. But they might be excused for their relative indifference to the farming community. Urban Canadians have gone through their own share of trouble in recent years. The economy in urban Canada was doing well in 2000, but it got there by going through a difficult decade of corporate downsizing, job layoffs and business bankruptcies. How can a miner who was laid off or a corner-store owner who was forced to shut down have much sympathy for Canada's farmers?

Some people, in fact, remain defiantly unsympathetic to the plight of agricultural producers. At the heart of their position is the fact that although farmers are cash poor, they are often asset rich. They may not be able to come up with the cash to feed their families, but most farmers are surrounded by hundreds of thousands of dollars' worth of land and equipment. On top of that, land, even in Saskatchewan and Manitoba, has appreciated 30 percent in value since 1993. What many people don't realize, though, is that even if farmers sold everything tomorrow, the grim requirements of debt financing would mean that many of them would walk away with little to show for their efforts.

On February 28, 2000, *Report: The Western Edition* noted that the average net worth for Canadian farms had climbed from $550,000 in 1993 to $650,000 in 1997. (That outcome was entirely predictable, as farmers continue to quit the business, leaving larger operators to take over their land.) The headline sarcastically declared: "Please don't feed the farmers: overall, according to net worth statistics, they're doing better than ever." The *Winnipeg Free Press* joined in the attack: "Farmer crisis never happened," it proclaimed on February 25, 1999. The Internet has been an escape valve for farmers who do not share the conventional wisdom in the countryside. There is a Web site derisively entitled "Poor Farmer" that includes a series of pictures of expensive cars and farm equipment, which is supposed to prove that farmers are doing just fine. The CBC's Internet talkback site, too, has provoked comments from farmers and others who reject the hard-luck stories: "The poor farmer is an urban myth"; "This thing is self-inflicted"; "The truth remains, agriculture is the most subsidized and specially treated of industries."

The Western Canadian Wheat Growers Association set back the farmers' cause by holding its 2000 annual general meeting in Puerto Vallarta, Mexico. It came as no surprise when the meeting made the front page of the January 6 *National Post* under the headline "Farmers' new cry: Two Coronas!" The image of four hundred farmers and agribusiness representatives frolicking in the sun and surf hardly corresponded with claims of an industry in crisis.

The fact remains, most farmers do not have the luxury of sitting on a beach in Mexico; they are desperately trying to stay on the farm. To lose a job or a business in the city is tough, but at least the displaced miner and the independent grocer do not lose their roots, their homes and their way of life in the process. That is what is happening to farmers today. They get no employment insurance in their time of need, no supports. Instead, they and their families are abandoned in a heartless form of social Darwinism that we do not embrace today in the rest of the country.

Beyond the basic human concern for others, the loss of farms has broader implications for urban Canadians. If family farmers disappear, chances are the land will still be used to produce the agribusiness products we find in Loblaws or 7-Eleven. One big McCorporation could technically oversee the production of all our grain. Of course that raises questions: Who would live on that vast expanse of land between Winnipeg and Calgary? How would the soil be managed for long-term sustainability? Would Canada be better off financially without family farmers on the land?

As our society grows older and increasingly health-conscious, we are becoming more interested in the nutritional value, quality and safety of our food. If it is produced by Canadian farmers, we can have more confidence in what we eat. Although self-sufficiency in food is not something we often think about, Canada surely does not want to become dependent on food imports from other nations—imports that could be interrupted in times of political strife or that are grown with pesticides not allowed in Canada.

What is happening to Canadian farmers is not a short-term, cyclical crisis caused by low commodity prices. Rather, it is a persistent, systemic problem that combines low prices with high costs. Aggravating that situation is a government that seems to lack agricultural policies beyond its focus on free trade and its appetite for deregulation and cost-cutting. Our system of agriculture is beginning to unravel under the combined assault.

It seems as if the federal government has abandoned farmers, left them to fight global adversaries on their own. Without saying so directly, it has turned its back on the family farm. It has quietly allowed a dramatic depopulation of an entire region of the country. In Western Canada the abandoned farms and towns stand as stark testimony to federal indifference. Is it a crisis? Well, the word "crisis" implies a situation that may improve. Sadly, this is a fundamental, structural change in agriculture that is dimming the lights on a way of life that defined Canada's very nature throughout the past century.

# Two

# Lessons of the Past

*April 28, 2000*

*My city car is dwarfed by farm traffic today on the gravel road heading up to the Wielers'. Grain trucks. Pickups. Tractors. Fierce-looking diskers and air seeders. The distant trees are still bare of leaves, but spring has officially come to the Manitoba countryside. The energy vibrates in the air as the first essential task of the farm growing season begins: seeding.*

*Gary Wieler is noticeably more cheerful today. The physical demands of spring seeding have erased his musings about the foolishness of modern farming. There are no thoughts about the irony of planting wheat when prices are too low to make it worthwhile. Instead, he is wearing his "serious work" uniform: blue coveralls and peaked hat, brim stained by oily hands. Revelling in the physicality of the work, he pilots his big second-hand 1986 John Deere tractor around an eighty-acre field. He is pulling two disk seeders, worth $8,500 each. They chew up the ground, leaving a ribbed corduroy blanket of furrows in the black soil behind him. The* *view from the enclosed cab of the tractor is expansive, stretching unbro-ken across the horizon. A single seagull swoops alongside, on a lazy look-out for a meal. Tiny funnels of dirt swirl in the dry spring winds.*

*Wieler will be going round and round this field in predictable and tightening circles today. This field is in the heart of the Red River Valley, some of the most fruitful land in the country. The soil is rich, dark and productive, the leftovers of a glacial lake. Gary's father and grandfather worked the land in the years before he took over the farm. The equip-ment was smaller then, but the critical requirement to get seeds into the ground each spring was just the same. It demanded the same determina-tion, the same grit, the same hope in the face of often challenging odds. The Wielers are farmers, bred in the bone.*

*Gary Wieler is not prone to sentimentality. It is only when he is asked that he adds up his family's years of service on the land. It is as if he has never done so before. He concludes with surprise in his voice: "Wielers have farmed this piece of land for fifty-one years."*

*In fact, the Wieler clan has been farming in Manitoba much longer than that. Gary's great-great-grandfather was among the first group of settlers to break an agricultural trail into the Canadian Prairies. Seeking religious freedom and the promise of exemption from military service, thousands of Mennonites emigrated from Russia in 1876. At first they lived in communal villages. However, by the turn of the century the col-lective system was breaking down, and individual ownership of land became the rule.*

*Diedrich Wieler, Gary's grandfather, farmed the land his grandfa-ther had broken near the town of New Hope. But in 1948, chafing under what it viewed as government interference on education, Diedrich's church organized a mass emigration to Paraguay. The strat-egy was to cut productive land out of the jungle and enjoy the bounty of two harvests a year. After six months the Wieler family concluded that the pioneer dream in the wilds of Paraguay was not for them. They came back to Manitoba and launched another new life, this time near the hamlet of Kane. Gary's grandfather bought a half-section,*

*320 acres, for $8,000. His hard-won purchase was the heart of today's Wieler operation.*

*He built a wood-frame house that served his family and his son's family until 1980. Gary, who grew up in the house with his two sisters, recalls without any resentment that there was neither hot water nor a septic system that could handle a toilet. When Gary and his father — also Diedrich — constructed the modern vinyl-sided house that is the Wieler home today, it was Gary's parents who first moved in. Gary and Lorna began their life together in a house trailer in the yard. When Gary's parents retired to Winkler in 1989, Lorna officially assumed control of the house. She still gets some good-natured in-law ribbing about the changes she has made — cheerful stencilling and blue-sponged paint over what was utilitarian beige.*

*Three generations of Wielers have shared the same yard and, evidently, the same philosophy. Gary often repeats his dad's rule: "Payments come first." Even in lean years, when others were having troubles, Gary's father paid his bills. No matter how hard it is, Gary will too. This is a matter of pride.*

*This year, for the first time, Gary and Lorna have rented out 160 acres. They will not have to pay to put in a crop in those fields — and they will get cold hard cash in return. They rationalize what was clearly a difficult decision by saying the farmer who is renting the land will be putting in beans, and beans are particularly good for building up nutrients in the soil for the next year.*

*There have been challenging years for the Wielers in their history of farming on the Manitoba plains. But family gatherings do not feature stories from the elders about how bad it was in the "old days." Even in the Dirty Thirties, they note, every farm was a mixed farm, with its own milk, chickens and pigs. The farm acted as a cushion against adversity. Although grain prices were low, a family rarely had to leave the farm for sustenance; everything they needed was right there, including a close-knit neighbouring farm community that was willing to share and help out.*

*More recent challenges underline this farm ethic of co-operation and support. Gary is almost wistful when he remembers the destructive 1997 Red River flood. It was his Depression, with all the mythology that goes with it. The Wieler home is miles from the river, but Tobacco Creek across the road swelled to a mammoth size when the waters of the Red overflowed its banks. The sandbags were piled three high around the house and just managed to keep the water at bay. But what makes Gary Wieler wistful is the memory of how neighbours the Wielers had rarely seen surfaced to help. For a short time there was a supportive farming community around Kane, Manitoba—just like in the old days.*

*On this April day in the year 2000, Gary Wieler's focus is not on the past but on the season that lies ahead. He has seeded the potholes only he can see and sown the corners of the field that might have been missed in the sweep of the diskers. He turns off the ignition and his tractor shudders to stillness. He is hoping a gentle rain will begin tonight as forecast, once he has finished harrowing this field, a rain that will moisten the seeds in their blanket of soil. "Let's hope this will be an exceptional crop, because that's what you need to break even," he comments ruefully, the real world of dollars and cents intruding on his satisfying physical labours.*

❧ Perched two metres above a churning motor on the dusty Manitoba prairie, Gary Wieler can be excused for not immediately recognizing his role in Canadian history. He is the latest in a long string of family wheat farmers. In many ways it was wheat farmers like the Wielers who defined Western Canada's early development. They were the ones who populated the West, extended Canada to the Rockies and gave the country a role on the world stage as an exporter of high-quality wheat. As Grant MacEwan, Western Canada's pre-eminent popular historian, wrote in *Between the Red and the Rockies*, "In a very real sense, wheat built a nation."

Agriculture is Canada's unsung national dream. It has always been the unassuming younger sibling to more dramatic nation-building ventures like the construction of the railway. The Canadian Pacific Railway (CPR) has taken on mythic proportions in the business of forging a nation, thanks to author Pierre Berton's *The National Dream* and song-writer Gordon Lightfoot's *Canadian Railroad Trilogy*. But even more than the ribbon of steel, it was the pure grit of homesteading farmers that changed the look of our country. Thousands of immigrants headed west, eager to carve a bright future out of the fertile Great Plains. They broke the virgin earth with hand-held ploughs and turned the wild prairie into neat, ordered fields. They built thriving towns and raised mighty grain elevators that were to stand for decades as sentinels of progress. The humble farmer endured, at the mercy of the rain and the sun and the most fearsome elements of nature's arsenal.

Farming may not be heralded as the national dream, but the individual tenacity of the pioneers has become part of the mythology that defines who we are. Songs, novels and films celebrate the grit of times past—the simple dwelling, often a sod hut on the windswept prairie; the austere diet, based on flour, oatmeal and potatoes; the plough slicing the earth, either pulled by gaunt oxen or wrestled by the pioneer farmer himself; the test posed by the natural calamities of hail, blizzard, frost, drought and desolation. Somehow this bleak picture has an attraction for us. Through the window of time, many see the frontier existence as a simpler life, where humans pitted themselves against the raw but honest forces of nature. When a Winnipeg film company put out a call in 2000 for two couples who would be prepared to live for a year like their forefathers had one hundred years ago, it was astounded to receive more than a thousand applications.

The real pioneers who found themselves on the sparsely treed plains of the West saw little romance amidst the austerity of their frontier life. Ronald Rees quotes some of the first settlers in his book *New and Naked Land*, who saw the prairie as unfinished—God's raw material. One immigrant, explorer and writer, William H. Butler, set the tone when he said: "This utter negation of life, this complete absence of history . . . One saw here the world as it had taken shape from the hands of the Creator."

Despite the desperate odds, the indomitable spirit of those earlier pioneers persevered. The past deserves to be remembered with a touch of admiration and, yes, even romance. After all, it gave shape to our nation, setting a course for the present—and perhaps the future.

There may have been grand plans, but Canadian agriculture began modestly enough. At first it was purely a subsistence industry carried out largely by white immigrants who grew what they needed to survive. The Native peoples in the eastern stretches of the country cultivated a little land and grew crops to supplement the wild meat in their diets, but the plains tribes depended almost exclusively on the hunt for their sustenance. Buffalo in particular provided food, clothing, shelter and fuel. When the buffalo failed, starvation was imminent.

Agriculture began in the East and moved westward. It slipped into the Canadian Northwest as the handmaiden to the fur trade. The wild stretches beyond the Great Lakes were the domain of Native peoples, Métis and the rough-hewn fur traders of the North West Company and the Hudson's Bay Company (HBC). A few vegetables and a little wheat and barley were grown on small plots for the sole purpose of supplying food to the occupants of the fur trade's forts or posts, but hunting continued to provide the primary nutrition in the West.

In the early 1800s the new Earl of Selkirk, Thomas Douglas, was deeply touched by the economic plight of the Scottish crofters who were being cleared from their lands to make room for sheep. He set out to find land in the New World that they could colonize. He eventually selected the forks of the Red and Assiniboine Rivers, the site of modern-day Winnipeg, probably because of its fertile soil, its proximity to the buffalo plains that stretched west of the Red River and its relatively easy access from the HBC's depot at York Factory.

The West's first experiment in organized farming began in the summer of 1812, when a ragtag group of Scots labourers arrived at Red River after having spent a miserable winter, near starvation, in makeshift huts on the shores of Hudson Bay. After another group of eighty Irish and Highland Scots showed up as hungry and unprepared colonists in October, it was the

Native buffalo hunt rather than any agricultural harvest that sustained them through another brutal winter.

The first years of the Selkirk Settlement were marred by inclement weather, debilitating illness, food shortages and persistent harassment by Métis acting on behalf of the North West Company. The North West traders were annoyed that the Hudson's Bay Company had allowed an agricultural settlement to be established at the confluence of its fur trading routes. The rivalry between farming and fur trading culminated in 1816 in a confrontation in a grove called Seven Oaks, where the Métis killed twenty-one Selkirk settlers. The overt friction between agriculture and fur trading was not resolved until the North West Company merged with the HBC in 1821 and the fur trade retreated to the Athabaska country. Then there was finally some peace and stability at the forks of the Red and the Assiniboine.

It was a slow, difficult start for the farming experiment. Fortunately, the Red River Settlement sat on the bottom of what had been a glacial lake enriched by rotting vegetation. The soil was fertile and there was the promise of future success. In 1831 the Selkirk settlers responded to the hard-won peace with a harvest that generated the area's first marketable surplus. By 1849 cultivated acreages were up by 35 percent. However, people still largely depended on wild meat for nutrition. Agriculture was for subsistence not commerce. At the same time, the owner of the vast tract of land surrounding the Settlement—the Hudson's Bay Company— was not convinced that it was in its interests to allow large-scale agriculture. Even after Selkirk's colony had taken hold, the HBC continued to distrust the concept of pioneer farmers. The Company and many of its Métis employees feared—correctly, as it turned out—that opening the rich land of the West to agriculture would lead to a wave of immigration that would ultimately destroy the fur trade.

The status quo remained largely intact until 1869, when the Canadian government offered to buy the HBC land—which included much of the Great Plains—and open it to settlement. That laid the foundation for government policies to build a nation. The master plan was that the millions of acres of Western real estate would serve as the commercial hinterland to serve the interests of "old Canada." The citizens of Ontario, and especially Toronto, hoped to open the West and enrich the East in one fell swoop. Their hope lay with pioneer farmers, who they imagined would initiate an economic trade-off, buying lumber, groceries and agricultural implements on the one hand while shipping grain on the other. Settlement, they argued, would consolidate the continentwide new nation and affirm Canadian sovereignty in the face of American pressures.

The national dream of Prime Minister John A. Macdonald's agricultural West took shape via specific government policies, the first of which was the Land Act of 1872. The geometric subdivision of the Prairies into a checkerboard of section blocks, each one mile square, formed the basis for future farms and towns. For just $10, anyone twenty-one or older could lay claim to a quarter-section, or 160 acres. Opportunity beckoned and thousands answered the call, attracted in part because of a recession that hammered the rest of Canada and its North Atlantic trading partners from 1873 to 1896.

It took several years before there were enough settlers to produce a harvest worth exporting to the East as the national dreamers had imagined. The West's export trade in wheat began unassumingly enough in 1876. A small shipment, just over 857 bushels, was placed on a Red River steamboat destined for the Steele Brothers seed company in Toronto. It made the laborious trip through Fort Garry, Duluth and the Great Lakes. It may seem a minor transaction by today's standards, but this was the first wheat to leave the new West. One year later, Manitoba wheat was shipped from Winnipeg to Europe. Over the next decade the fledgling grain trade grew hand in hand with increasing production, although farmers could not boast that theirs was a lucrative business. Within ten years production had almost tripled. In 1884 the Manitoba wheat crop was 6.1 million bushels.

Farmers were able to produce a crop worth exporting, and it was a variety of wheat much favoured in Europe, but the means of shipping the harvest was arduous—overland through the United States. The federal government was eager to provide an all-Canadian transportation option to assert Canada's claim to the Northwest against American competitors. Macdonald managed to put together a Canadian syndicate of private interests, with strong financial support at home and in the international investment community, to build the Canadian Pacific Railway.

The construction of the rail line was accomplished with astonishing speed under the direction of William Van Horne. It presented a monumental challenge: 1,000 kilometres through the swamp and rock of the Canadian Shield, 1,300 kilometres across comparatively easy prairie, and 700 kilometres through near-impenetrable mountains to the west coast. The last spike was driven on November 7, 1885, at the meeting place of the east and west lines in Eagle Pass, just three years after work had started. The event was marked by Van Horne's anticlimactic five-second speech: "All I can say is that work has been well done in every way." Regular service began the next year, with scheduled traffic from Montreal to Vancouver.

The domination of the western trade route through the United States was over. However, it became apparent that Eastern Canada could not deliver enough homesteaders to settle and work the broad expanse of land that had suddenly become accessible. The CPR, eager to do its part to bring in settlers and carry out a grain harvest, initiated an active campaign for immigration. It bombarded the British and Continental press with information on life in Western Canada. The CPR carried the gospel of emigration to distant corners of the British countryside. No railway station wall or hotel lobby was free from one of the CPR's posters. Agents for the railway, called Canadian crackers, earned a dubious reputation by spinning webs of words to describe an idyllic farm life in the New World, with no mention of winter or mosquitoes.

Despite the CPR's efforts, rates of immigration remained disappointing. Many who left Britain and the Continent chose to go to the U.S. or Australia, or even Argentina or Brazil—that is, until Clifford Sifton of Manitoba became the federal minister of the interior in 1896. He launched an ambitious and elaborate effort to encourage emigration from unconventional places. Looking for hardy pioneer material, less fickle than the

British, he set his sights on the crowded and impoverished peasant lands of the Austro-Hungarian Empire. Thanks to Sifton's immigration efforts, Canada's population grew as much between 1900 and 1910 as it had in the preceding three decades. In 1909, for example, 18,500 entries for homesteading were filed with the Dominion Land Office in Moose Jaw alone.

Wheat had become "the keystone in the arch of Canada's national policy. Its production and sale made possible the construction of transcontinental railway systems, and the extension of political control across the Prairies to the Pacific," wrote W.T. Easterbrook and H.G.J. Aitken in *Canadian Economic History*. The economic potential of farming attracted the flush of settlement to the Prairies, finally fulfilling the national dream of a country extending from sea to sea.

The next phase of Canada's agricultural history was the era when wheat ruled. "King Wheat," as the precious commodity was affectionately called, was so plentiful that Canada became the biggest wheat-exporting nation in the world, a distinction it held from 1920 to 1935. Canada was dubbed "the breadbasket of the Empire" for its work in feeding the far-flung colonies and dominions of the British Empire and supplying Britain's allies during the Boer War and First World War. And Canadian farmers were celebrated for their industrious wheat growing: Canada's yields per acre were consistently higher than those in the U.S. in the first decades of the twentieth century.

It was a heady time for the wheat economy and one that inevitably attracted a new breed of entrepreneur. The arrival of grain barons with names like Richardson, Searle and Peavey launched a period of corporate domination of the grain trade. The conflict between the growers and the grain establishment became the stuff of legend. There were many stories about the virtuous, hard-working farmer pitted against the capitalistic grain barons. Whether or not farmers truly were the embattled victims of grain-handling monopolies, their unity of purpose eventually led to an exceptional new co-operative movement.

The conflict between grower and grain establishment began almost as soon as the new lines of steel thrust their way across the farming frontier, punctuated almost immediately by the grain elevators of the handling companies. In the early days of prairie wheat production, grain had been loaded by hand into bags, a laborious process; there was no other way of doing it. That changed when the W.W. Ogilvie Milling Company built its first elevator at Gretna, Manitoba, in 1881. That new structure on the prairie horizon signalled the start of a complex grain-handling system and the beginnings of the conflict between farmers and grain entrepreneurs. The massive slope-shouldered structures rose on the horizon every 15 kilometres or so—the distance easily managed by a horse and cart. Designed to clean, dry and gather wheat, a country elevator could store 25,000 bushels of grain and then unload them into rail cars using the basic principle of gravity. These prairie sentinels soon dotted the landscape, markers of the wealth of the burgeoning wheat economy.

As the elevator and milling companies grew, so did the conviction of many farmers that these businesses were abusing their power by lowering the price paid to farmers and giving elevator companies preference over farmers in the event of rail-car shortages. The elevator companies further provoked producers' suspicions by coming together to form the North West Elevator Association, which ended up controlling two-thirds of the elevators on the Prairies. Farmers believed the Association was "the syndicate of syndicates" and was linked to the Winnipeg Grain Exchange—known to farmers as "the house with Closed Shutters." In reaction, farmers created the first incarnation of the co-operative movement—the Territorial Grain Growers Association—in 1902, following it up soon after with the first attempt at co-operative grain marketing, the Grain Growers' Grain Company, formed in 1906.

The Grain Growers' Grain Company merged with the United Farmers of Alberta in 1917 to form the United Grain Growers pool system. Its counterpart in Saskatchewan was the Saskatchewan Co-operative Elevator Company. Together they owned 650 local elevators, about half of the shipping points on the Prairies, and controlled about one-third of the terminal capacity at Thunder Bay. Farmers had revolutionized the competitive commercial grain industry by controlling the pattern of elevator services and the prices offered to grower owners.

The production zenith of Canada's Western grain industry came during the years of the First World War. That was when the Prairies truly earned the accolade "breadbasket of the Empire" by supplying wartorn Britain with necessary stocks of wheat at a time when conditions had shut down transport from Australia and Argentina. In 1917, Britain created a single wheat import agency for itself and its allies. With only one purchaser in the market, the Canadians and Americans were forced to set a shared wheat price. In Canada this was managed by the Board of Grain Supervisors, set up under the War Measures Act by means of an Order-in-Council.

Canada's effort to increase her wheat output under the stress of war succeeded brilliantly. Assisted by favourable weather, the 1915 crop produced a record volume of 395 million bushels. By 1917 the country had 17.4 million acres cultivated with wheat, compared with 10.3 million in 1910.

After the war the governmental controls lapsed, and in 1919 the private trade was not ready to resume marketing. So in 1919 the government set up the first Canadian Wheat Board to market that year's crop. With Australia and Argentina back in the game, the artificially high prices of the war soon began to slide. The government had no intention of getting into the wheat business and eagerly restored the wheat trade to private hands.

When wheat prices collapsed soon after Canada abandoned the Wheat Board, farmers concluded that the private grain trade was to blame. They campaigned hard, but to no avail, to restore government marketing of wheat and eliminate the futures market. When it seemed Ottawa would not comply, they turned to their second option: the pools. Farmers were watching the visible success of co-operative marketing movements in Europe, Australia and the United States. A persuasive enthusiast from California, Aaron Shapiro, gave speeches throughout the Prairies promoting the idea of a made-in-Canada pool system that would crush the grain exchanges.

He struck a chord in the Canadian farming community. Under the pooling system a pool had to sign up at least one-half of the producers in a geographic area. Farmers had to agree to sell all their produce through a central organization for a set period of time, usually five years. Each farmer would receive an initial payment when he delivered his crop, and the grade and quantity would be recorded. An interim payment would be made to the farmer according to the average price his quality of grain received over the year. The pool's promise was that it would avoid the annual autumn glut on the market, and as a result of its orderly marketing eliminate middlemen and speculators, thereby increasing the average return to the farmer.

Theory became reality when the Alberta Co-operative Wheat Producers was organized in 1923, followed the next year by the Saskatchewan and Manitoba pool systems. The three pools then combined to create a Central Selling Agency, with offices overseas, and they also began to buy up elevators. Within three years, they were handling half of Canada's wheat trade.

The Winnipeg Grain Exchange tried to hold back the tide of reform. It bought a Yorkton radio station to combat the pools' organ, the *Western Producer* newspaper. The battles between the grain men and Western farmers became intense. But the 1920s were fat years, with stable prices and expanding markets; both the pools and the traders flourished.

The farmers' co-operative energy led to political change too. The Progressive movement developed as the vehicle for people to express their dissatisfaction with the two long-standing parties. Western farmers provided a key plank for the Progressive campaign through their fight for reduced tariffs, branch lines, the regulation of grain grading and weighing practices, and competitive elevator and grain-buying systems. In Alberta, the United Farmers of Alberta, under Henry Wise Wood, came to power in 1921. In Manitoba, John Bracken's United Farmers of Manitoba also assumed office in the 1920s and held on to power for almost three decades. T.A. Crerar, the founding president of the United Grain Growers (UGG) in

1917 and federal agriculture minister under Robert Borden's Union government, led a national farmers' movement, the Progressive Party.

In the late 1920s optimism on the farm was fuelled by impressive yields and prices, along with confidence in the marketing system. The family farm and the rural infrastructure were operating much as their designers might have dreamed. The complex structure of grain handling—the elevators, the rail lines, the grading systems—was accepted. By 1920 most of the arable prairie land had been brought under the plough. And wheat production, already in excess of 360 million bushels in the bumper crop of 1915, was poised to exceed half a billion bushels by 1928. That year produced the Prairies' "wonder" crop—the best in fourteen years.

Incredibly, the flush days of prairie agriculture were about to come to a sudden, dramatic end. And so would the heady days when Canadian farmers successfully worked together for economic and political gain. At no point in the future would Western farmers manage to repeat the confident, co-operative triumphs of those days.


The pool concept as a marketing innovation collapsed in 1929 with the crisis in the world economy. The pools were caught with more wheat than they could sell. At the same time, they had guaranteed higher prices to farmers. Whether a case of poor circumstances or poor management, they were sucked into bankruptcy. The federal government intervened to help the banks that had lent the pools money, but the pool innovation was essentially dead.

And then, when it seemed things could not get worse, the rains stopped. Nowhere were the hardships of the Depression more keenly felt than in the Canadian West. Prairie farmers suffered a bitter confluence of circumstances: agricultural price declines, failure of foreign markets and drought. Had these lasted just two or three years, the hard times would have been forgotten as they had in the past; but the unfortunate combination of events ensured the Depression would hang on for a decade, even when the rest of the world was recovering.

At the heart of the crisis was the deflation of the world wheat economy. From a high of $1.60 a bushel in 1929, the price of No. 1 Northern plummeted to less than 40 cents in just three years as international markets collapsed. With this kind of commodity price drop it became apparent that Western farmers were overly dependent on wheat: 60 percent of their crop income came from wheat.

Worst of all was that most unpredictable of factors—the weather. The climatic conditions on the Prairies in the 1930s were a sobering reminder that weather can be the most capricious of considerations for farmers. It stopped raining in 1931 and hot, dry winds began to blow. Then the dust storms began. The precious topsoil that should have been nurturing seeds lifted on the gusty winds, blackened the sky, smothered gardens and crops, and settled in doorways and windowsills. It was especially bad in the many areas that should not have been tilled in the first place because conditions were too dry and the soil too thin.

As the dust storms reduced visibility to a few feet, lakes went dry and farmers cut Russian thistle in a desperate effort to prevent their cattle from starving. And the drought denied the most basic of pleasures, repeatedly forcing the cancellation of that essential social highlight of the rural calendar—the country fair. Barry Broadfoot in *Ten Lost Years* quotes farmers who remember the biting grit in the air. One recounts: "That dirt that blew off my hand, that wasn't dirt, mister. That was my land . . . The land just blew away."

Unbelievably, 1936 was worse still. It was the coldest winter on record, the cruel temperatures combining with blizzard after blizzard. The summer that followed was the longest and hottest yet, with temperatures regularly exceeding 100 degrees Fahrenheit. The subsequent winter was again unusually cold, the next summer hot and dry.

The drought then delivered a plague of near-biblical proportions. The dry weather offered ideal conditions for grasshoppers to grow and multiply. By the end of the decade they were a critical problem on several hundred thousand square kilometres of the Canadian Prairies.

When the economists counted up the yields and incomes, they provided stark conclusions about the extent of the disaster. In the 1920s the average harvest produced 350 million bushels—about 17 bushels an acre. From 1933 to 1937, harvests produced an average of 230 million bushels—9.5 bushels an acre. In 1937, Saskatchewan produced an average of 2.6 bushels per acre. According to Barry Broadfoot, "farming was a slow way of starving."

Calculating the human costs of the catastrophe was impossible. Rural relief provided food, fuel, clothing, shelter and the necessities of farm life: seed, feed, tractor fuel and supplies. Relief was often necessary, but it was accepted with humiliation by a population that had prided itself on its hard work and independence. By the end of the 1937 crop failure it was estimated that two-thirds of the farm population were destitute.

One response to the crisis was to leave. About 250,000 people, beaten down by the dust, the wind and the hunger, moved out of the Prairies between 1931 and 1941. It was a dramatic exodus for a region that had so recently been settled.

Despite everything, the essential backbone of the prairie grain-handling system had survived. The agricultural economy, however, was severely hurt. The federal government was anxious to repair some of the damage wrought by the natural and economic calamities. In 1935 it set up the Prairie Farm Rehabilitation Administration to reclaim the worst-hit areas of the agricultural economy. The government agency's programs taught farmers how to deal with soil drifting, water conservation and land reclamation. Grants and engineering advice created community irrigation schemes and encouraged thousands of farmers to dig dugouts and build dikes to collect and store water for their livestock. Abandoned land that many say should not have been ploughed in the first place was transferred to the Crown, fenced, seeded with grass and turned over to local community pasture associations for livestock grazing. The Farm Assistance Act was passed to offer a small measure of aid to farmers suffering from low yields through no fault of their own.

The university extension services were set up as a way to provide essential research to farmers.

It was small consolation, but farmers finally won the fundamental intervention they had been demanding since the First World War. In early 1935, Prime Minister R.B. Bennett yielded to the pressure to relieve the burden on farmers by proposing a reincarnated Canadian Wheat Board. His government owned 234 million bushels of wheat, acquired when the pools collapsed. He began by musing about the nationalization of the entire Western grain elevator system, and would have created a monopoly agency for the sale of major field crops—wheat, oats, barley, rye and flax—both at home and abroad. After a vigorous debate, Bennett settled on a compromise: the Canadian Wheat Board would be an optional marketing channel for wheat only.

Although it was a compromise, the creation of the CWB did signal an important turning point in the grain business. The federal government was going to market grain and, most importantly, guarantee a minimum price to farmers. It was a vital and essential policy statement in the midst of difficult times.

Four years later, facing a situation like that of the First World War— the necessity of maintaining a continuous grain supply for the Allies—the government gave the Board the monopoly many farmers had long demanded. In subsequent years the Board's monopoly was extended to oats and barley when Mackenzie King's government faced election and had reason to be worried about Western support. Prairie wheat farmers still had political influence.

Ironically, the ten-year-long economic and climatic disasters of the Depression years, which left the West resembling a scarred battleground, were ultimately relieved by war. But agriculture would never rebound to its former glory. In the decades that followed the Second World War, the agricultural landscape underwent a dramatic shift. It was a period of painful readjustments that would have astounded the original settlers or the determined farmers who had survived the winter years of the Depression.

The 1950s saw the beginning of a significant shift from country to city. Prairie society became much like the rest of the country—more urban than rural, less dependent on agriculture. Saskatchewan, the most farm-based of all the provinces, ceased to grow in population after the 1930s. In 1941, eight of every ten people in Saskatchewan lived on farms and in villages; by 1981, only 400,000 people, or four of every ten, were classed as rural. The countryside was emptying. Rural schools, churches, ball teams and sports days ceased to exist. The number of farms was cut in half during the forty years after the war. At the same time, although fewer people were farming the Prairies, they were cultivating a larger area than when the rural population was at its peak. The size of individual farms increased dramatically. Individual farmers were physically capable of handling larger acreages thanks primarily to the development of more sophisticated machines and chemical fertilizers and pesticides.

Family farms were turning into "commercial farms," in the language of economics. However, incomes remained low. Statistics Canada reported that one-quarter of farms recorded operating losses in 1996. By the end of the twentieth century the family farm was increasingly seen as a business rather than a way of life. It was a capital-intensive industry, with mechanized production techniques, focused almost entirely on creating greater and greater yields. The image of the family farm as a co-operative unit of fathers and sons, mothers and daughters, all working together, began to fade.

Dismantling also began of the system that had served Western farmers so well in the glory days of wheat. Most visible was the abandonment of the elevators and the 33,000 kilometres of branch lines that snaked throughout the Prairies. There were 5,758 elevators in 1933; only 600 remained by the late 1990s, with more slated to come down. They have been replaced by huge concrete inland terminals and elevators. The basic concept remains the same: elevate grain, then allow it to flow into bins and rail cars using gravity. But the new versions are massive structures where grain is measured in tonnes rather than bushels. The Canadian Museum of Civilization has even paid tribute to what has been lost by building a version of an old country elevator in its Canada Hall.

The prairie farmers of the 1920s would have been appalled at the corporate consolidation that has occurred in recent decades, making competition an elusive dream. In 1921, sixty-seven companies controlled country elevators, yet farmers of that time were convinced there was little competition. By the late 1990s, after a series of mergers and consolidations, there were only five of the original elevator companies left, including the remnants of the once powerful pools. Nevertheless, there was little protest. In the last few years of the century, large transnational companies began stepping into the Canadian market; ConAgra and Louis Dreyfus began building new grain collection facilities.

It would have pained the early co-op movement to see how the co-operatives have transformed themselves to fit into a world of "big business" and "competitiveness." The United Grain Growers, the very first farmer co-operative, became a publicly traded company in 1992. Then UGG took its new corporate ethic one step further when it announced a strategic alliance with Archer Daniels Midland, the U.S.-based grain giant. The Saskatchewan Wheat Pool began selling shares on the Toronto Stock Exchange in April 1996, although control still technically rested with its seventy thousand farmer-members. It still bills itself as a co-operative—the country's largest publicly traded co-operative. However, it has not been doing well financially: it lost $90 million in 2000, and shares that were originally priced at $12 traded for $2.40. In 1996 the last remaining true farmer co-operatives, the Alberta Wheat Pool and Manitoba Pool Elevators, merged to form Agricore. It was an attempt to get big enough to survive in the new competitive agribusiness environment.

The Canadian Wheat Board was stripped of some of its scope in 1989 when the government pulled oats from its authority. In the late 1990s it was further assailed by demands from farmers who argued they would be better served if the CWB's monopoly were eliminated. Farmers were finally polled on whether a so-called dual marketing system should be supported. They voted instead for the continued existence of a government marketing monopoly, but the CWB was left bruised and battered by the recognition that farmers no longer spoke with a united voice.

At the turn of the twenty-first century, the winds of change that are blowing across the Prairies are as strong in some ways as the dust clouds of the 1930s. In those days drought battered the land and the morale of those who worked it. However, many farmers persevered, calling on the frontier determination of their forefathers. Today the winds of a fundamental economic transformation are sweeping the Prairies clear, rattling the clapboard signs on the abandoned buildings in towns that stand as skeletal reminders of how farming once ruled the West.

The Perkins restaurant on Pembina Highway in Winnipeg's south end was the scene for a meeting I had with an observer who is well qualified to pass judgment on the transformation in agriculture. On that June day, Clay Gilson, the dean of Canadian agricultural economists and an influential adviser to a series of federal and provincial governments, came for coffee. Handsome and tanned, with a shock of white hair, he gave no clue that he would pass away suddenly just a few weeks later. In fact, he was distracted that day by the condition of his brother, who was in hospital. But Gilson was true to his reputation as someone always prepared to talk agriculture—and to educate.

Gilson was an agricultural economist, but he had a reputation for applied research and practical application. For example, he was one of those recruited to help develop a crop insurance plan. Gilson was no mere keeper of statistics, lacking appreciation of what those statistics meant for farmers. After all, he grew up on a farm in Medora, in western Manitoba, and lived through the Depression. All that was left of Medora, he noted not with nostalgia but with regret, was the cemetery and the church; the school had been granted a second life as a grain bin. Amidst the clatter of coffee cups and the din of a suburban hangout, he admitted it was too late for Medora and countless other prairie towns.

Gilson said short-run problems like low commodity rates have distracted farmers from time to time. But the changing shape of agriculture over the past fifty years was culminating with the new millennium in a "fundamental structural transformation." For years the change had been incremental and manageable to a degree. Some level of change, he acknowledged, was inescapable. "To deny the inevitable change is like putting your finger in the dike," he said. However, the pace of farming's transformation into an industrial system at the beginning of the twenty-first century seemed unchecked.

In 1970, in the report of the Federal Task Force on Agriculture, Gilson recommended assistance for farmers who he could see would be forced off their farms by structural change in the industry. He foretold the future when he argued then that failure to deal with the farmers' plight would not only maroon that generation of farmers but the next as well. Many years later, in a noisy chain restaurant on the edge of Winnipeg, on the edge of his own life as it turned out, the man who served on numerous government inquiries could only admit that Ottawa had not come to the rescue.

He said the past offered a lesson about the nature of communities, co-operation and determination. It was a lesson the federal government had to learn before it was too late for the last remaining towns and farmers on the Canadian Prairies. At a time when there was nothing there but raw, open grasslands, John A. Macdonald had a national dream to build an agricultural West that would sustain a nation. "We had a vision that lasted a century. My grandparents built a country," said Gilson. Keeping in mind all those settlers who were invited to the West, and who returned the invitation by developing the world's most productive wheat economy, he said it would be shocking to see the once fertile farmlands revert to empty spaces. He argued it was time for some clear direction from government. "Don't tell me it can't be done. We need some nation building."

*Three*

# Desperately Seeking Readlyn

May 18, 2000

The tiny A.C. Barrie wheat sprouts push their way through the heavy, black soil, straining for the sun. They emerge into a field of fellow seedlings shaking their heads in the gentle spring breeze. Together, they cast this field in a flush of the freshest green. The buds on the trees of the Wielers' windbreak have swollen and unfurled a curl of leaves. The grass is greening in the warmth of the sun; young Nicholas Wieler is circling the lawn on the riding mower. This is already the second trim of the year. The entire landscape is coloured in spring green. It is the hue of another season's promise born from the warming soil of a prairie spring.

There is a calm in the countryside, now that the seeding rush is over. It is almost as if the rural populace has slowed down to listen to the sound of the fledgling canola, flax and wheat popping through the soil.

There is no traffic today. The only vehicle to confront me on the gravel road leading up from Highway 23 is a grain truck with Gary and *son Thomas on their way to the Paterson elevator with a load of wheat. The Wielers are shipping as much of last year's wheat as they can in an effort to clear their bins and get a little necessary cash. This is the third load today; one more tomorrow. Lorna is outside, shovel in hand, exertion staining her cheeks red. She has been shovelling the bottom of the flat-bottomed grain bins, scooping the wheat the auger could not reach. Although it is only 20 degrees Celsius, it is warm enough to make her breathless. When Gary returns from Kane, she rewards herself with a glass of lemonade on the patio in front of the house.*

*We sit silently on the new plastic patio chairs, overlooking a broad expanse of prairie. The endless vista evokes a kind of lethargy. There is only one clump of trees in the distance — the prairie marker of a settled home. "It's the Germans," Gary, a man of few words, explains, describing some European newcomers who have the necessary capital to manage in today's prairie agriculture.*

*When I ask them what Gary's parents might have seen from this spot, the Wielers become animated. "There were farms everywhere. Neighbours right over there." Gary points just across the road. "Another farm every quarter-mile. Little yards everywhere." They show me the township map — a checkerboard of quarter-section blocks as they were first laid out in 1872. Discreet little dots indicate where there are actual farmyards. According to the map, there are now only three farmyards in the sections adjoining the square where the Wieler home stands; that is, "the Germans" along with a childless couple and a yard without a home. Gary explains that the rural municipality issues a new map every year because the landscape changes so frequently. This map, drawn up in 1999, is already out of date.*

*The map verifies what a glance across the horizon suggests. There are no neighbours, as we understand the term, on the skyline. There are no neighbourhood kids the boys can play with. No opportunity for a coffee klatch. Instead, the entire family has to practise a self-reliance that would be unknown in the city, or even in the country itself a generation ago. Philip, fourteen, is off today doing yard work at a farm close to Kane.*

*Nicholas, twelve, has the mower assignment. Thomas, with huge, absorbing eyes and an animated expression under his peaked hat, trails his father in obvious admiration.*

*Not so long ago there were five schools within an 8-kilometre radius of the Wieler home. A marker stands in the field across from one of Gary's wheat fields as a tribute to the long-gone McNab school. These days the boys find their friends scattered throughout the countryside, the school bus the glue that binds them. Eight-year-old Thomas is on the bus forty-five minutes each way to and from Roland, 15 kilometres from the Wieler home. Philip has graduated to high school, and to a longer trip still.*

*Kane, just 8 kilometres away, still has a Paterson elevator. Reflecting the sense of depressing inevitability pervasive throughout the West, the locals speculate on when it will close—like the UGG elevator did in 1996. This fall? Next year? For now, much of the grain collected here is trucked to a high-throughput elevator in Morris. And the truth is that N.M. Paterson & Sons is not closing elevators as quickly as some of the other grain companies, so Kane's Paterson elevator may have a longer lifespan than the rumour mill forecasts.*

*It is entirely predictable that gossip will turn to the fate of the elevator. It is, in fact, the only commercial structure left on Kane's single street. The school closed in 1973. It briefly enjoyed a reincarnation as a community centre, but after ten years there were fewer and fewer plays, band practices, anniversary celebrations and fall suppers. The 4-H club could not sustain operations on its own and the community centre experiment ended. The only store in town has became a private home. The John Deere dealership disappeared altogether, as did the garage. Even the historic Bergthaler church, once the spiritual centre for the area's Mennonite community, could not sustain a congregation by the 1970s.*

*Today there is no place in Kane to buy a soft drink. Only the old KANE sign on the road hints of its former status as a town.*

Assiniboia, a few days later. I am staying at the Wheel Inn, a lanky strip of rudimentary boxes glued together end to end. The view from my motel room, over the tops of the cars parked in front, is of the row of elevators across the road that proclaim the farming fame of southwestern Saskatchewan. I have a free morning, so the first order of business is a hearty breakfast at the Bar-B Inn. Just about every table is taken, mostly by older farmers and farm wives. The non-smokers are directed to the dark interior; the smokers score the booths by the sunny windows. The sound of clattering cutlery and energetic gossip underscores the fact that this town has not only survived the transformation in prairie agriculture, it has thrived.

I mustn't dawdle over my bacon and eggs and snippets of other people's morning conversations. It is a perfect, clear, sunny Saskatchewan day. A beautiful day for a drive.

I have been warned that the highways in southern Saskatchewan are in bad shape. Sure enough, just out of Assiniboia on Highway 13E—the former Red Coat Trail—signs with ominous warnings begin to appear along the ragged shoulder of the road. CAUTION. BROKEN PAVEMENT FOR 50 KILOMETRES.

I am in search of Readlyn. A bizarre goal perhaps, since Readlyn, like many other small towns, apparently vanished when the four elevators closed, along with the school, the church and the other amenities of small-town life. I was told that Readlyn now has a population of two. But Readlyn had been granted a second life of sorts when former resident and now Calgary businessman Art Hazle spent his earnings and his time renovating and hooking up electricity to the old store and the telephone services building. About five hundred curious people came to see what was done and to celebrate Readlyn's one-hundredth birthday in 1998. Curiosity is driving me too.

Sure enough, there is a sign on the road—official government green—that points the route to Readlyn down the next gravel road. The road is long and winding, snaking through a gold and glowing landscape. Those who travel only on the Trans-Canada would never guess that this too is

Saskatchewan; it is far too hilly. No other sign appears to help me find Readlyn. Instead the road ends in a T, flanking a rise overlooking a deep coulee. There, in the scrub brush, is a tiny hand-painted sign that says READLYN. 2 KM. It neglects, however, to point the way. Oh well, it is a beautiful day for a drive.

I choose left. Several kilometres down the road, behind an incongruous electric fence, sit an amazing number of decrepit tractors and farm implements, along with a fading church and a little red shed—too small for the equipment and too tawdry for the church. This must be the "museum" I have heard about. I must be close. Across the road is an ancient garage—closed, of course. There is a copse of trees over the next hill, signs of habitation.

As my rental car crunches up the drive to the house trailer, the occupant appears. She is an elderly woman, curious, not anxious, about the rental car that has been bumping aimlessly through the landscape. She is the former teacher at the Readlyn school. She remembers her first class of thirty-two; now, she says, the bus picks up only one child. She asks me not to use her name—not because she is afraid of publicity, but because she does not want to seem flashy. "Readlyn," she says, pointing over the rolling hills, "is there. Past the museum. You can't miss it."

I should have turned right, not left. Oh well, the sun is still shining. Back to the relics' museum, and one kilometre farther along, tucked behind the road, there it is: Readlyn. No sign. There is a neat white fence around the collection of buildings, placed within spitting distance of one another, breaking all the prairie rules about ample space. The buildings of reconstructed Readlyn are neatly arranged, a parody of rural life. There is no sign of life in this "town"—except for the yellow dog at the nearby farm that begins barking in protest at my arrival.

I stop the car in the middle of "Centre Street" and step out to explore a way of life of times gone past. A peak in the window of the false storefront rekindles distant memories of two-penny screws, bolts of cotton fabric and licorice babies lined up in the cubbyholes of the long shelves that hang on the walls. Children have carved their names on one corner of the building—an old-fashioned, country-style graffiti.

I go back to the car, turn the ignition—and nothing. Wait. Try again. Wait some more. Still nothing. Check out the store again. No, I am not delusional, the engine of this brand-new Honda rental will not turn over. I, the urban writer, check out my purse and find a nail file, a tangle of safety pins and a notebook, not exactly useful for an automobile break-down in the countryside. Even if I had a cell phone, and even if it worked, how would I describe where I was?

So I begin to walk. The hound who discovered me lurking about in abandoned Readlyn guides me to his house. He must want company, for there is no one at home. A bicycle lies sprawled on its side. There is another farm, not far up the hill, but as I trudge up I see a combine pulling away over the crest of the hill, disappearing into the distance. No one is home there either.

I am running out of options. There has been no movement on the gravel roads in this quiet corner of the province the entire time I have been bumbling along in search of Readlyn. So I set off down the road, purposefully now, not sure how far I will have to walk before I see the next sign of modern life. Oh well, it is a beautiful day for a walk.

It serves me right. I remember all those times I played devil's advocate and asked prairie farmers, "What does it really matter if there is no one left in the countryside?" They shrugged and smiled. "Well, what happens if your car breaks down?" I dismissed the idea then, but now I am paying the price. There is hardly anyone left on this prime Saskatchewan farm-land to help a damsel in distress, much less to maintain a way of life.

Then I hear it. The rumble of a truck engine. A cloud of dust is rising on the gravel road. It is approaching me. I abandon urban niceties and plant myself in the path of the oncoming vehicle. Two men and a woman, shirted in near matching lumberjack plaid, invite me to jump in. No doubt they would have helped me even if I hadn't forced them to stop. With the skill of those used to fixing broken tractors and combines, they spot the loose cable of my battery in no time, securing it with pliers ever ready in a back pocket. I offer my hapless story. I know the account of the silly writer in the city Honda will make the rounds at the Bar-B Inn. But it seems that offering myself up for good-natured ridicule is the least I can do in return for the grace and skill that have been granted me in this forgotten corner of the Prairies.

It is tempting to dismiss the fate of towns like Readlyn or Kane as an inevitable side effect of economic evolution. Farming has, after all, been undergoing a radical change, but other industries have gone through change too. However, when a business transformation confronts those industries, it is usually those directly involved who have to adjust. When a hardware store in Toronto or Hamilton or Vancouver closes its doors in the wake of the arrival of a Home Depot, the owners and the employees are the ones affected; the city itself simply breathes deeply and adjusts to the new commercial reality. In contrast, agriculture's transformation from a family-based way of life to an agribusiness enterprise is straining the very definition of rural Canada. When the farmers go, the businesses and towns go too. There is no one left to buy groceries at the local store, no one to tank up at the small local gas station, no children to send to the town's school. As farmers abandon the land, the social fabric woven of people, towns and businesses is irrevocably torn.

The current crisis on the farm is accelerating the trend of the last fifty years. There has been a massive depopulation in rural Canada, especially in the West, which is almost tantamount to an economic cleansing of these regions. At the last census count in 1996, there were only 276,548 farms left in Canada. The people who live on them make up less than 3 percent of the country's population. In comparison, there were 733,000 farms in 1941. There will be no official count of how many more farmers Canada has lost until the 2001 census is tabulated.

The pressures on farmers began decades ago, with the development of new machines that replaced the pure physical brawn of the horse-and-buggy days. The "Green Revolution" brought the development of new chemicals and seeds that further improved farmer productivity. Yields rose, but obversely, there was less need for people to work the land.

Farms got substantially bigger. Canadian farms are now 22 percent larger than they were twenty years ago. This is particularly true on the Prairies, where farmers depend on cash crops. Between 1936 and 1996 the average-size farm in Saskatchewan increased from 400 acres to 1,152 acres. It is not unusual to see farms of 5,000 acres.

In the past five decades on the farm, change has guaranteed the survival of the fittest at the expense of those who could not adapt. However, at the turn of the new millennium, it is not just the marginal farmers who are being pushed out; it is those who survived the staggering interest rates of the 1980s, the grasshoppers of the mid-1990s, the floods of the late 1990s. During the last "farm crisis," in the 1980s, there were massive rallies and farm gate protests against foreclosures. This time the crisis is more subtle, with smaller operations quietly being absorbed by larger ones. Debt, long hours of work on the farm and at off-farm jobs, and an overwhelming sense of powerlessness in the face of low commodity prices, rising costs and unfocused government policy compound a profound sense of despair on today's farm. These days it is often the stable operations—run by the kind of farmers who would have made the homesteaders proud—that are boarding up their windows in defeat.

Nowhere has the revolution in agriculture cut more deeply than in Saskatchewan. Between 1936 and 1996 the number of farms in Saskatchewan dropped steadily, from 142,391 to 56,995. Agriculture and Agri-Food Canada predicts Saskatchewan's realized net farm income will stay at negative levels until at least 2003. In the wake of these non-incomes, one in three remaining farmers are expected to quit.

The broad open prairie, the unencumbered winds, the co-operative sense of community, have defined Saskatchewan from its start. The prairie life has inspired the likes of Guy Vanderhaeghe, W.O. Mitchell and Sharon Butala, and animated the political zeal of Tommy Douglas and John Diefenbaker. The small-town hockey rinks of the Canadian

Prairies produced Gordie Howe, Wendell Clark and Theo Fleury. The depopulation of Saskatchewan is now stripping the province of the rural roots that gave rise to a distinct creative, caring and hard-working spirit. As farming becomes more marginalized, banking, public administration and other service industries are taking over the Saskatchewan economy. We are witnesses to the virtual loss of what Allan Fotheringham once described as "the most Canadian of provinces." The loss of the fundamental rural fabric of Saskatchewan is felt even by those who live far away.

In early 1999, Gail Forbes was on the protest circuit. Young, articulate and direct, she offered an unflinching view of what farming was like. She and her husband, Murray, farmed 1,800 acres near Senlac, in western Saskatchewan. When their work on the farm was combined with an oil-field delivery business they ran on the side, it left them, as Gail puts it, "no life." The three Forbes children were basically raising themselves as their parents scrambled in a desperate attempt to make the farm pay.

In the 1998 growing season the Forbeses saw not a drop of rain. It was the bitter continuation of three years of drought in the area. Gail remembers Murray, the perpetually optimistic farmer, consoling her by saying "the rain will come." "No it won't," replied Gail with a healthy dose of scepticism. And it did not. It left them with a disastrous year. Neighbouring farmers were in the same situation, so Gail organized a petition asking for government help. Then came a local rally, and another, and finally protests on a grand scale. Fuelling her was her steadfast belief that the federal government would help if only it understood what was happening on the farm. But to her disillusionment she found that her farm operation did not qualify for the federal-provincial Agricultural Income Disaster Assistance program that was touted to be the salvation for farmers in trouble. There would be no financial help for Gail and Murray Forbes. Hope was replaced by despair.

A sense of foreboding, brought on by the persistently low commodity prices, hung over her as they put in the 1999 crop. Thanks to benevolent weather, this crop looked great—yields of forty, even fifty bushels an acre. A once-in-a-lifetime harvest. However, because of low grain prices, that ended up meaning very little. The best the Forbeses could hope for was to break even.

One fall evening under a sky of breathtaking beauty, as they were eating their dinner in a swaying, golden field of nearly worthless grain, Gail screwed up her courage and approached Murray. "I've had it," she told him. Much to her surprise, he agreed that it was time to give up the farm. Neither their kids nor their parents made any effort to change their minds.

In the year 2000 the Forbes family became another of Ottawa's faceless statistics. They sold four quarter-sections of land, rented out another three, and converted another three to grass. They were ready to sell the homestead—eager, in fact, to make a clean break—but they could find no buyer for the beautiful house, treed yard and quarter-section of land around it. They still had a few acres, but for the most part Gail and Murray Forbes had quit farming in the wake of insurmountable odds.

Quitting farming is not just a case of losing a job. If that happens in the city, it is an undeniable shock, a disappointment, a loss; the task is to find another. And until something new comes along, there is always employment insurance and other government support programs to cushion the pain. It is very different on the farm, where home is the workplace. There is no EI here. And it is not just a question of lost income, it is a lost way of life. To lose a job on the Canadian farm means losing everything: the place you live, the life you lead, your family heritage.

For Gail and Murray Forbes, thankfully, there was a parachute. Even while they were full-time farmers, they ran an oil-field delivery operation to help make ends meet. Now they are putting almost all of their efforts into the oil supply work and finding, much to their wonderment, that hard work does indeed finally pay. Gail says she doesn't look back. Does she regret their decision? "Absolutely not. There was no point in trying to keep it going. The government wants to see big business take over farming. It's really very sad, but they don't care about the family farm."

It has been a relief for Gail Forbes to be free of the stresses of farming. But, as for many others, farming was at the core of Murray's being. The only life he ever imagined for himself involved sitting on his tractor with the spread of the land rolling beneath his wheels, working under a blazing prairie sunset, toiling the crop according to his own schedule. During the tough times, says Gail, he was in "absolute denial." He is still having some trouble adjusting.

Of necessity, every farmer is a jack of all trades. A farmer must be able to solder a piece of farm equipment, understand the agronomy of the soil, recognize an animal that is ill, do the books and finish off the day by hooking up to the Internet to check the state of world markets. These are, unfortunately, skills not much valued in our job-specific economy. Murray was lucky to have access to the burgeoning oil industry; other farmers have fewer options for life after farming.

Saskatchewan has the oldest population in Canada: nearly 15 percent are over the age of 65, and 7 percent are over 75. Farmers are no exception to the rule. In Saskatchewan, the average farmer is 58 years old. That means it is not uncommon to see producers in their seventies or even eighties shuffling around the farm. Retirement is not a viable option for many of the veterans of the agricultural wars. They have had to use their savings and equity, which were supposed to cushion them in their golden years, to support the farm. Their children have already moved on to nine-to-five, full-benefit, holiday-pay, employment-insurance-eligible jobs in the city.

Many farmers are not particularly well educated. A grade 10 education is typical. Unfortunately, education is crucial for success in the new knowledge-based economy. Saskatchewan already has the least educated workforce of any province in Canada. According to the 1998 Canada Labour Force Survey, just over 55 percent of employed workers in Saskatchewan have a high school diploma; that is 10 percentage points lower than Nova Scotia, British Columbia or Quebec. In February 2000 the *National Post* came up with a derogatory label that spoke volumes about Saskatchewan's preparedness for the new economy: "Mississippi of the North."

Given their options, many farmers simply soldier on. They try to cope in a world where they earn significantly less than the minimum wage and have to dip into the savings and equity they once thought would carry them through retirement. History and circumstance have equipped them with a stoic personality that ironically does them more damage than good. The countryside is populated with strong, silent, independent types—the kind who are unwilling to admit difficulty and ask for help. Many feel shame if they have to confess an inability to make it. This kind of determination served their forefathers well. In the homesteading days, to claim land, the homesteaders had to stay on their quarter-section for three years. Only four out of ten pioneers had the requisite stamina to stick with it. Doggedness was celebrated as the essential farm asset. Today it is a recipe for an increasingly outdated and irrelevant existence.

The modern family farm cannot sustain itself without off-farm income. A two-thousand-acre grain farm has become an after-work chore. In 1971 off-farm earnings accounted for about $3,000 of a farmer's annual income. Now, that amount is about ten times greater—crucial for any chance of survival on the farm. The Centre for Rural Studies and Enrichment found that in 1996, 77 percent of total average family farm income came from off-farm sources. "Farm families have no choice but to seek off-farm employment; in many cases, managing the farm is done after a full day's work off the farm," the Centre's *Compare the Share* report concluded.

Under the new order, the woman of the family invariably works off the farm. Gone are the days of the farm wife who spent her days cleaning the house, baking bread and collecting the garden harvest for the winter. Now she also drives a school bus, helps at the local nursing home or even works in the city.

Belinda Kerda lives the life of a typical modern farm woman. She farms with her husband, Rob, near Dominion City in southern Manitoba. She is up at five to make lunches for her four boys and husband, before setting off for a shift in the artificial insemination laboratory of a hog barn. Then it is home to work in the fields, make dinner and do what has to be done to hold the family together. She charges through a typically harried day with extraordinary cheer. She does all this by practising the power of positive thinking. When I ask her how important this season is for the family farm, the pretence falters, she bites her lower lip and says, "I don't want to think about that."

Farmers used to talk about passing on the family farm to the next generation. Having a family of four boys, like the Kerdas, was exceptionally good fortune; surely at least one of them would stay on the farm. Now, children are actively discouraged from dreaming of a farm life. Instead, just like in the city, parents try to steer their kids to university. Agriculture schools do attract interest, but almost all of the "aggies" in the class of 2000 at the universities of Saskatchewan and Manitoba plan to go where the money is and get jobs with agribusiness companies.

It is impossible to know how many farmers are leaving the land. For the most part they do so quietly, like Gail and Murray Forbes, renting out their land before finally selling. Unlike during the crisis of the 1980s, bankruptcy numbers are not sounding an alarm. Farmers are leaving the land without the showy foreclosure auctions of the 1980s or the shame of bankruptcy. However, some estimate that as many as 15,000 of Saskatchewan's 55,000 farmers will quit during this current "crisis." In just one week in 1999, eight families in the Swift Current area all decided enough was enough.

At what point is the critical mass lost—that magic number of people needed to maintain the service industries of nearby towns, the infrastructure of schools, hospitals and highways, the tax base, not to mention the stewardship of the land itself? The countryside between Winnipeg and Calgary is already dotted with abandoned homes, the once brightly painted siding quickly greying in the prairie sun and wind.

Farming today requires a skill not taught in any university—the ability to cope with nearly fatal levels of stress. It manifests itself in high divorce rates, depression, alcohol and drug abuse, family violence and suicide. In the spring of 1999, eleven farm families in southeastern Saskatchewan put themselves on a kind of suicide watch, calling each other every day to see if they were close to the breaking point. The Mennonite Central Committee reported in 2000 that it knew of eight suicides in Saskatchewan and another two in Manitoba. It is difficult to say how many other suicides were simply not logged as such.

The increasing reports of petty vandalism, crime and theft are an indication of the level of stress undermining the values that used to define rural life. Graffiti is appearing on grain bins; churches that have never been locked are now in danger of being ransacked; broken beer bottles appear with increasing frequency in roadside ditches. This is happening in a landscape where most farm families used to leave the back door open so any passing stranger could go in the house and use the phone.

There were no protests, road blockades or tractor demonstrations in the summer of 2000. But in Saskatchewan, no one interpreted the silence as a sign that the situation on the land was improving. Instead, the realization of the continuing crisis prompted a full-court press by various agencies and government departments in Saskatchewan. Twenty-two organizations, such as the Farm Health and Safety Council and the Agriculture Development and Diversification boards, came together in an attempt to devise strategies to help farmers. The Centre for Agricultural Medicine in Saskatoon aborted its planned program promoting skin health when it woke up to the recognition that its efforts in 2000 must be directed at farm stress. It called in Lynda Haverstock, clinical psychologist and former leader of the Saskatchewan Liberal Party, to assess the situation and make recommendations.

Haverstock knew that the "farm crisis" of the 1980s resulted in an increased number of suicides, accidents and injuries, visits to physicians, marital breakdown, family violence and the subsequent loss of family farms. She suspected the current economic situation would do more of the same. The Centre for Agricultural Medicine became the co-ordinator for an effort that included distributing twenty thousand copies of "A Rural Stress Toolbook" to farmers. This workbook was designed to get producers to assess their own stress levels by gauging their reaction to sixty-one differ-ent high-pressure situations and then learning some relaxation techniques to deal with their anxiety. Some farmers suggested that if the money for the initiative had been given directly to farmers in the form of financial aid, this would have gone further towards easing stress.

The Saskatchewan government also ran a Farm Stress Line where farmers could be counselled anonymously over the phone. The hotline received significantly more calls in 2000 than it had in the previous year. Calls in January 2000 were up 30 percent over 1999; calls in February were up 39 percent. By the summer, organizers were sure they would field more calls than the 1,800 they had received in 1999. More than 600 callers identified financial concerns as their primary reason for calling, while "stress burnout" prompted another 233 people to phone. There is at least one call a week from someone considering suicide.

Sharon (the farmer/counsellors here do not give their surnames) takes a lot of those calls. She farmed in northeastern Saskatchewan until two years ago. That was when she and her family decided they had had enough of hard work that returned next to nothing. She had been one of the stress hot-line's callers; now she says she is able to give a little back. Not surprisingly, she says, farmers frequently ask her a lot about what it was like to get out.

Sharon's husband was also lucky, finding work in the oil industry. The new working life, says Sharon, has been a relief. But she admits it is hard to leave the farm behind. One thing she knows for certain is that they will never move to the city. For now they live in a cottage, so they can still taste the rural air.

Her in-laws were disappointed to see the family quit. "Our parents prob-ably would have hung in there," says Sharon, in reference to the dogged determination of many earlier generations of farmers. The next generation felt let down too. Her kids idealistically talked about carrying on the family farm—even though they are grown up and pursuing their own careers. In the end, neither stoicism nor romance could save this family farm.

•  •  •

The rural infrastructure of the grain-handling system, which was so laboriously developed over a century, has disintegrated along with the family farm. Elevators were initially built every 15 kilometres along rail lines that ran like veins carrying the essential lifeblood throughout the Prairies. More than 5,700 elevators stood in the West in 1933, 3,000 of them in Saskatchewan. Towns like Kane grew up around them. Now there are only 600 elevators left—and the number drops every week. In place of the short trip of old, farmers now have to truck grain 80 kilometres or more to a concrete superelevator. And the elevator towns, many having already seen their school and hospital close, have now lost their economic heart as well.

Something about prairie grain elevators touches our emotions. They are much more than mere storage containers with the capacity to weigh, clean and load grain; they are a potent symbol of the social and economic lifeblood of the region. Many children's picture books feature the slope-shouldered lines of the prairie sentinels, silhouetted against a sunset or against wheat-field gold. Grain elevators have inspired all kinds of arts and crafts; they have been immortalized in stained glass, landscape painting and wood carving.

But the real thing is disappearing. The demolition of an elevator tugs at some memory, some emotion, that lies within each of us, no matter how distant our connection to the land. Perhaps part of our reaction is shock at the ease with which an elevator is flattened. An ordinary caterpillar claws at one side of the base of the structure. The massive building, built by hand with heavy timbers a hundred years ago, somehow—impossibly—balances on its good side, a chewed hole exposing its innards. Then the cat gently pushes on the whole section, much as a lumberjack would fell a tree. The structure tips over in a cloud of dust, a century of grain scatterings and memories crumbling to the ground and exploding into the air. There are always onlookers—photographers, the locals, the curious, the disappointed—when history comes crashing down.

The classic elevators have become so rare that the town of Inglis in northwestern Manitoba has won historic designation and the accompanying funding for its row of five grain elevators. The Inglis elevators technically have a historic value equivalent to Louisbourg or the Plains of Abraham. The elevators are all closed now, and so is the rail line that once serviced them. Fortunately, someone with foresight got to them before the grain companies were able to knock them down like a row of dominoes. They stand cheek by jowl, a remembrance of the past, of a time when Inglis warranted the competitive energies of five elevators. The hope is that tourists will take the detour to Inglis to see what agriculture was once all about. The farmers who still work in the area now have to truck their grain past the "historic site" to a concrete version of progress 30 kilometres away.

Less visible but just as significant to the grain-handling of the past was the network of rail lines that connected the prairie elevators to distant ports. Branch lines became less necessary as trucks appeared on the scene that could ship directly to grain-handling facilities on the main line. For decades, branch lines were politically protected by federal policy. Canada's two railways, Canadian National and Canadian Pacific, were allowed to abandon only 4 percent of their system each year. The brakes came off in 1995, when the federal Liberal government killed the Crow benefit—the Western Grain Transportation Act (WGTA)—which set freight rates along with service and infrastructure levels. Canada had already lost 17 percent of its branch lines from 1968 to 1995. Now the two major railways identified a further 20 percent of lines they intended to discontinue while they maintained the high traffic main line and secondary lines. By the end of the century the Prairies had lost 30,000 kilometres of branch lines.

The changes to government legislation accelerated the rationalization of the two main railways and shifted the economic gain from farmers to the railways. In 1995 CN suffered a loss of more than $1 million. By the next year, after a round of downsizing, it logged a profit of $142 million. CP's fortunes were just as good. In 1995 it registered a loss of $592 million; in 1996 and 1997 it turned profits in excess of $400 million. Nearly one hundred years ago, prairie farmers rebelled against the railways for much less provocation.

There was one tiny bit of consolation for farmers: the railways started to sell some branch lines rather than just tearing them up and leaving untended gravel paths in their wake. For example, the fate of four lines—550 kilometres through the plains south of Swift Current—had been in doubt for years as grain companies diverted grain to their big new terminals along CP's rail line to the north. A long and vigorous campaign by local farmers and communities to retain rail service evidently persuaded CP to sell the lines to a homegrown company.

The essential service industries of rural life are disappearing along with the infrastructure of the grain-handling system. Bank branches, which used to serve all but the smallest towns have closed. Between 1990 and 2000, the five major banks closed fifty branches in the Prairie provinces. Many Canadians, both rural and urban, have had to deal with the disappointment of losing the convenience of a local branch, but small towns in Western Canada have had to cope with the virtual death sentence that comes with the loss of a bank.

In the 1980s the banks were criticized for pushing farmers into bankruptcy by recalling loans made at staggering interest rates. Now the banks are searching for ways to blunt the pain. In fact, the Farm Debt Moratorium Board reports that it is not banks that are demanding payment these days; it is farm equipment companies. The Bank of Montreal set new cooperative standards by reaching an agreement with the credit unions of the Prairie provinces, whereby the bank closed some of its branches and passed the accounts on to the credit unions. Richard Nakoneczny of Credit Union Central in Manitoba says credit unions are perhaps better suited for today's agricultural community because they have a different definition of "profit." Nakoneczny says that, far from closing branches, credit unions are opening new operations, even if only part-time branches in smaller towns. Credit unions across the Prairie provinces started up 387 operations in the 1990s. Saskatchewan, however, took a hit, losing 86 of the 757 credit societies it had at the start of the decade.

Canada Post rationalized savagely in the late 1980s and early 1990s, closing more than 1,300 post offices, many in small rural towns. The move provoked a furious backlash by a movement that called itself Rural

Dignity. That in turn led to a moratorium on branch closings. In 1995 a review of the system held public hearings and commissioned research that proved the obvious: "the post office is a social hub of small towns, and that mail service is a vital communications link." Decima Research did a survey for the review that found that 80 percent of respondents in communities of less than ten thousand agreed "when a post office closes, the community it used to serve loses some of its identity and distinctiveness." It was too late for many towns, but Canada Post agreed that no more of its four thousand rural branches would be cut and that the kind of delivery standards common to big cities would also apply to smaller rural communities.

Canada's health care system, established by Saskatchewan's own Tommy Douglas, is hugely troubled even in its birthplace. One study claimed that an ill person in Ontario will get to see a specialist fifty days before a similarly ill person in Saskatchewan. There was a brutal rural hospital rationalization in Saskatchewan in the early 1990s that left only one in three hospitals open. The Plains Hospital in the south end of Regina was closed even though it was where most rural patients were referred. Today, emergency wards at rural facilities are rarely open past midnight. A general practitioner is a rare commodity in Canada's small towns. There is a joke going around in Saskatchewan that people don't die in towns that have no doctors, so being doctorless has become a claim to fame of sorts. Of course, people do not generally die at home; they invariably go where the health care is, which means they die in the larger town that merits the hospital.

Schools are another key indicator of a community's health. Rural kids now routinely have to travel two hours a day to get to and from school. When a school cannot come up with enough students even by plumbing the far-flung farming community, the prospect is grim. There is no future in an area lacking young families.

It takes an extraordinary resolve to fight that sense of inevitability. The town of Inwood, population seventy-five, is one of the rare communities that has been able to marshal its energies to stop what might have seemed like irreversible decline. Inwood School, in the Interlake of Manitoba, used to bus its senior-high students 20 kilometres to the modern collegiate in the town of Tuelon. The arrival of principal Thomas Kowalchuk in Inwood changed all that. He held back the students in grade 10 to form the nucleus for Inwood's new high school program. By 1999 those five students were ready to graduate. It may have been the smallest in the country, but the town of Inwood held its first graduation in thirty years. Everyone in town came to the community hall where the graduation services were held in tribute to the five grads and the town itself. Inwood had reclaimed its high school and a piece of its past. Change was apparently not as inevitable as it seemed.

But many rural people have only themselves to blame when local stores, co-ops, farm machinery dealers and garages disappear. Many would rather drive the 30, 50 or 70 kilometres to a franchise operation in a distant town than shop in the old local hardware store. Driving has become the new way of life in the rural West, although the highways are beginning to buckle under the strain of grain trucks rumbling past towns on their way to "high-efficiency" grain terminals elsewhere.

Bob Langdon is the Lutheran minister in Earl Grey, a community of three hundred about 70 kilometres northeast of Regina. It is nestled in rolling country with bush and bluff, well suited to mixed farming. Sheep, a rare sight on the Canadian Prairies, are visible as smudgy white dots in the pastures. Thanks to the diversity of their mixed operations, farmers here are not fatally dependent on falling grain prices. And the town itself is close enough to Regina to be considered a bedroom community.

Nevertheless, Langdon believes the crumbling agricultural economy is the single biggest stress on his congregation. He says farmers have no confidence in the business or government—"zero confidence," he says to emphasize the point. Those who have stayed on the land have become very bitter. He says one farmer told him he was hoping for hail so he would be able to collect crop insurance. As a minister, Langdon has had to counsel farmers on the growing incidence of abuse and family discord, and on the rash of problem drinking that seems to have hit the community. Several farmers have been plagued with thoughts of suicide. Most importantly, Langdon says farmers have to learn not to become too attached to the land. It is ironic, because love of the land is what conserved and enhanced the soil to the point where it was able to create a productive agriculture.

"There is a lot of pain, but it is under the surface now," he says. He likens the situation to an active volcano, burbling and hissing and ready to erupt. Will it explode or implode? Will the trails of lava score Canada forever? He does not know, but he is sure a "judgment," so to speak, will come. If farmers survive this time, he says it will become "their Depression," worthy of the same kind of stories and mythology that defined those earlier days.

Langdon has a unique perspective on agriculture because he was once a farmer himself. He ran a farm northwest of Moose Jaw for thirty years. After two bad years in a row he had what he calls a nervous breakdown. He passed the farm on to his two sons and took the unusual step of starting seminary school. He graduated in 1993 at the age of fifty-five.

These days, the farmer turned preacher drives 3,000 kilometres a month in his effort to service his widely dispersed parishioners. Like most rural clergy he has to do double-duty, ministering to the church and congregation at Southey as well. He does it, quoting early twentieth-century Swiss Protestant theologian Karl Barth, by "holding a bible in one hand and a newspaper in the other." Both communities are going through a quiet panic as a result of the transformation in farming. In Earl Grey the school is under threat of closing and there is no physician. But, despite the challenges, Langdon says his calling now is blessed compared with his previous life in agriculture. "It just gives me the chills to think of farming now."

• • •

The depopulation of the Canadian West involves more than the loss of a romantic mythology from our past; there are also economic repercussions for those who live far from the troubles. Cities are invariably stuck with absorbing the ex-farmers. There has been no effort to quantify the public cost of farmers leaving their way of life, but it is fair to assume that welfare and/or job retraining will be involved in many cases.

There is a school of thought that promotes the idea of "exit programs." Federal and provincial governments are quietly developing such programs to help farmers "exit'" agriculture for greener, often urban, pastures. It is not a politically popular idea in a country where keeping farmers on the land is a sacred cow. But University of Manitoba agricultural economist Daryl Kraft, for one, says that basic human decency demands there be government supports to help farmers make the transition out of the business. He says many producers he sees have the skills to become effective, productive members of Canadian society. As an example he mentions a one-time farmer who now runs a cellphone franchise.

Exit programs will not be helpful in regions that do not have jobs, however. There are simply not enough new jobs being created in places like Saskatchewan to accommodate farmers leaving the land. In 1999 Saskatchewan produced about twenty-nine thousand new jobs, about half the number generated in neighbouring Manitoba and considerably fewer than P.E.I., which has only one-tenth of Saskatchewan's population. Saskatchewan's high-growth industries like uranium and potash mining are capital-intensive but employ few people. The province has a misleadingly low unemployment rate—less than 6 percent—largely because so many people leave the province in search of work. At one time Saskatchewan exported wheat; now it exports people.

Some observers are offended by the notion of government applying its energies to helping farmers leave the business. Clay Gilson, professor emeritus of agricultural economics at the University of Manitoba and long-time government adviser, passed away suddenly in the spring of 2000. In an interview just before his death, his lips tightened noticeably when he spoke about transition programs. Although he acknowledged it is too late for many communities, like the one he grew up in, he said developing transition programs for farmers is a sign of giving up on agriculture. "We should stop talking about exit strategies. Exit programs are a way of ignoring the plight on the farm. The challenge," he said, "is to find a way to preserve the family farm even in the face of the current structural crisis."

Prairie towns like Readlyn and Kane are little more than road signs today as farmers give up their way of life in the face of unmanageable forces. Bob Langdon, Gail Forbes and Sharon, the stress-hotline counsellor, are among those who have "exited" agriculture, leaving the stress of their farming days behind. Their faces present the new look of modern agriculture. But although relief from pressure has quickened their smiles, they still cannot quite believe the government let them go. They ask in a virtual chorus: if family farmers like ourselves are pushed out, who will take care of the land?

*Four*

# The Cost of Doing Business

*June 3, 2000*

*The Wielers are up at 5 a.m. By virtue of being eight, Thomas gets to sleep in. So does Philip as the designated babysitter. But for Nicholas, Lorna and Gary there is time only for a quick bite before heading out to the canola field. The morning is blessed with an unearthly calm, the calm that comes just after dawn. By midday the prairie winds will blow again, just like they have for the past week. The sky is clear now, but by afternoon the rain clouds will open up, leaving the fields of southern Manitoba sodden.*

*The Wielers have to spray their Roundup Ready canola with Roundup. For the past week either wind or rain has kept them from the field. The canola is now about thirteen centimetres tall, and weeds are beginning to compete with the tiny plantlets for soil and sun. It is high time for the spraying — it should have been done a week ago. Gary Wieler has no experience to draw on when it comes to this genetically modified variety of*

63

*canola. Roundup Ready canola has been commercially available for three years now, but this is the Wielers' first attempt. The canola has been spliced with a gene from another organism that is resistant to Monsanto's popular herbicide. In theory, within three days, the wild oats, the mustard and everything else touched by the Roundup will wither—that is, except for the gene-spliced canola armed with a new resistant gene. It will stand bright and green in a sea of shrivelled, greying weeds.*

*Gary's chemical spray system is very basic. There is no global position-ing satellite system here or even a specialized hi-boy sprayer. Instead, he uses a rudimentary contraption. A big plastic tank sits behind the tractor and feeds the sprinkler-like nozzles along the sixty-eight-foot-wide rig. The sprayer is twenty years old, but the tank is brand-new. Gary bought it for $650 last week when the old tank sprang a leak, then another.*

*Gary needs Lorna and Nicholas to help direct him. This spraying process is a low-cost option, but it carries high labour requirements. If Gary crosses his path as he goes up and down the field, some strips will receive too much herbicide, others not enough. The mistakes will not be apparent until later, when the multicoloured weeds infest the field in a curious zebra pattern.*

*Gary lays out a grid of orange flags across the field by criss-crossing the 160 acres on the all-terrain four-wheeler, planting little wire stakes topped with plastic banners every fifteen metres. He lines up his row of stakes with Lorna and Nicholas, who stand at twenty-one-metre inter-vals along the edges of the field. Then, with his tank full of Roundup hooked up, Gary carefully follows the orange markers.*

*The procedure takes all morning. Then the sprayer is cleaned and tucked away in the farthest corner of the yard, behind the grain bins, to discourage curious kids. The weary family opts for an early lunch, or din-ner as it is often called in the country. Today the order comes for the quickest thing possible: ham sandwiches that the boys build themselves, and a big bag of chips plopped on the table. Fortified from lunch and armed with rubber gloves and the four-wheeler, Lorna and Nicholas head out again to pluck the flags out of the soil.*

## The Cost of Doing Business

*That just about completes the second major requirement of modern, industrialized agriculture on the Wieler farm. Except for a field of peas, the herbicide spraying is done. The Wielers finished treating their four hundred acres of wheat on Monday with a tank mixture of Target and Horizon chemicals to combat the broadleaf weeds and wild oats. The wheat is now about fifteen centimetres tall, quivering in the beginnings of a prairie breeze. It takes a practised eye to see the weeds. They are mere shoots, curling twisted broadleaf and stringy slender fronds. The wild oats are erupting with extra energy because Gary did not spray for them last year and this year's early seeding encouraged their growth.*

*It has been tricky getting the spraying done. Then again, it always is. On average there are about eight good "spray" days in southern Manitoba, and this year has been no different. Every time Gary got set up for the chemical application, the wind would suddenly change. He had to stop spraying altogether for two days to avoid drift into other fields. "We have to look out for the neighbours," he explains.*

*Lorna has carefully placed the bills for the chemicals on the office desk. They total $14,000 and are all due within thirty days. It will take some inventive juggling to pay those bills in time. Perhaps the Wielers will have to access the $10,000 operating loan they collected from the bank this spring. Or they may have to dip into their Net Income Stabilization Account—a producer and government funded program to help stabilize incomes. Or they could draw some extra revenue from some odd jobs or from Lorna's cleaning business. On Wednesday, Lorna and Gary intend to apply for a position as a custodial/cleaning team for the Roland elementary school.*

*It comes as no surprise that the Wielers don't much like the chemical bills. But they are also uncomfortable with the widespread chemical use for philosophical reasons. They have explored the idea of going organic but found it would be difficult to earn organic certification in an area where conventional grain farming, with its chemical use, is well entrenched. As on many farms, the garden intended to serve the household's needs never sees any sort of pesticide. If the striped, voracious potato beetles attack Lorna's garden crop, she will commission one of the boys to pick them off by hand or she will resort to a home recipe and douse the bugs with a rhubarb-based brew. She has no proof that pesticides leave any kind of residue, but just to be safe she scrubs her store-bought apples with vegetable and fruit soap until the waxy finish disappears down the drain.*

*"Nobody likes to spray," Gary adds matter-of-factly. "We try to keep it to a minimum." But he acknowledges that a farmer must use herbicides to remain competitive in today's industrial agriculture. Gary says it all comes down to how much a farmer can tolerate seeing even a single weed amongst the broad stretches of their crops. In the past week, Lorna says, the skies over southern Manitoba were alive with planes spraying the crops from the air—a sign of farmers who cannot abide any weeds. Gary Wieler says he has learned to accept a few weeds. He prefers to spray late, not out of any noble environmental concern but because he hopes to get by with paying for only one spraying.*

*The prairie wind is beginning to roll in from the northwest when I leave the Wielers for my re-entry into city life. A black, moisture-laden cloud is not far behind. The window for spraying is about to close.*

*As I head along the gravel road to Highway 23, a white-tailed deer bounds alongside, keeping pace with my car. Then it speeds ahead, sprints over the road and across the fields into the distance, oblivious to the chemical rain that came before it.*

&. For the Wielers, chemical spraying is a necessary evil of today's industrial agriculture system. It plays a crucial part in keeping yields up—in remaining competitive. As it is with other farmers, the cost of chemical fertilizers, herbicides and pesticides is the Wielers' single largest operating expense.

Chemicals and farm equipment are the essential "inputs" of the industrial model of agriculture practised in the developed world. "Inputs" is, in fact, an industrial term. In its early days agriculture largely defied industrialization. It was difficult to manage agricultural biology by using the techniques that had created smokestacks, assembly lines and factories. But by the 1920s the mechanized tractor was beginning to be seen on the farm landscape. Mechanization, new seed varieties and new chemicals finally managed to bend nature into yet another industrial system.

What we have now is a biological assembly line, with inputs coming in one side and commodities going out the other. The development of bigger, more intensive systems on the farm, following the principles of modern industrial production, resulted in total industrialization by the end of the twentieth century. Huge tracts of land were farmed with the aid of machines and chemicals in a system that closely resembled an open-air factory. Industrialization was particularly obvious in animal agriculture, where animals were raised in confinement barns that from the outside looked like factories that had strayed into an isolated rural setting.

Although nature still exerts its power from time to time, farming in the developed world now takes its cue from industry and manufacturing rather than the traditional roots of agriculture. This industrialization has succeeded at lifting both rural and urban society out of subsistence living. It is the huge productivity gains that have lowered food prices to the point where Canadians spend such a small part of their incomes on groceries. But industrialization has achieved these successes at the expense of the people who live on the land. Henry Ford once observed that the biggest problem with running a factory is that you have to hire whole people when all you need is two hands. In agriculture it took fewer people to run the new, highly productive industrial system. Many of those who farmed simply became redundant.

Farmers are leaving the land these days in ever-increasing numbers because of the marriage of low commodity prices and high input costs. It is often said that farm incomes are low because subsidies paid to farmers in other countries increase production, which in turn lowers commodity prices. But farm incomes have fallen to Depression levels not just because of low commodity prices but also because of rising costs. Between 1974 and 2000 gross farm incomes actually tripled, rising from $9 billion to

$29 billion. However, any gains farmers might have made were wiped out by a staggering increase in the cost of running the farm. Between 1947 and 1997 prices for wheat seed rose 35 percent and seed corn went up 69 percent. In the same period the price of a tractor rose 481 percent. Since 1975, farmers' input costs have climbed more than four times. It is accepted thinking on the modern farm that these inputs are all essential. It is no wonder that farmers overwhelmingly identify high input costs as the number-one obstacle to achieving a profit on the farm.

In the United States, farmers spend about $10.5 billion a year on chemicals, $9.4 billion on farm equipment and $3 billion on seeds for major crops. There is no comparable national monitoring of input prices and farm expenses in Canada. Statistics Canada used to check on price increases four times a year, with Agriculture and Agri-Food Canada financing that research to the tune of about $1 million a year. Then, in 1999, the financing and the work came to an abrupt end. Now, Statistics Canada offers a yearly farm input price index that provides significantly less detail. That index shows that for every $100 farmers spent on seeds, fertilizers, chemicals and fuel in 1992, they paid $121.60 in 1999.

The Alberta government is the only provincial government that reviews input prices. It found that equipment costs rose by 6.6 percent in just one year. A typical self-propelled combine cost $210,000 in 1999, compared with $198,000 the previous year. Alberta Agriculture, Food and Rural Development also found that the price of a 100-kilogram bag of treated canola seed had risen 20.9 percent in the same year. Diesel fuel, which cost $27.45 per 100 litres in July 1999, cost $40.51 in July 2000.

The Centre for Rural Studies and Enrichment, a research and development office found in the heart of small-town Saskatchewan, undertook a study in the late 1990s to assess where the retail food dollars were going. *Compare the Share* found that farm input costs increased by 16.5 percent during the 1980s while farm product prices rose only 0.2 percent. During the 1990s farm input costs rose even more—by as much as 28.9 percent. Between 1986 and 1998 machinery costs went up as much as 56 percent, fertilizers 21 percent, pesticides 30.2 percent, seed 28.9 percent, feed 16.8

percent. In the same period, farmers earned a little more from what they produced—7.9 percent more. Clearly, that was nowhere near enough to offset the rising input costs.

The first "input" to arrive on the Canadian farm was the tractor. In the pre-Depression glory days of prairie grain agriculture, the farm demanded pure physical brawn. The toil required of a prairie farmer would twist the back, spring sweat on a furrowed brow, blister overworked hands. The best strategy for a farmer of that time was to have a large family, where each child could be counted on to feed the chickens, direct the oxen at seeding or stook the sheaves of grain. With this kind of unpaid labour a farm could maintain ten people for a year. But the physical costs were huge. A pioneer farmer is said to have trudged 5,280 miles (8,497 kilometres) behind a plough or horse in working a single section.

Then along came liberation: the tractor. The tractor was the symbol of new agrarian mechanization and the first step along the path to industrialization. In one generation, from 1920 to 1950, the tractor transformed the farm, exchanging dependence on draft animals for dependence on mechanical power. It forced farmers to alter the production techniques they had perfected and begin experimenting with new strategies. All around them farmers could see a society that was being transformed by machines. And they were eager to become part of the revolution. A tractor on the farm proudly proclaimed to the world that the farmer was progressive and up-to-date.

At first, mechanization came slowly, as equipment broke down easily but could not be that readily fixed. And the cost of the new industrialization seemed prohibitive compared with the expense of feeding a couple of horses. But for many farmers the tractor represented the emancipation from drudgery. It promised something they had never known before: free time. Individual farmers soon became capable of handling larger acreages. About three hundred acres had seemed the optimum in the pre-tractor days; with mechanization, about a thousand acres became the norm. In

1930 it took an hour of farm labour to produce a single bushel of grain; today that bushel is generated in less than a minute.

However, mechanization was a double-sided coin. On one side it offered relief from the grind of farm toil, but on the other side it forced many farmers off the land by introducing crippling new input costs and creating oversupplies. The tractor was the means that allowed production to expand while the labour supply shrank.

With the arrival of the high-priced tractor, many farmers stepped into indebtedness for the first time. Much as they are now, early farmers were forced to borrow money to purchase up-to-date equipment. That indebtedness intensified their vulnerability to the downside of cyclical crop prices. As a result, farmers were often unable to meet their bank payments. Foreclosures were anything but rare.

With mechanization, it also cost much more to begin farming. In 1952 the cost of a tractor, equipment and other purchases necessary to start in the business were far greater than the potential life savings of the average individual. The traditional agricultural ladder by which an energetic young farmer could pull himself up was destroyed. Today that situation is even more pronounced. The high cost of start-ups explains why there are so few young farmers on the rural landscape.

Few commercial farms operated long without mortgage encumbrances. Mechanization and expansion were two mutually complementary trends—and both required capital. A larger scale promised more rewards, but it also placed the farmer's entire equity in jeopardy. The tractor had promised more leisure, but "saved" time often had to be reinvested to pay off the mortgage.

Ironically, mechanization was a benefit that would harm many farmers. It caused overproduction, which increased supplies and in turn lowered commodity prices. By displacing animal power, farm equipment prompted millions of acres to be released from the requirement to grow feed for draft horses and oxen. One-quarter of a typical early producer's land had been dedicated to growing food for his animals; now all that land began producing crops for human consumption. The tractor further increased crop yields by granting producers a little more time and opportunity to be productive. With a tractor, for example, the harvest might be completed before that drenching storm on the horizon arrived. Hours of work were extended past sundown or past the time draft animals would have been tired.

Mechanization sharply reduced the requirement for labour in the farm fields of the country. The total amount of farm labour displaced by the arrival of the tractor in the United States between 1909 and 1938 is estimated at 785 billion person-hours a year—about 10 percent of the labour required for annual crop production. The introduction of the power-lift alone cut one million person-hours of work a year. A 1941 survey reported that "almost every farmer who migrated to the city blamed the tractor for his fate."

And mechanization changed the social framework for those left on the land. There was no longer an economic argument for large families. The tractor was much more efficient than another child could ever be.

Advances in farm equipment have continued to improve the technology on the farm and at the same time tax the financial capabilities of farm families. The Farm Debt Mediation Service, the agency that works to help farmers restructure their debt in order to avoid bankruptcy, reports that it is farm equipment dealers that most often call for payment of loans, thus forcing farmers into debt mediation. Dean Vey, the general manager of the mediation service, says implement dealers often move on farmers even if they have missed just one payment. In 1999/2000, 4,564 actions were initiated by equipment dealers for non-payment of loans, compared with just 260 by banks and credit unions.

The equipment dealers are aggressive in trying to get payment, yet they are equally forceful in making the original sale. Promotional material boasts of implements "that will make the farm pay." There are now specialized machines for just about every task on the farm. John Deere, the major farm implement manufacturer in North America, offers dozens of tractors, combines and every imaginable piece of farm equipment. A new combine can cost as much as $260,000. The Enns Brothers

John Deere dealership in Morris, just 30 kilometres from the Wieler farm, reported that in 2000 it sold five 425-horsepower tractors on tracks, like the equipment seen in the construction industry, for $250,000 each and eight of the massive combines worth more than $250,000. Some farmers in the fertile watershed of the Red River valley are clearly doing well. But even with these kinds of sales, the dealership's general manager, Murray Thompson, says commodity prices have to come up if the farm equipment business is to manage. What happens if they stay down? "I don't even want to think about it," he says.

For many farmers, new is not an option. That is why there is a brisk trade in used equipment. But even second-hand prices are enough to take your breath away. In a recent edition of the *Western Producer*, farmers offered a 1988 combine for sale, with 2,492 hours of service on it, for $67,000, or a 1994 combine for $135,000. The prices of mechanization make it clear why farmers like Gary Wieler have to look past the new and the shiny . . . and make do one more year with the equipment they can afford.

Robert and Judith Harrison have the love-hate relationship with their equipment that is typical of Canadian farmers. They love the power, efficiency and specialization that farm equipment offers. But they hate the price of it.

There is no doubt that machines have transformed life for the Harrisons on their farm west of Carmen, Manitoba. The two-storey house is essentially the same as it was in Robert's father's day, but everything else on this century-old farm has changed dramatically.

In 1971, when Robert and Judith took over, the farm was just four hundred acres. Harvesting was usually contracted out to custom combining operations. Otherwise, Robert's father had to manage with a 65-horsepower tractor. "Now, anything less than 150-horse is considered a toy," says Robert, quantifying the change.

Like many of their generation, Robert and Judith set out to make the farm bigger, more modern. That called for mechanization. They bought their first rotary combine in 1977, then traded it in for a newer version three years later. That one, along with $11,000, bought them another new one after three years, and *that* one was traded in for the fourth generation for just $17,000. An investment tax deduction made the regular upgrading of combines feasible. But the cycle stopped in 1985 after a couple of bad crop years. Now the Harrisons just make do with the old; they still have that combine they bought in 1985. If they wanted a brand-new combine now, it would cost them $150,000 along with the trade-in, and that is out of their reach. "The equipment is like me—aging," says sixty-three-year-old Robert with a laugh.

Today the Harrisons seed 1,300 acres of corn, wheat and edible beans. They could not have developed an operation of this size without buying every imaginable implement to make their work a little easier. This year they bought a new corn header, a machine that slices the heads off the plants during harvest. It lists for $38,000. Robert does not even want to think about what he might have spent in fuel over the years. "Diesel fuel is over ten times what it was in 1954," he says reflectively.

Like farmers across the Prairies, the Harrisons are quick to voice opinions about freight rates, grain-handling companies or rural depopulation. But they do not question the mechanization that has transformed their lives. Although they may complain about the high cost of the technology, they are convinced that becoming bigger has made their farm viable—a farm they hope they can pass on to the next generation.


While mechanization has been responsible for much of the transformation in modern agriculture, the truly astounding increases in productivity were sparked by what has been referred to as the Green Revolution or, in less complimentary terms, chemical agriculture. The 1960s witnessed significant new developments in breeding and chemicals that transformed agriculture once and for all into a big business. The Green Revolution spawned new hybrids—virtual miracle crops—that used nutrients more efficiently, prompting higher yields. Coupled with mechanization and the introduction of chemical fertilizers, fungicides, herbicides and pesticides, a new hyperactive agriculture was born. It essentially tripled yields of corn, rice and wheat between 1950 and 1980.

Modern North American farmers are hugely dependent on chemicals. Fields are prepared by chemical fertilizers, then swept clean of bugs and weeds by chemical pesticides. Disease often demands yet another chemical solution. Chemicals are now being used as desiccants to replace the old-fashioned requirement for swathing before harvest. The bigger a farm gets, the more it has to spend on chemicals and equipment.

The appetite for chemical solutions has made North America the world's largest regional market for pesticide and fertilizer sales. The U.S. market for farm chemicals reached a high of $10.4 billion in 1995, and it is expected that agrochemical purchases grew by six percent each year through 2001.

The World Wildlife Fund estimates that there are about six thousand pesticide products registered for use in Canada. The WWF has also calculated that at least 50 million kilograms of herbicides, insecticides and fungicides are used in Canada each year, at a reported value of one billion dollars. Regrettably, definitive numbers on chemical sales are not available from either the companies that produce them nor the governments that monitor those sales. Both claim that such details are proprietary corporate information.

Farmers today generally seem to accept the chemical use that industrialization has prescribed for them. But they are annoyed with the rising costs—and even more annoyed when they hear how prices jump without apparent justification. The cost of anhydrous ammonia is a good example. This chemical, a source of nitrogen, is the fertilizer of choice for many fields. It is applied in the fall before the winter's numbness sets in. It is made with natural gas. A review by the National Farmers Union found that anhydrous costs rose 41 percent between 1994 and 1998, even though natural gas prices fell 16 percent in the same period.

Clearly, anhydrous ammonia producers did not raise the price of the fertilizer because of rising gas prices. Nor could rising labour costs be blamed for the galloping charges. In fact, labour costs had remained relatively stable during that time. The National Farmers Union concluded that fertilizer prices rose because wheat prices rose.

Anhydrous ammonia prices kept pace with wheat prices in the 1994–95 and 1995–96 crop years. Unfortunately, when the price of wheat and other commodities subsequently dropped, anhydrous ammonia prices did not immediately follow suit. Suppliers and distributors were evidently eager to take advantage of good markets, less eager to lower their prices when times were tough. "Farmers, lacking market power and dependent on purchased fertilizer, have few options but to pay the price," the NFU wrote in its submission to the July 1998 meeting of federal and provincial agriculture ministers. A classic case of what the market will bear.

In the fall of 2000 natural gas rose again significantly, and anhydrous ammonia prices rose in step. The cost of the fertilizer climbed 40 percent—that is, 22 cents for a pound of nitrogen compared with 16 cents a pound in 1999. This time prices rose despite what the market would bear.

It may be tempting to dismiss increasing input costs as corporate greed in action. Yet one of the biggest costs facing farmers— about 25 percent of what they have to pay out each year—is due to action by the federal government, not the private sector. At issue is the fact that government has virtually eliminated all supports that used to cushion farmers against the high cost of shipping their grain to ports for export.

The labyrinthine details of the "Crow rate" and its successors are enough to clear a room when the topic is raised. But it has been regarded as a birthright by Western farmers since 1897. The elimination of the

Crow benefit on August 1, 1995, marked a momentous shift in Canadian agriculture. Without many Canadians noticing, Jean Chrétien's Liberal administration ended a century-old policy of subsidizing the shipment of prairie grain to port.

The Crowsnest Pass rate, as it was called, began in the late nineteenth century as part of a deal with the Canadian Pacific Railway to help it build a rail link through the Crowsnest Pass in the Rockies and into southeastern British Columbia. It promised prairie settlers artificially low freight rates "in perpetuity." By the 1970s Canada's two railways, CP and CN, were complaining bitterly that they were losing hundreds of millions of dollars each year and that vital rail improvements were being neglected as a result. Some farm economists also argued the subsidy skewed agriculture away from value-added processing. They said the freight subsidies had long encouraged raw grain to be shipped offshore, whereas the marketplace would have advanced livestock production or other value-added activities by making it cheaper to keep unprocessed grain at home.

So the Liberal government finally agreed in 1983 to adjust this linchpin in the Western Canadian economy. Transport ministers Jean-Luc Pepin and, later, Lloyd Axworthy scrapped the historic Crow rate and replaced it with the Western Grain Transportation Act (WGTA), under which prairie producers would be protected from rising freight rates and excessive inflation by a "safety net." While rates for farmers would rise somewhat—from 13 cents a bushel to 25 cents a bushel over four years—they would not rise to market levels. The railways were to be paid a "Crow benefit" worth $658.6 million a year that would make up for the cap on producer contributions. This marked the beginning of the end of the fixed-shipping-cost era of Western grain production.

Once the initial blood had been drawn, the grain-handling system was suddenly open to assault. Brian Mulroney's Tories cut the level of the subsidy paid to the railways under the Crow benefit. Then, Jean Chrétien's Liberals administered the final blow. Amid the frugal cost-cutting times of the mid-1990s the government announced the total elimination of the Crow benefit to the railways. Farmers would have to pay the entire commercial rate of shipping their grain to port, subject to an annual cap on rates set by the Canadian Transportation Agency.

From the government's perspective, ending the Crow benefit would diversify prairie agriculture by encouraging value-added sectors like canola crushing and cattle farming. It would also eliminate what some on the international stage viewed as an export subsidy. Opponents of the policy shift felt it would give too much power to the railways and send transportation costs sky-high.

After killing the Crow benefit in 1995, the Liberal government spent years tinkering with the grain-handling system in an effort to appease aggrieved farm groups. It appointed retired Supreme Court judge Willard Estey in 1998 to conduct a one-year review of the handling and transportation system. He laid out a plan for a much more market-driven scheme, even recommending the Canadian Wheat Board's role in transporting grain be eliminated and it simply act as a "port buyer"; it would then become the job of the grain companies and the railways to get the right grain to port at the right time. Estey also recommended removing the cap on rates in exchange for a promise from the railways to reduce the total freight bill over a set number of years.

Transport Minister David Collenette announced the federal government would implement the Estey report, minus the controversial limitations to the Wheat Board. He appointed retired civil servant Arthur Kroeger to determine how the changes should be brought about.

In the spring of 2000 the Canadian Transportation Agency complicated the mix still further by announcing it would allow farmers' freight rates to rise by 4.5 percent. That would cost a farmer in central Saskatchewan shipping to the west coast an extra $1.45 per tonne of grain. The CTA said it was legally obligated to announce the maximum rate that railways could charge for the new crop year. It made this calculation based on higher costs of fuel, labour, material and capital, but it did not take into account that both railways had just announced healthy first-quarter profits.

The prospect of a sanctioned rate increase coming in the midst of anticipated reform horrified farm groups. Opponents said the rate-setting mechanism was flawed and that grain transportation reform must begin immediately. The federal government then confused agricultural observers by ignoring what had been its stated intention, to deregulate the system. Instead, it did an about-face and began implementing policies that seemed to assist Western farmers. The federal cabinet began by assuring producers that the CTA freight increases would not take effect. Then it introduced a bill to cap the railways' grain revenues and lower hauling charges, and forced it through the House of Commons and the Senate so it could be enacted by August 1. Now, hauling charges for producers would actually be reduced by $178 million for a typical annual thirty-million-tonne prairie harvest, despite the joint protests of Cargill, Agricore, United Grain Growers, Saskatchewan Wheat Pool and James Richardson International. The Wheat Board would be involved in organizing and allocating rail cars for the portion of its grain that is supposed to be shipped commercially.

To put things in perspective: the Bloc Québécois denounced the government's bill as election bribery for Western farmers. If the envy of Quebec is any indication, it seems federal legislators at last paid some heed to the persistent voices from the West.

In the early years of the twenty-first century it makes sense to ask if the cost of farming in Canada will continue to rise. There is, after all, a constant push for new technologies and innovations. This "progress" will certainly cost farmers more.

Precision farming is the latest stepping stone along the industrialization path. It is a capital-intensive trend that will put still more price pressure on producers. Precision farming uses computers and global positioning systems (GPS) to monitor and assess huge amounts of information. Meteorological stations measure weather, soil character and nutrients. Yield measurements are taken every three seconds during the harvest. It offers perhaps more information than most farmers can assimilate.

Proponents of precision farming claim it will boost efficiency by helping to reduce input costs. In theory, farmers would have to apply chemicals only where the system indicates they are needed. Some critics, notably Steven Wolf from the University of California, Berkeley, say precision farming simply attempts to legitimize chemically based agriculture in an era of rising environmental concern. It is, he says, first and foremost designed to advance industrial modes of production.

It costs US $15,000 to $20,000 to buy a yield monitor, global positioning receivers, and computer software and variable controllers for the application of chemicals. So far the new technology has failed to capture the imagination of most farmers. The most basic piece of precision farming equipment is found on fewer than ten thousand of the six hundred thousand combines in use today. But observers insist this new high-tech method of farming is on its way to agricultural fields.

University of Manitoba agriculture professor Rene Van Acker is sceptical about the benefits of embracing such new technology. He says old-time farming was in fact "precision farming," in that a farmer knew every knoll, every pothole in every field. By asking that producers keep their eyes on their GPS instead of on the sun and the horizon, precision farming devalues farmers' knowledge of the land, building instead further dependence on the agrochemical industry. He says it reduces the traditional farm role by substituting capital and technology for valuable agronomic knowledge and farming skill. "The best way to have precision agriculture is to have more farmers," he says.

Will Oddie has been an organic-crop producer near Swift Current, Saskatchewan, since 1989. He made the move to organic production for philosophical reasons; but in 2000 he saw four of his neighbours make the switch in the face of the debilitating input crunch. He thinks of it as the "right move, for the wrong—though justifiable—reason."

Many farmers are bucking conventional wisdom and taking up the challenge of producing food with fewer inputs, defying the trend to industrialization. Huge numbers of farmers are switching from conventional to organic methods, making the move not for environmental reasons but for economic ones. They are tapping into a consumer movement that has seen demand for organic foods rise by as much as 15 to 20 percent a year over the past decade. Organic production accounts for only a small proportion of the food that is grown in Canada, but at least it offers signs of growth—something Canadian farmers rarely find nowadays.

Robert Gehl is one of Oddie's neighbours—one of those who watched Oddie at first with derision and then with admiration. Gehl runs a long-time family farm with his brother Bill; together they crop nine quarters. In 2000 they began the three-year transition to organic production on two of those quarters. To be verified as organic a field has to be certified free of chemicals for three years. That means the Gehls are not allowed to use chemical fertilizers or pesticides on the fields they hope to have certified organic, but at the same time must sell their 2000 harvest on the conventional market, not the organic one. They are preparing themselves for yields that will be down 40 to 60 percent. "The painful part is the transition," explains Robert Gehl. That is why the two brothers are doing the changeover slowly, over about five years.

Robert Gehl is a practical man, and he does not hesitate to say that high inputs were the key reason they decided to make the move to organic. "It was just crushing us. It is horrible." On their conventional "industrial" fields they have to spend between $85 and $115 per acre to bring a crop to harvest. If they are lucky, they will get $150 an acre in return. In comparison, the input costs for organic crops are almost negligible. But there is a requirement for much more babysitting of the crop. Gehl admits there is a "steep learning curve" to become skilled at farming without the ease and convenience of chemicals. If he just let the crops grow without intervention, the fields would soon be mottled with the hue of weeds.

Other farmers are also looking to reduce their chemical use but without opting for full organic certification. They are buying fewer fertilizers and pesticides and looking for low-cost, natural alternatives to purchased inputs, for example, planting peas or clover to add nitrogen to fields instead of purchasing anhydrous ammonia or granular fertilizers. Another thirty-seven Manitoba farmers responded to an advertisement from University of Manitoba researchers organizing a program called Pesticide Free Production (PFP) Canada. The farmers made a commitment not to use any pesticides while their 2000 crop was in the ground, although fertilizers before and after the crop was seeded were permitted. The idea is that this system of farming is more flexible than strict organic production.

Orla Nazarko, the master's student overseeing the farmers participating in the PFP program, said 75 percent of the farmers were able to go through the season without breaking the no-pesticides rule. The others were so overwhelmed with weeds, they felt there was no way they could do without. Nazarko says there is no easy way to characterize the farmers who took part. They were both young and old, interested for both environmental and financial reasons. The one conclusion she could draw was that the producers tended to farm more marginal land, where they were used to trying different techniques to get a good crop.

Pesticide Free Production and organic production lower input costs for beleaguered farmers, and even small savings in inputs translate into huge increases in net income. Estimates have shown that if farmers cut their input costs by just 15 percent, their net incomes would double. Yet there is little institutional support for those initiatives. Research invariably looks at how to create more and "better" inputs. Farmers who want to manage without those inputs are often left to their own devices. Whether organic or reduced pesticide use, all these farmers are trying to cure their bank account blues, but in the process both strategies also create a more stable ecosystem, in which the chances of pest outbreaks and the development of pesticide resistance are reduced. The environmental benefits are a bonus. The motivation for the farmers may be more economic than environmental, but the benefits to society may be doubly significant.

•   •   •

Although it would never admit it, government tacitly supports the private sector and its rising farm input prices. It does so by funding chemical- and fertilizer-intensive agricultural research while underfunding research that offers alternatives to purchased inputs. Van Acker of the University of Manitoba's plant science department says public sector research at universities is tied to private sector support. Typically, that comes from companies hoping to earn profits from the sale of inputs. Under current research plans just about every dollar awarded by government agencies has to be matched with a private sector contribution. That is easy when the university researcher proposes to work to develop a genetically engineered crop with a tolerance to herbicide; Monsanto or other life sciences companies are likely to be interested. But it is more difficult to find funding to research low-input systems such as, for example, one that would explore the value of intercropping (growing two crops in one field).

Van Acker is interested in how weeds invade, establish themselves and compete with crops, and how to curb them naturally without using herbicides or genetic engineering that gives plants a built-in resistance to herbicides. Van Acker says his approach is to produce knowledge that producers can own to avoid high-cost inputs. The biotechnology revolution is certainly overwhelming interests like his. As a result, Van Acker's discipline is often seen in agricultural circles as the "low-tech" or "old-fashioned" approach to problems. He says he is lucky to have the support of his department, although he notes that his dean has gently reminded him not to get "nostalgic" for the old days.

Van Acker says public research should be focused on the producer, as it was when Agriculture Canada still saw itself as an extension service. The government department called Agriculture Canada became Agriculture and Agri-Food Canada in 1993 and, as part of the continuing deregulation of services, it seems more interested in directing money and supports to the private sector than to producers. Van Acker is blunt in his indictment. "If Agriculture Canada had focused more of their information on producers, there would be more farmers." Agriculture and Agri-Food Canada is the largest agricultural research arm in

Canada. In Winnipeg, four hundred people work at what is still collo-quially called the Ag Canada research station. These days one of the station's key projects is working with Monsanto to develop wheat resistant to glyphosate or Roundup.

The National Farmers Union agrees that the Canadian government could do a lot to help farmers by funding "least cost" agriculture. Research could help farmers who now find they have to try out innovations on their own. For example, farmers are using clover, which suppresses some weeds, to add nitrogen and organic matter to the soil. They are seeding clover and cereal crops like wheat in alternate rows, harvesting the wheat in the fall and letting the clover grow into the summer of the second year, when they plough or disk it into the soil. These farmers would benefit from the development of varieties of clover that would not grow as tall as the wheat in the first year, would add more nitrogen to the soil and would better suppress weeds.

If this kind of research were done by the public sector, the fruits of the research would be in the public domain and available to all farmers—a high return for a low-input option. Farmers have no say in how corporate input manufacturers spend their money. However, governments do have the opportunity to direct their efforts to serving the public good.

There are significant pressures on Canadian farmers to mechanize more, to focus on chemical or biotechnological inputs, and to embrace high-tech strategies like precision farming. But more and more farmers in the agricultural landscape are now asking when enough is enough, and who benefits from these strategies, because it is clearly not them.

Industrialization has not been a successful model for agriculture from some perspectives. It has increased productivity, but it can hardly be termed a success if farmers cannot afford to stay on the land. As examples in this chapter have shown, "advances" in agricultural technologies may have done more damage to the ecological and social resource base of rural areas than any societal benefit they generate from more "efficient" food production. This system generates great wealth from the countryside but returns poverty to farmers.

Agricultural industrialization is now losing its momentum. It was spectacularly successful in expanding food production for nearly half a century, but that is coming to an end. Grain production rose 40 percent per person between 1950 and 1984; but from then until 1995, it fell about 15 percent. In the past two decades neither the output nor the number of people supported by an acre of land have risen as quickly as they did before. It seems the soil no longer responds in the same way to chemical fertilizers. The Green Revolution is coming to a close.

The continuing push for high-input agriculture is impoverishing farmers. The only winners in this system, it seems, are the big companies that get cheques from farmers who can hardly afford to pay.

*Five*

# Follow the Money

June 17, 2000

*Every morning and every night, Gary Wieler goes out to the louvred weather box close to the cattle corral to check the temperature and the amount of precipitation there has been. He logs his readings carefully in a register that goes to Environment Canada once a month to help the government agency make assessments on the state of the weather. His local reputation as the "weatherman" means he routinely gets phone calls from other farmers who want to know precisely how much rain came with that ominous cloud that swept overhead.*

*Environment Canada will soon pronounce that June 2000 was cursed with twice the amount of rain that typically falls in the month. A quick look out the kitchen window would conclude much the same. It has been raining too hard for too long. It is not the kind of socked-in rain that sometimes passes through the Prairies for a day or two. This June's precipitation has been totally uncharacteristic. Every day for the past two weeks the skies have abruptly opened up, drenching the land in a hard, soaking rain, sometimes accompanied by the kind of electric light show most Westerners would expect after a hot, humid summer's day. Then the skies shut off, oblivious to the damage they have wrought. But the capricious rain leaves the trees swollen with moisture, the fields sodden with precipitation they cannot absorb.*

*Gary tells a story of one farmer who got twenty-two millimetres of rain in a single downpour. It will only get worse. The newspapers will soon tell of the town of Vanguard in southwestern Saskatchewan that suffers an odd flash flood. More than a year's worth of rain will fall in just ten hours, submerging the community and washing out two bridges. Twenty-three southern Manitoba municipalities will apply for disaster assistance for farmers whose cattle were cut off by pastures transformed into lakes. Crops will be drowned in water the clay-based soil can no longer soak up.*

*Gary has not been able to spray that field of peas he had hoped to get to nearly two weeks ago. He could not take his tractor into the field without tearing the earth. The weeds are now defiant—about ten centimetres tall. He has to subdue them now or they will begin to choke his field. He is especially silent today, thinking with a farmer's quiet intensity about how to resolve a practical problem. He decides he must spend the money to have herbicide sprayed by air or custom hi-boy. It will double his spraying costs on this field, but he feels it has to be done if he is to have a crop. He heads off to see the crop consultants at the Agricore agro-service centre on Highway 23. They dispatch two men who operate a hi-boy spraying outfit to tail Gary back to the field. They conclude they will be able to get their lightweight rig into the weed-challenged crop, but only if they buy new, taller tires.*

*For now, it is deceptively beautiful out, one of those peculiar periods of calm in the continuing storm. There are clouds overhead, but for a while we pretend it is a classic prairie summer's day. The cottonwood trees rain down their fluffy seed in a virtual snow. Daphne, the corgi-collie cross, has been shorn by No. 5 clippers, a summer cut. School will be out soon—this coming Thursday for Philip, the end of the month for Thomas and Nicholas. Just to get his parents in the mood for summer, Philip's entire class will spend Thursday evening at the farm. And on Friday, Thomas's Beaver troop plans to overnight it outside. "I'm going to be grouchy," Gary offers in his deadpan fashion.*

*Tomorrow is Father's Day. Along with the new office chair he gets from the boys, Gary will receive a practical and welcome gift. The Agricore crew comes with its Rogator high-clearance sprayer and blankets the field of peas with an even layer of MCPA Sodium Salt herbicide, an old standby in the chemical arsenal. They will leave a few ruts in the field, but their new tires help them avoid getting stuck. In just a few days the weeds will shrivel and fade.*

The extra money Gary Wieler has to spend to get his peas sprayed will squeeze his bottom line, but Agricore will earn extra money from his misfortune, as will the makers of the herbicide that Gary chooses. In modern industrial agribusiness, *someone* is making money, even if farmers are not.

There is, after all, money to be made from the production of food. Behind the farmer stands a staggering array of industry players. Unlike the situation of a hundred years ago, when consumers were often directly linked to the farmer, today many people stand between the farmer and the consumer, transforming the product of the farm into what we now consider food. For example, to make a loaf of bread, we need not just the farmer but the miller, the baker, the truck driver and the retailer. All those players—except for the farmer—are earning a lot more than they did twenty years ago.

Producers are earning what they did during the Depression. They are being squeezed today from both ends of the agribusiness chain: on one side by all those who provide the inputs of farming—the fuel, seeds, fertilizers, chemicals, machinery and implements used in the running of the farm; on the other side by the grain companies, railways, packers, processors, retailers and restaurants. Almost every link in this agribusiness chain is dominated by transnational corporations. Each one routinely earns revenues equivalent to those of all Canada's farmers combined. The farm crisis is not affecting them.

Today, most consumers spend little of their time assembling meals out of raw ingredients, never mind canning, pickling or freezing the necessities of life in preparation for a long Canadian winter. Instead, we opt for prepared "convenience" foods—instant pasta sauce and noodles, all the pleasure of a pizza in a box of hamburger helper, ready-to-heat chicken cordon bleu in a frozen vacuum pac. The taste of modern Canada is for foods that can be heated in a microwave or ordered takeout. A drive-through window is now designed as an integral part of a doughnut shop so that the modern coffee drinker need not get out of the car, never mind share a convivial cup with a neighbour or friend. The "accidental tourist" who wishes to avoid unnecessary surprises can dine on McDonald's from Beijing to Paris.

In our industrialized world, food has become a business activity in which we participate as workers, customers and consumers, and if we're lucky, as corporate shareholders. There was a time, not that long ago, when food was at the heart of our culture. A wedding party, a birth, a funeral—these life passages were all marked by food grown and prepared very close to home. Today it is often difficult to tell where our food comes from. We still use it to celebrate, but a meal in an ethnic restaurant bears little relationship to a feast lovingly grown and prepared at home. Most days, food is simply fuel to further our busy modern lives. The depressing reality is that farmers are seen simply as the providers of raw ingredients that will ultimately be transformed for the sake of convenience, speed and consistency. Financial compensation is, unfortunately, dispensed according to this logic. What is rewarded is the global agri-food system that prepares, processes and delivers the food of today. What consumers seem to want is what corporations can give them: processed foods that make life easier.

It is a reflection of our tastes and of the industrial agribusiness industry that we spend 10 percent of our income on food, 24 percent on entertainment. In the 1950s and 1960s we spent 25 percent on food and 10 percent on entertainment. Our priorities have shifted significantly. In fact, the average consumer has earned enough by February 7 to pay for all her food costs for the year. The Canadian Federation of Agriculture designated that day Food Freedom Day in an effort to draw attention to how little consumers actually pay for food. It is based on the public relations success of Tax Freedom Day, the day in July when taxpayers are said to be finished working for the government and can begin working for themselves. Farmers' Freedom Day would come even earlier in the calendar: the average Canadian earns enough to pay a farmer his annual income in just eight days.

Ironically, most Canadian shoppers would say they are paying a lot for their food. They are probably reacting to the fact that their weekly supermarket bill has gone up significantly in the last twenty years. For example, retail beef and pork prices rose 131 percent between 1978 and 1998, and a loaf of bread costs 84 cents more than it did in the early 1980s. Judging by what they pay at the grocery store checkout, consumers can be forgiven for assuming that farmers are earning more.

Although retail prices have gone up in the past two decades, wholesale and farm prices have remained virtually unchanged. There have been no windfalls for hog or beef producers, although prices have gone up significantly at the meat counter. The price of one bushel of wheat stayed the same from 1975 to 1999, although consumers continued to pay more for their bread. Today a loaf of bread costs about $1.50, of which 10 cents goes to the farmer. For every bushel of malt barley produced and sold to a brewery, the farmer takes home $4 (before expenses), the government $213 and the retailer $193.

In 1991, former federal MP and agriculture minister Ralph Ferguson tried to analyze how the food dollar is divided. In his *Compare the Share* report Ferguson found that farm gate prices and retail prices were closely aligned during the 1970s; but from 1980 to 1990, what a farmer was paid rose very little while the prices consumers paid increased dramatically.

The price gap widened even further during the 1990s. That was the finding when the Centre for Rural Studies and Enrichment, a research and development office located at St. Peter's College in Muenster, Saskatchewan, updated Ferguson's work. Its analysis found there was increasingly little connection between the prices farmers were paid and what consumers had to pay at the supermarket. Retail beef prices rose $6.14 per kilogram between 1977 and 1998, while farm prices rose only $1.57 per kilogram. The price of a box of cornflakes rose $2.44 in the same period, while the price of the corn used to make that box increased only 3 cents. In 1998 an Ontario farmer would have received 1 cent less than he had twenty years earlier for the white winter wheat that went into a box of crackers; shoppers, meanwhile, had to pay $1.17 more for those same crackers.

The analysis shows that the marketplace is clearly failing farmers. And perhaps it is also failing consumers, by charging them prices that are unrelated to the cost of growing the food in the first place. It seems the only ones really winning from our global system of agribusiness are the corporations that stand between the producers and the consumers.

Why can't farmers exact a greater share of the consumer food dollar? Well, they are competing for their share with corporations that are thousands, if not millions, of times larger than they are. Every player in the food production line is a corporation, except for the farmer. Control and direction of the food system has passed from those who grow and eat the food to fewer and fewer people in fewer and fewer corporate boardrooms. The focus of these global food merchants is returning comfortable profits to shareholders. The companies farmers have to deal with routinely report double-digit returns on equity, while farm returns have fallen to less than 1 percent. As an example, the George Weston company earned a 37.3 percent return on equity for a profit of $773 million in 1998.

The Canadian retailer is not an anomaly. Cargill's revenues in 1999 were $75 billion. Philip Morris—the parent company of familiar labels like Post, Kraft, Kool-Aid, Jell-O, Maxwell House, Marlboro and Miller— had revenues in 1998 of $109 billion. Philip Morris likes to say that one dollar in ten spent in a U.S. grocery store is used to buy a Philip Morris product. Founded in 1847 as a tobacco company, Philip Morris only became a food company in 1985 when it purchased General Foods. Nestlé, the makers of Stouffer's, Maggi, Libby's, Nescafé and Perrier, was also doing well, despite the farm crisis: in 1998 it had revenues of $76 billion. In comparison the gross revenues of Canadian farms were tiny: all 277,000 farms together earned revenues of $29 billion before costs in 1998.

Not only are the companies huge, but there are fewer and fewer of them. Corporate consolidation is happening at a frantic pace in the agribusiness sector, much as it is in other, more high-profile industries. All eyes may be focused on the likes of the AOL–Time Warner merger, but similar consolidations and mergers are happening with companies that control our food. For example, Cargill, the world's largest privately held company and the biggest U.S. grain exporter, announced its intention to buy Continental, the second-largest grain exporter south of the border. There was next to no public outcry. It was left to those inside the system to point out that the merger would have a significant, perhaps stifling, effect on competition.

In the second half of the twentieth century there was significant merger activity in the food sectors of most industrialized countries. Canada, however, had the dubious distinction of experiencing higher levels of corporate concentration than the U.S., Japan or Germany. As early as 1968, the OECD noted that the food business was one of the most concentrated sectors of Canadian industry.

Every link in Canada's agribusiness chain is dominated by just a few companies—and they are usually transnational players. The Canadian National Farmers Union documented all the consolidations of recent years in a report it presented to the Senate Standing Committee in February 2000. *The Farm Crisis, EU Subsidies and Agribusiness Market Power* was the work of several NFU researchers who were convinced that the government's focus on international subsidies missed the point. NFU director Fred Tait is certain the farm income crisis "is all about the domination of corporations. We are questioning the single-minded strategy of the government."

The NFU found that when farmers like Gary Wieler buy herbicide, chances are it is produced by one of only a handful of firms. When they buy Poast, Edge, Treflan or Prevail herbicides or Lorsban insecticide, they are buying from Dow Chemical. Revenues in 1997 for Dow reached $29 billion, equal to the gross revenues of all Canadian farmers combined. Dual, Horizon, Target and numerous genetically engineered seeds are all the product of the European multinational Novartis—1997 revenues of $31 billion. (Novartis has since merged with Astrazeneca to form Syngenta.)

Gary Wieler has to buy his oil, gasoline and diesel fuel from one of the three retail companies that handle most Canadian fuels—Imperial Oil, Petro-Canada and Shell Canada. Together they earned revenues of $17.5 billion in 1999.

Three companies control 71 percent of Canada's nitrogen fertilizer production. Agrium, North America's largest nitrogen fertilizer producer, controls 45 percent of the market. Saskferco, a joint venture between Cargill and the government of Saskatchewan, and Canadian Fertilizer Ltd., a partnership between Western Co-operative Fertilizers and CF Industries, control the rest.

Chances are that Gary Wieler buys his insecticides, fungicides and herbicides from the seven chemical companies that market most of the products used in Canada. Worldwide, the top ten companies control 85 percent of the $45.4-billion market in chemicals. Because of patent protection, there is even more concentration in specific categories of pesticide. For example, Monsanto, the maker of Roundup, and one or two other companies sell the vast majority of non-selective herbicides in Canada.

Although there seems to be a huge number of seed options for farmers, they are actually produced by an ever-shrinking number of companies. Four companies—DuPont/Pioneer, Monsanto, Syngenta and Dow—

control 69 percent of the North American seed corn market and 47 percent of the soybean seed market. While Canadian figures are not available, Monsanto probably controls up to one-half of the canola seed market with its Roundup Ready varieties. Genetically engineered canola made up at least 60 percent of the canola grown in Canada in 2000.

Two farm equipment manufacturers dominate the Canadian and North American market: John Deere and the new Case/IH–New Holland merger. For antitrust reasons, the U.S. required New Holland to spin off its Winnipeg tractor plant to Buhler Industries. In early 2001 that Winnipeg plant, the last remaining tractor plant in Canada, was locked in a labour dispute and its future was uncertain.

Five banks control Canadian agricultural credit, with some participation by the federal Farm Credit Corporation and a network of relatively small credit unions.

After farmers like Gary Wieler grow the crops and produce that we once called food, a series of corporations step in to get those "agri-food products" to market. And once again we see the same kind of market concentration.

Two railways, CN and CP, haul Western Canadian grain. Most farmers are captive to one or the other railway by virtue of where their farms are located. There is continuing pressure on the railways to grow. CN announced in 1999 it wanted to merge with Burlington Northern Santa Fe to create a supercarrier. When the U.S. government indicated it wanted to review the consolidation, CN and BNSF backed out of the deal. However, observers say it is an indication of what the future may hold.

There are five primary grain companies—Agricore, Cargill, Pioneer, Saskatchewan Wheat Pool and UGG—that currently control most of the grain collection in Canada. Analysts predict that mergers and takeovers will soon leave as few as two. Deregulation that has allowed U.S. companies to step into the Canadian marketplace will be behind some of the expected consolidations. The Dominion Bond Rating Service told the *Winnipeg Free Press* in the spring of 2000 that it forecast a giant shakeout in the grain industry. Most vulnerable are the companies that have not earned as well as expectations might demand. Agricore's earnings dropped to $1.3 million in 2000 from $7.6 million in 1999 and $65.4 million in 1998. The Saskatchewan Wheat Pool too has problems; it recently had its credit rating downgraded to "negative" from "stable." UGG continues to register what the business pages call unimpressive profits, despite its partnership with the U.S. giant Archer Daniels Midland. The big concern is that the American multinationals like ConAgra, ADM and Cargill will survive, while the Canadian companies that once dominated the landscape of the pioneer farmers will fail. Those grain-handling corporations are beginning to see that their future may be tied to producers' fortunes.

At first glance it seems as if the next step in the food chain has been spared the consolidation seen elsewhere in the industry. After all, there are a reasonably large number of big food processors in Canada. However, the NFU analysis shows there are only a few companies producing each specific item. For example, three large firms produce pasta in Canada. Borden (Catelli, Lancia) produces 39.2 percent of Canadian pasta. RJR Nabisco, the makers of Primo pasta, account for another quarter of Canadian plant capacity. Italpasta has another quarter.

On the milling side, four companies produce 80 percent of Canada's flour. The biggest player is the American giant Archer Daniels Midland, which bought up the Ogilvie Milling division of John Labatt as well as McCarthy milling from George Weston. The U.S.-based multinational now controls 46.3 percent of the country's wheat-flour milling. Of course, most of the wheat grown on the Canadian Prairies is exported raw for processing in other countries.

On the red-meat side, consolidation's impact is very clear. Two multinationals, IBP and Cargill, dominate the beef-packing industry in North America. Together they control 74 percent of Canadian capacity, with two mega-slaughterhouses in Alberta. In pork, Smithfield Foods dominates the U.S. industry, and Maple Leaf in Canada.

Three companies manufacture the bulk of our soft drinks, four produce most of our cereal, a handful process coffee, and a small number make frozen french fries.

Five companies control food retailing in Canada, which is neatly divided up between them. Pattison/Overwaitea and Safeway control British Columbia. The Weston-Loblaws-Westfair partnership and Safeway dominate the Prairies. The Ontario market is dominated by Weston-Loblaws-Westfair, Sobeys, Metro-Richelieu and A&P. Metro-Richelieu, Empire-Sobeys and the Weston conglomerate control Quebec. And two companies—Empire-Sobeys and a Weston group—share Atlantic Canada.

Restaurant chains increasingly control the business of eating out. The ubiquitous McDonald's corporation had worldwide revenues of $118.3 billion in 1998. Tricon, which operates KFC, Taco Bell and Pizza Hut, boasted 29,700 franchises in a hundred countries.

The list of these power blocs is long and numbing but also crucially significant. Even a playlist could not help you stay current with all the acquisitions, mergers and consolidations. For example, many will not have noticed that ConAgra purchased International Home Products, which used to be the food division of American Home Products. And Unilever swallowed up Bestfoods. Unilever and Bestfoods had combined global 1999 revenues of $52 billion, providing a profit of $8.6 billion. Bestfoods is the corporate name for products we know as Skippy peanut butter, Mazola corn oil and Entemann's bread. Philip Morris got even bigger in 2000 by closing a deal to buy Nabisco Holdings Corp. for $14.9 billion. Kraft and Nabisco had operating profits totalling $5.5 billion in 1999. Kraft Canada is one of the largest processed-food companies in the country with 3,900 employees and sales of about $2.1 billion a year. The merger of the two giants was supposed to result in cost savings of about $600 million by 2003. Only a naive observer would imagine that those savings will be passed on to consumers or farmers rather than delivered to the parent company in the United States.

With reduced competition comes market power and the ability to say "take it or leave it." Antitrust or competition laws are supposed to stop this kind of bullying, but it is difficult to prove collusion or price-fixing amongst invisible cartels. It is natural to conclude that if there are only a few players, a quiet conversation may be enough to ensure everyone co-operates. However, it took several years for the courts to find Archer Daniels Midland, together with several Japanese "competitors," guilty of price-fixing on lysine, a synthetic amino acid added to pig and poultry feed. The case against ADM was ultimately carried on the evidence of the former president of the company's BioProducts division, who had actually been an FBI mole for twenty-two years. He acquired incriminating video and audio tape evidence that implicated ADM, and the company ended up paying hundreds of millions of dollars in court awards in response to the class action antitrust suit brought forward by about six hundred lysine customers. Although this kind of evidence is difficult to get, it is possible that some such level of co-operation takes place amongst other corporations too.

William Heffernan, a professor of rural sociology at the University of Missouri, has spent years studying corporate concentration. In his report for the U.S. National Farmers Union in 1999, called *Consolidation in the Food and Agriculture System,* he says the point of consolidation in the agribusiness world is not to be the only corporation left standing, but to find a way to dominate the food chain by controlling every link "from gate to plate." Mergers, joint ventures, partnerships, contracts and agreements happen as companies attempt to develop "clusters" with the power to dictate the entire global market, from genetic research designed to develop new seeds through to the creation of new processed food products for the dinner table. Heffernan says the whole global agri-food system is woven together by a host of working relationships between firms. Watching clusters develop as new relationships are formed and old ones are broken, says Heffernan, "is like watching a chess match and trying to anticipate the player's next moves." For example, ADM lacked access to farmers, which they could get from Novartis's farm connections in chemicals and biogenetics, while Novartis benefited from ADM's grain-processing facilities. So when Novartis and ADM teamed up, it was a corporate match made in heaven. (Astrazeneca has since merged with Novartis.) Heffernan says other global food clusters are beginning to be formed: Monsanto and Cargill have shared interests, as do DuPont and Pioneer Hi-Bred.

In 1978, when Canadian society still seemed to care about such things, the federal government appointed a Royal Commission on Corporate Concentrations. The report of that commission warned: "Enforcement of the Combines Investigation Act has been ineffective in discouraging mergers that increase concentration within an industry." Since then neither legislation nor political will has toughened Canada's legislation on corporate concentrations.

Multilateral trade rules also facilitate rather than restrict consolidation in the agribusiness sector. Nowhere in the debates on agriculture and trade at the World Trade Organization has the concentration of market power in commodity markets even surfaced as an issue for consideration.

Not only are corporations becoming the dominant players in Canada's agri-food system, but foreign companies are taking over the sector at rates not seen in other countries. It is generally agreed that as the number of competitors drops, foreign players become dominant. Canada has a virtual open-door policy to takeovers by foreign corporations, which means that the pace and direction of the sector is being determined beyond our borders.

In the future the world's food production will be controlled by a handful of companies. There will be significant pressure on the only independent operators in the chain—the farmers—to join in the corporate web. Farmers will be coerced to contract directly with corporations, becoming an essential link in a seamless chain of food production. They will provide labour, land and equipment to companies, yet will still have to deal with the risks imposed by the vagaries of nature. Farmers will have to give up the independent streak that has always defined them. Experts, even leaders of the new co-op movements, are telling farmers that giving up their independence and joining an alliance is the only way to survive in the new corporate order.

This kind of farming represents a huge change in how agriculture operates. Companies, not independent farmers, will be making management decisions, such as when seed is to be planted, which chemicals are to be used, and when and how the crop is to be harvested.

This corporate contract system is already largely in place in broilers and hogs in the United States. About 95 percent of chickens south of the border are produced under production contracts with fewer than forty firms. Farmers are expected to borrow money to build huge concrete barns according to company specifications; chicks of the company-selected breed are then delivered, as is the feed and medication. The farmer's assignment is simply to fatten the chickens to the prescribed weight until it is time to ship them off the slaughterhouse of the company's choice—usually one controlled by the company. The farm manager has to apply little independent judgment. In many ways he is simply a cog in a system dictated by corporate headquarters. The Rural Advancement Foundation International is even blunter. RAFI describes the contract farmer as little more than a modern-day "serf."

The livestock industry in the United States is rife with stories of contract producers who overextended themselves by building corporate-directed barns, or who complain that the mother corporation sends them chicks in poor health, which could never be fattened to specifications.

In Canada the contract system is beginning to develop in the livestock sector, particularly in the pork industry. McCain's is already following this model in potato production. It controls the potato system from its position as a major world processor, with fifty production facilities in nine countries.

The movement to contracts is now beginning in field crop production as well. In theory the grower provides labour, land and equipment; the contractor provides seed, chemicals and management. Several technology trends are hastening the move to full vertical integration, the most significant being genetic engineering.

Monsanto, the leader in the development of genetically modified organisms (GMO), requires any farmer using its biotechnology to sign a

Technology Use Agreement. Under the TUA, the farmer agrees not to save seed from a Monsanto engineered crop for future use and to allow Monsanto representatives to inspect the farm at any point over three years in search of errant seeds. Monsanto has waged an aggressive campaign against farmers who violate its TUAs. In the late 1990s it set up "tip lines" to allow people to offer up information about their neighbour's farming practices. Private security guards, hired by Monsanto, were spotted sneaking through farmers' fields, Baggies in hand, collecting samples of seeds for analysis. Apparently, hundreds of farmers accused of "stealing" proprietary technology quietly settled with Monsanto rather than contest the claim.

Percy Schmeiser of Bruno, Saskatchewan, was not prepared to slip away quietly in the wake of Monsanto's allegations. He went to court in the spring of 2000, insisting that whatever Roundup Ready canola Monsanto investigators had found in his fields had got there by mistake, not design. Monsanto accused Schmeiser of using the genetically engineered seed without the appropriate TUA—a deliberate patent infringement. Schmeiser in turn asserted the Roundup Ready genes ended up in his fields through wind action, cross-pollination and spillage from passing trucks.

By late 2000 the federal court judge who heard the case had not yet rendered a decision. However he rules, the case will have a significant impact on how biotechnology companies use contracts to control crop production. That is because Monsanto alleged Schmeiser did not have to know he was planting Roundup Ready canola for his actions to constitute an infringement on their patent. On that basis no farmer could save seed from year to year because there is no way of knowing if a seed contains any stray genes that are under patent protection.

From a corporate point of view the most irritating thing about field cropping is that farmers can save seed from one year to the next. It is a fact of nature, and 1.4 billion farmers around the world take advantage of this basic principle of biology. But there is no money to be made by those selling seed if producers insist on saving it. The seed industry has already developed hybrids in an effort to short-circuit this biological reality; farmers have to buy hybrids every year. Almost all corn varieties are hybrids, but wheat has stubbornly defied hybridization.

The seed industry is now working to develop what it calls "sterile seed technologies." Critics call this technology "the Terminator" because it is intended to terminate a seed's natural ability to propagate in a subsequent year. RAFI has been watching the progress of this technology most closely. In 2000 it reported that life sciences companies had filed more than thirty patents to develop seeds that would commit suicide before being planted again. To their credit, the companies have put a voluntary moratorium on the use of those seeds. However, Agriculture and Agri-Food Canada is also working on this technology, and so far it has not said it will not use it in publicly bred varieties.

Another scientific advance that would serve to lessen farmer independence in a corporate system is precision farming. With the global positioning technologies it will no longer be necessary for farmers to have personal contact with the land. Decisions are made in the farmer's office as a big truck with a computer on board reads from a satellite. The so-called farmer will not have to know much about the fertilizer or chemicals being applied to the field, as this will be done automatically. Precision farming will be like doing piecework.

The corporatization of agri-food will sap both the independent spirit of farmers and their economic well-being. A University of Nebraska study found that when 10 percent of pork production is controlled by corporate contracts, pork packers pay 6 percent less to hog farmers than they pay when the corporate presence is minimal; when half of the hogs in a given area are produced under contract, the price paid to the independent hold-outs falls by 26 percent. A Virginia Polytechnic Institute study shows independent farm production of hogs offers many more economic benefits to the local community than does the corporate contract system. Independent farmers were found to produce 10 percent more jobs, 20 percent more retail spending and 37 percent more local per capita income.

The experience in the United States stands as a cautionary example for the Canadian producer. Nevertheless, many cash-strapped Canadian farmers will probably not be able to withstand the pressure from corporations to step into contract production. Many farmers will be reduced to franchisees, dependent for all their inputs on a few corporations, and liable for royalties to those same corporations on everything they produce. The vertical integration of the food system, from seed to table, will be complete.

In the early 1970s federal NDP leader David Lewis introduced the phrase "corporate welfare bums" into the Canadian lexicon. It struck a chord then, earning the NDP an influential role in Pierre Trudeau's minority Liberal government. Thirty years later, corporate domination of our economy is seemingly accepted without question, reported dispassionately in the news pages, celebrated in the business pages. No one likes to suggest that corporations should be denied the right to make money, so protest about corporate control in the food sector has been left to the National Farmers Union, an organization often dismissed for its left-leaning views. Vice-president Fred Tait admits that the reaction to the NFU's report was "a little hostile."

However, a negative reaction to domination by multinational corporations has been making itself felt. Witness the protests that disrupted the World Trade Organization meetings in 1999 in Seattle or the Biosafety protocol in Montreal in early 2000. There is an inclination to dismiss the activists as rabble-rousing students, but no matter what their age, they seem to reflect a growing concern.

In the United States, Senator Byron Dorgan, a Democrat from North Dakota, has always been seen as a maverick. He has been thumping the tub against corporate concentration in the agriculture sector for years. Several years ago Dorgan and members of the Coalition of Americans for Anti-Trust released a white paper stating the federal government was under-equipped and falling behind in enforcing antitrust laws. Now his message is touching a nerve. As chairman of the Democratic Policy Committee he called a hearing in early 2000 on the lack of competition in agricultural markets. Then in April Dorgan amassed support from twelve other farm senators, including Senate Democratic leader Tom Daschle of South Dakota, to introduce legislation to fight anti-competitive practices by giant corporations. The Farmers and Ranchers Fair Competition Act would establish a special counsel at the Department of Agriculture, require any agribusiness with sales of more than $100 million a year to disclose ownership of any other agriculture-related business and establish a commission that would compensate farmers for injury caused by inappropriate corporate actions. The bill had received second reading in the U.S. Senate by the end of 2000 and was being reviewed in committee.

In Canada the question of corporate concentration is beginning to surface in unexpected corners. Loretta Smith is a director with the Ontario Federation of Agriculture and a farmer who finishes two thousand hogs each year near Thorndale, Ontario. Although she has not seen much pressure for contracts from vertically integrated companies in her area, the prospect alone is enough to provoke a tangible fear. Two years ago, when hog prices bottomed out, she noted there was no drop in prices at the local store. She was paid just $36 for a 235-pound pig. On that basis, she says, a Christmas ham in the store should have cost just $3. Well, that was not the case. She says the cynic in her wondered if the packers who dominate the industry got together and said, "How low should we let them fall?" She remains assertive and defiant. "Convince me that the four packers didn't talk to each other and say how low could it go."

So it was Smith, young, polished and poised, who rose at the February 2000 general meeting of the Canadian Federation of Agriculture to introduce a resolution calling on the CFA to lobby the federal government for legislation "limiting multi- and transnational corporate ownership of agricultural resources and commodity production facilities." There was a slightly pained expression on the faces of agribusiness representatives in the room, but the resolution easily won support. To the CFA's credit the organization carried the resolution further. The International Federation of Agriculture, which represents sixty nations, has now put together a committee to look at corporate domination in the global food system.

Loretta Smith is quietly hopeful for change. She thinks people are ready to put some sort of controls on corporations. "Have you ever come across a multinational corporation that gives you quality for a low price?" She says Canada may have cheap food, but what people seem to care about most of all is safety and quality. "I see people not looking at prices, but reading labels."

Smith and other producers are beginning to demand their fair share from an agribusiness system dominated by global corporations. They must feel some degree of envy when they look at their colleagues in supply-managed sectors. The *Compare the Share* study concluded that farmers in agricultural sectors regulated by supply management saw their prices track retail prices, and farmers tended to retain a higher percentage of the retail price. For example, the price of eggs increased at the same rate on the farm and in wholesale and retail outlets. In unregulated sectors like grain and pork, farmers received lower prices in 1998 than they did for their products in the 1970s, while retail prices increased.

But the expansion of supply management is unlikely, so farmers must find some other strategy to either acquire market power or limit corporate influence. Either way they need the support of the people who consume the food they grow. Despite their disconnection from the farm and their appetite for homogenized convenience food, most consumers are not prepared to sacrifice Canadian farmers for the financial well-being of transnational corporations. Consumers are citizens of a broader society. Most would not welcome a food chain where control lies in a few corporate hands. Monsanto-in-the-Fields is not everyone's idea of an ideal agricultural community. How much corporate control we allow is a reflection of the kind of country we are going to become. The family farm today is like the canary in the mineshaft for the global economy. The farm crisis shows in stark terms what happens to our lives, our communities and our values when we bow down before multinational finance. Is this the economy we want?

*Six*

## The Business of Farming

*It's official: summer is here. The Wieler kids are home from school for their two-month break, and the essential tasks of an agricultural spring—seeding and spraying—are done. In the past week the sun has begun to caress the land, offering the warmth the crops need to stretch and grow. A wave of green now shimmers across the flat, expansive fields of southern Manitoba.*

*The town of Kane is marking the coming of summer with a party. Although only a handful of people live in the town now and there is no place to buy a soft drink, Kane knows how to throw a good party. This weekend's celebration is supposed to commemorate the school, closed since 1973. Local matriarch Dora Hildebrand explains, "Our community is closing down, but we haven't quite closed the books."*

*More than four hundred people have come from across the country to witness the unveiling of the Kane school marker and to share stories of*

*their early days in the one-room schoolhouse. The town is teeming with
people. Because there are no roads in Kane, the cars are parked helter-
skelter along the shoulders of Highway 23, stretching almost as far away
as the place the German POW camp stood during the war.*

*As usual this year, the sky is moody, threatening rain. Environment
Canada promised a hot, sunny day, but things have already cooled off
dramatically. Rain begins to spatter. Still, folks are gathered in the fes-
tive white tent, staked where the school used to be and where, these days,
a few cattle normally roam. The partygoers are listening to country
music and gossip from long ago, oblivious to Mother Nature's ill-timed
intervention. The cairn was unveiled a few hours earlier. It is handsome
black granite but looks, unfortunately, like a tombstone. As one cele-
brant notes, only time will tell if it is a tribute to a prosperous past or a
grave marker for a dying town.*

*Sunday is the one day off Gary Wieler allows himself in the farm work-
week, but he and Lorna and the boys are not here. They are what Dora
Hildebrand calls "the younger people who don't remember Kane as a community." Instead, the Wielers are using their Sunday to visit grandfather
Diedrich at the Health Sciences Centre in Winnipeg. He suffered a serious
heart attack a week ago. He was moved from the Morris hospital to the city
health centre with the thought that he might need an angioplasty.*

*His condition is a worry on a personal level, but the farm will suffer,
too, from the loss of the help he was able to offer in past years. The imme-
diate family will have to do double duty to pick up the slack. Lorna has
cleared her calendar and the boys are getting older and more capable of
doing their part. The Wieler farm is definitely a family affair.*

*For the next week or so the Wielers will have a chance to revel in that
rare summertime pause on the family farm, between seeding and harvest.
The first family assignment for the "summer holidays" is for Nicholas
and Philip to somehow transform their recalcitrant young steers into
show cattle for the upcoming 4-H meet at the Carman Country Fair.*

*After that the cycle of the seasons will resume—haying, cattle, har-
vesting . . . Gary, Lorna and the boys are all prepared to work hard. It is,*

*after all, the way of life they have chosen for themselves. But it does rankle a bit when someone in Carman says to Lorna in an offhand, unlistening way, "Why don't you give it up so someone else can take over and make some money at it?"*

❧ Even with a sure hand on the wheel and the solid traction of his late-model 4WD truck, it takes nearly an hour for Warren Jolly to make it to the outer reaches of his 6,400-acre farm. It truly does stretch as far as the eye can see, over the dips and swells of the rolling southwestern Saskatchewan prairie. Jolly is one of the 20 percent of Canadian farmers who grow 80 percent of the country's grain. And he is the epitome of everything the Canadian government defines as successful in modern farming: efficient, competitive and big. For Jolly, farming is first and foremost a business.

Between 1936 and 1996, Canadian farms got progressively bigger. What was a typical four-hundred-acre farm in Saskatchewan in 1936 has now tripled in size. Many farms are five thousand acres or more. Statistics Canada confirms the continuing trend to what it calls "commercial farms," that is, farms with revenues of more than $250,000 a year.

The Western Wheat Growers Association, which tends to be made up of large and self-described "innovative" producers, echoes what is popular agricultural economic thinking. It maintains that farmers have only been able to stay ahead of the financial crisis by increasing their land base and the size of their machinery. A policy paper by the association, entitled *The Business of Farming*, says farmers have essentially two options for survival: they either get an off-farm job or increase their land base.

Former U.S. secretary of agriculture Earl Butz would agree. He set the tone for the industrialization of agriculture in the early 1970s. "Get big or get out," he told American producers, imagining a landscape populated with farmers like Warren Jolly. He was not the first to offer that rough-and-tumble bromide to farmers. Some say Ezra Benson, secretary of agriculture in the 1950s, started the "get big or get out" message. In the 1960s, John Kenneth Galbraith's common wisdom that "bigger is better" attracted a significant following. By the time Butz came around, "agriculture" was already becoming "agri-food," and the get-big philosophy was central to modern thinking. "Adapt or die" is another favourite phrase Butz liked to use to describe the structural changes he saw confronting North American farmers. Canadian politicians were not so blunt as the outspoken Earl Butz, but in their quiet way they too expressed the wisdom of the times that getting big was the way to achieve the efficiencies demanded by our industrial system of agriculture.

The industrial model flourishes on Warren and Paula Jolly's farm. An operation of this size can only be managed with large equipment, routine use of chemical fertilizers, pesticides and herbicides, and hired farm labour. The Jollys own three combines—two with the latest GPS technology—three 425-horsepower tractors (the biggest that John Deere makes), a $200,000 1998 air drill, a tandem grain truck and an assortment of gargantuan grain bins dotted throughout the landscape. The implements sitting in the yard down from the house alone are worth $2 million. There are massive granaries looming on the horizon, shrewdly situated on the outskirts of Jolly land. Two are lined up next to a weathered barn, complete with a spire. It is a picture of the old and the new cheek by jowl.

During this year's seeding and harvest the Jollys employed seven farmhands. Finding staff is one of the biggest challenges for the operation. It is increasingly difficult to find people who want to work in an area that has no towns, no hospitals, no schools and no services.

Paula Jolly's assignment is to make those jobs more appealing. She does that in the kitchen. Meals are a perquisite of a farm labourer's job and are expected to be good. A svelte and sophisticated grandmother at forty-five, Paula works in the kitchen for hours each day, like the farm women of earlier generations. And then she spends up to two hours on the road, delivering hot meals to the field.

The picture of the farm wife toiling in the kitchen to feed the menfolk may belong to earlier times, but this is not the kind of place most people think of when they hear the term "family farm." Nonetheless, Warren Jolly is the third generation of his family to farm in this corner of the world. The old homestead, a solid-looking two-storey structure, is just down from where Warren and Paula have built their impeccably landscaped, comfortable brick bungalow. Warren's father farmed 1,400 acres. When Warren took over operations in 1968, he immediately started adding to the holdings. "Dad was afraid I was getting into trouble," he remembers with affection. "But he never told me to stop." Warren admits it was risky to embrace a philosophy of getting bigger; in thirty-two years of operation, he says, "there has never been a debt-free day."

There is no doubt the Jollys' expansion has been possible only because so many others have left the business. The old idea of co-operative neighbourliness that defined the Canadian Prairies through much of its history has faded. Instead, it has become a dog-eat-dog world, where survival depends on others failing. Some might describe Jolly's actions as ruthless; others say he is just a good businessman. With his intense, unsmiling presentation, Warren Jolly knows that many of his neighbours might be a little apprehensive around him.

At fifty, Warren Jolly can personally attest to many of the changes that have transformed the southwestern Saskatchewan he grew up in. The statistics tell some of the story: from 1936 to 1996 the number of farms in Saskatchewan dropped from 142,391 to 56,995. There are not enough people left farming on the Prairies to warrant the continued existence of the small towns that once erected false fronts on their buildings in a declaration of importance.

The gritty, painful story of the Prairies' transformation is told in places like Congress. Just 15 kilometres down the highway from the Jollys' home, Congress is now the location of one of UGG's high-throughput elevators. The UGG motto, "Investing in the West; Meeting Farmers' Business Needs," is emblazoned on the most important sign in the town. The concrete silos of the terminal loom over what was once a thriving community. Now, Congress is a collection of about a dozen house trailers and unassuming homes. The only other business in town is a café that apparently does not have the energy to put out a sign; business hours are scrawled in felt pen on the window. A young boy playing in the dirt in his backyard looks up and waves as an unfamiliar car goes by. Courtesy is still alive and well in this town.

Mossbank, the closest community to the Jollys' and the place that shaped Warren's youth, has survived as the area's primary rural service centre. There is still a John Deere dealership in town. Two food stores. A co-op. Even a wheat-weaving studio. But the competition from Moose Jaw, an hour away, is beginning to sap the town's energy. There are plenty of spots to park up and down the gravelled thoroughfare that bills itself as Main Street. An unattended Yorkshire terrier is sprawled lazily on the sidewalk. He rises to sniff my tires and meanders out into the street, apparently confident that traffic poses no real hazard.

Warren and Paula, among the other locals, admit they are partially responsible for the lack of traffic on Mossbank's Main Street. They get in their cars and trucks and make the drive to the city, where the Wal-Mart offers more selection and better prices than the Mossbank hardware store. Last night the Jollys had dinner in Regina—half an hour beyond Moose Jaw. Warren Jolly notes the passing of towns like Congress and Mossbank with no particular sentimentality. With a shrug of his shoulders he says, "That's life."

Unlike the family farmers we may picture, Warren Jolly does not spend his time duct-taping aging farm equipment. He says he rides each piece of machinery he owns for an hour every day, but he is not likely to get bleary-eyed in the combine as daylight dissolves. Instead, his job as manager of a business invariably brings him to the office, a room off the garage entrance cluttered with faxes and e-mail printouts. Paula describes Warren as someone who understands bookkeeping, who always knows from day to day exactly what the financial state of the farm is. A businessman through and through.


Warren Jolly may have his eye on the balance sheet, but he admits low commodity prices have hurt big farmers just like small ones. Farmers have become more businesslike, yet they are still losing money. According to the 1996 census, 10 percent of large farms—those with revenues of $100,000 or more—recorded operating losses. Many farmers overextend themselves as they grow by borrowing money to buy more land and equipment and then find they cannot repay what they have borrowed.

This is what scares people like Gary Wieler. He looks with longing when chunks of land go on the market or at the massive machines sold by the John Deere dealership in Morris. But he does not share Warren Jolly's willingness to assume the risk of debt. He does not want to become one of the 10 percent of farmers who try to grow and cannot make it work. Gary knows the bank would probably lend him money to buy land or equipment, but "How would I repay those loans?" he asks, not expecting an answer.

The Jollys have not succumbed to the perils of ill-advised growth. However, Warren says getting big is no insurance against the current downturn in the farm economy. Last year, 1999, was their most productive ever, yet it took all their earnings just to pay the bills. Jolly says $1 million goes through the farm every year; in 2000 he spent $40,000 on fuel, $250,000 on chemicals. He admits that the stress of operating under continually poor financial conditions is eating away at pure enjoyment. Warren contends that "getting big has helped us," but he does concede size is not the panacea some economists might have thought it was. "You can be large or small. It doesn't matter. The trick is to be businesslike."

He does not imagine corporations will move in to farm the land. Instead, he thinks foreign buyers will flex their muscles on the Canadian Prairies. (Saskatchewan was just in the process of opening up its foreign ownership laws at the time of this writing.) He says only foreign interests will have sufficiently deep pockets to handle the absurdly low return on investment that defines Canadian farming. "There is no other business that would be satisfied with our returns on investment." The average farm return on equity stands at less than 1 percent.

• • •

As Warren Jolly says, in agriculture, big is not necessarily beautiful. The larger a farm gets, the more likely it is to embrace monoculture systems, that is, growing huge tracts of a single crop. Monoculture—the deliberate choice of uniformity and the continual production of a single crop—is an essential characteristic of today's industrial agriculture. Machine harvesting requires that every plant in a field be ready for harvesting at the same time and by a single process. The requirement for uniformity demands that plants mature simultaneously and be roughly the same size and shape. Chemicals are an integral part of the equation to deliver uniformity and consistency. Modern agriculture has abandoned diversity in favour of productivity.

However, those requirements open up sections of the country to crop failures and disease. The Irish potato famine of the nineteenth century is the classic lesson about the perils of relying on just one variety. In that case, blight decimated the potato crop, which was largely planted to one type of the tuber. About two million people died of starvation over five years as the nation's staple food item disappeared.

The decline of genetic diversity, or biodiversity, is now universally recognized as a problem, and there is less diversity now than there was even a few decades ago. History has repeated itself. In 1970 the southern corn leaf blight destroyed $1 billion worth of the U.S. corn crop. Some southern fields were totally decimated. It is sobering to contemplate what kind of a swath a disease like that could cut today through Canada's Prairies. Modern industrial agriculture seems to have ignored the lessons of the past, instead urging farmers to rely on an ever-narrower range of crops. It seems to hold that agriculture's problems are "simple," that they can easily be fixed through the logic of industrialization.

North American agriculture rests on a very narrow genetic pool. At the beginning of the 1990s six varieties of corn accounted for 46 percent of the entire American corn crop; nine varieties of wheat made up one-half of the wheat crop; and two kinds of peas made up 96 percent of that crop. Few people realize when munching their fries from McDonald's that the corporation's insatiable appetite for potatoes has encouraged the widespread planting of just one variety. Even though there are more than two thousand species of potato, Russet Burbank now composes half of the world's harvest.

The monoculture philosophy thrives on the Jolly farm. Most years Warren plants every single acre with one variety of durum wheat. This year he tried something new—600 acres of chickpeas. But that leaves 5,800 acres in durum. With one variety and with the massive equipment parked on the hill down from the yard, the wheat fields can be easily planted, sprayed and harvested in a system managed from the farm office.

Jolly is not particularly concerned about his monoculture crop being susceptible to disease. He shrugs with indifference. He says it is not as if every other farmer in southwestern Saskatchewan has planted the same variety of durum. And he dismisses the suggestion that repeated planting of the same crop has sapped the soil of its nutrients. Conventional wisdom holds that you must rotate your crops from field to field every year, allowing the land to remain fallow, or idle, for a year and then planting a crop like beans to fix nitrogen in the soil. Jolly says his single most productive piece of land is a field that has been continuously cropped with durum wheat for twenty-seven years. He knows that defies all expectations. This field's surprising staying power even attracted the attention of university researchers, who came to collect some soil samples. They speculate that this field does not see much snow in the winter, which might protect diseases, yet experiences a deep killing frost.

Industrial agriculture is built on a foundation that assumes big is better, that monoculture economies of scale are more efficient and that chemical use is needed for high productivity. These assumptions have worrying implications for the environment.

Probably the key concern for most consumers is the use of chemicals in the production of food, whether hormones in livestock or pesticides in fruits, vegetables and grains. Despite assurances about the safety of pesticide use, consumers continue to be apprehensive. A poll conducted for

ABC's *20/20* early in 2000 found that 45 percent of consumers believed organic foods were more nutritious than conventional foods. Perhaps more surprising, 57 percent thought that producing organic food was better for the environment. A Canadian poll by Environics in 1995 indicated that 89 percent of Canadians supported the objective of a 50 percent reduction in pesticide use within five years, even if this practice resulted in produce costing more and looking less attractive. And in an Angus Reid Group poll in early 2000, 23 percent of respondents identified chemical use as the most important issue facing agriculture, virtually tied with genetic modification of food and the sustainability of agriculture itself. Proof of our concern comes in the marketplace. The organic food market is growing at dizzying rates—as much as 25 percent a year. Regardless of the assurances they are given, many consumers are convinced that the chemical practices of industrial agriculture are bad for themselves and the environment.

Much of our anxiety can be traced back to Rachel Carson's groundbreaking 1962 book *Silent Spring*. It blew the whistle on DDT, a pesticide that was being heralded in those days as both useful and benign. Most notorious chlorinated pesticides like DDT have since been banned in Canada, as their disastrous effects on wildlife and the environment were conclusively proven. The "crop protection" industry, as the pesticide business likes to call itself, declares that the chemicals used today are much less harmful, leaving few residues in the soil. But the World Wildlife Fund says it is naive to think pesticides have no impact on any living things other than those they are designed to kill. Like the birds that fell silent in Rachel Carson's day, a whole host of wildlife species are affected by today's more "gentle" chemicals. The loggerhead shrike, the prairie chicken and the swift fox have all virtually disappeared in the wake of chemical rain, according to the WWF.

The burrowing owl ended up on the endangered species list as a result of carbofurans used to counter grasshopper infestations. Liquid carbofuran was banned in 1995, the granular version in 1998. The WWF has been pressuring the federal government to ban lindane (with which some canola seeds are coated) as a pesticide toxic to wildlife and humans. Lindane, as well as its sister compounds, has been classed by the U.S. Environmental Protection Agency and others as a "possible carcinogen." In Canada, the Pest Management Review Agency launched a "special review" in December 1998 that could take years. Atrazine, an endocrine disrupter that has been blamed for the disfigurement of frogs in the St. Lawrence River valley, has been under review for years. Atrazine, the most popular of the family of triazines, is routinely used for the management of weeds in field crops, although not commonly in Western Canada. The World Health Organization has noted that atrazine causes breast and testicular tumours in rats, and it has been outlawed in several European countries.

Agriculture has also taken a toll on the soil. Although many of us take it for granted, the land is a non-renewable resource that has taken thousands of years to develop. When the bison roamed the Great Plains, the root structure of the prairie grasses formed an impenetrable web even the constant winds could not dislodge. When the steel edge of the first plough cut that interlocking mesh, it set in motion a cycle that carried the precious prairie topsoil on the tails of the wind. Since we began farming in Western Canada nearly one hundred years ago, we have depleted 40 percent of the soil. The Dirty Thirties were so dirty in part because the soil, particularly land that should never have been tilled, was ploughed. Under agricultural conditions it takes about five hundred years to make twenty-five millimetres of soil, and you need fifteen centimetres of soil to grow crops. So it will take a very long time to replace what has been carried away.

The movement of soil off the land and into waterways can cause serious problems for fisheries, transportation and land drainage. Sediment can actually clog up streams and ditches, prompting flooding. Because soil usually carries nutrients, like nitrogen and phosphorus, drifting soil can ruin fish habitats by clouding water with algae. And of course when soil dirties the air, it can cause problems for people with breathing difficulties such as asthma.

An awareness of farming's effect on the soil is growing. Fewer farmers are simply putting a match to the stubble left in their fields after the crop has been harvested. Instead, stubble is more and more often left on the land to stop the wind from blowing the soil away. This is called conservation tillage. Reduced tillage practices have gone a long way to preserving the soil. Instead of turning over the soil to control weeds, farmers plant directly into the stubble left from the year before. In 1998 it was estimated that 35 percent of crops in the United States were grown using conservation tillage.

In many ways industrial agriculture deserves credit for the introduction of conservation tillage. For example, Warren Jolly could not run the acreage he does if he had to cultivate all of his land. It is much easier to seed and fertilize directly into the previous year's crop stubble. Because conservation tillage demands specialized equipment, is has become the purview of the big. On the downside, to curb weed growth, conservation tillers tend to rely on broad-spectrum herbicides such as glyphosate, which they apply in the spring before seeding. No-till strategies may go a long way to resolving soil erosion, but they also require significantly more herbicide than a conventional acreage would.

The more chemicals farmers apply to the soil, the more energy they use circling their fields. The amount of energy required to produce a calorie of food is constantly increasing. At issue is not just the fuel required to do all the mechanized work on the farm; energy is also needed to manufacture fertilizer and chemicals at the front end of the process, and to transport and refrigerate food in the final stages of its delivery to the consumer. In comparison, most non-industrialized societies' agricultural sectors are net energy producers.

Agriculture also plays a role in the production of greenhouse gases. Carbon dioxide, nitrous oxide and methane gases are produced from livestock, farm equipment and the basic tilling of the soil. According to Agriculture and Agri-Food Canada, farming was responsible for releasing 67 million tonnes of damaging carbon dioxide equivalents in 1996. Most of this was nitrous oxide, which has a particularly long life in the atmosphere and an especially harmful impact on the ozone layer. Nitrous oxide is generated by soils that are ploughed for farming and then boosted with chemical fertilizers. One study showed a fertilized barley field near Quebec City had nitrous oxide emissions as high as seven kilo-grams per hectare per year, compared with negligible amounts from untouched soil in a nearby forest.

Agriculture has also been implicated in the pollution of waterways, aquifers and wells. Nitrogen fertilizers, which are routinely used on today's farms, can run off fields into rivers and streams, or leach into shallow aquifers. This effect is particularly marked if it rains shortly after application. Nitrates in water systems can cause the familiar green algae bloom. While it may be unsightly for us, it is often fatal to fish and other marine creatures. A study by Agriculture and Agri-Food Canada found that 87 percent of the surface water it tested in Alberta had nitrate levels above those specified for aquatic life.

Government scientists and university professors are producing volumes of research on whether industrial agriculture is increasing environmental damage. To be fair, it cannot be assumed that environmental problems result from farming having followed an industrial model. When one traces the reason for any specific environmental accident, it is often a case of a producer making a bad decision, whether spilling a jug of chemical near a well site or over-applying chemicals to a field before a rain. Accidents can happen on a small family farm as well as a large industrial operation. However, it is more likely that problems will occur when systems encourage the kind of thinking we might see in a factory. A family farmer loves and cares for his land, hoping to pass it on to the next generation; a farm manager may not have that kind of ethic. Although government has been an enthusiastic promoter of the industrial model, even a joint federal and Alberta review of water systems concluded: "It is generally accepted that the greater the level of agricultural intensity, the greater the risk to groundwater and surface water quality." The link between industrial agriculture and environmental damage is most easily made with intensive livestock operations, where hundreds of barns are crowded into a small space—as they are in Alberta's "feedlot alley."

·  ·  ·

The waitress in Picture Butte's Red Cactus Grill comes blasting through the swinging doors from the kitchen with the confidence of someone who knows no one will dare cross her. She bears down on my table with a Coke in hand. I would prefer a cup of coffee or tea, but I am not about to make her day worse. She has already told me she was in at six-thirty this morning, boiling water for the day shift. "I wouldn't want to live in the olden days. No way," she says reflectively. "I would come in half an hour early and start boiling water so it's ready for the girl that comes in at seven o'clock and we just had to continue boiling water throughout the day." Since local health authorities discovered dangerous microscopic parasites in the water ten days ago, everyone in Picture Butte has been under orders to boil their tap water. It is a major inconvenience for this town's favourite coffee spot, and a potential health risk for the burghers of Picture Butte.

This was December 1997, long before the water in Walkerton, Ontario, became fatal. Picture Butte was in fact the second community in the 200-kilometre stretch north of Lethbridge, known locally as "feedlot alley," to be told it could no longer drink its tap water for fear that disease would strike its young, elderly and infirm.

Although its name may conjure up images of a picturesque town nestled in rolling hills, Picture Butte, population 1,000, looks a lot like most farm communities on the Prairies. Not exactly a "picture," it is low-slung and serviceable to half-ton traffic. Nor did I see a butte in town. Picture Butte's true claim to fame is emblazoned on the sign leading into the community: THE LIVESTOCK FEEDING CAPITAL OF CANADA.

A quick drive out of town takes you to that classic southern Alberta landscape, undulating with grassy hills swept clean of snow by warm and strong chinook winds. Buttes and coulees overlook the deep, treeless ravines that the Oldman River cuts through the scenery. But off the well-travelled routes, tucked behind the hills, are the livestock operations that give this area its nickname. There are about 1.3 million animals in feedlot alley: 500,000 cattle, 600,000 chickens and 200,000 hogs. It represents one of the highest concentrations of livestock in all of Canada.

The animals here generate as much waste as a city of eight million people—and all of it is untreated. The manure is simply sprayed onto farmers' fields with a giant gun or slopped out the back of a truck. The concern is that manure will wash into the Oldman River, which supplies the irrigation canals that are the lifeblood of this parched, windswept corner of the world. The irrigation canals are also the source of water for local towns like Picture Butte.

From the perspective of a visitor like me, this is another story of a self-evident conflict between economics and the environment. But there are subtleties here that are specific to a rural community. Leading the charge for the environmental concerns is not your typical young urban activist, but a retired, long-time resident of Picture Butte who appreciates the economic benefits of the livestock industry. Ed Malmberg started up a petition demanding "clean air and clean water" and for a short time became a media star, talking to radio, TV and newspaper reporters from as far away as Calgary. Then, when he got a little pressure from local business, he toned down his environmental talk. "I never knocked any of them down. The only ones I ever put pressure against is the local government and the government of Alberta. And not to put the industry down whatsoever. I want to see us all get our heads together and get this straightened out for our next future, because if we don't, we're in trouble," he says defensively in the neutral ground of the local volunteer firehall.

Rick Paskal runs a cattle feedlot just north of town—one of the places the formerly fiery Ed Malmberg would have been concerned about. It fattens about seventeen thousand cattle each year, in the last stage of their life before dispatch to the packing plant. Paskal is a businessman who spends much of his day in the feedlot offices, protected from the brisk chinook winds, co-ordinating the movement of cattle first to the feedlot and then to the slaughterhouse. The cattle are outside, enclosed in pens measuring about 30 metres by 30 metres, a couple of hundred to a pen. They walk about sullenly, probably having been deposited here after enjoying the relative freedom of some open rangeland in southern Alberta. Their hooves squelch through urine and dung, creating a thick muck that makes movement difficult. The highlight of their day now is when the feed truck comes rumbling down the access road, dropping a shower of dry, dusty pellets in the long trough that flanks the pens.

There are cowboys here like those we know from the romantic mythology of Alberta's past. They are in spurs and boots, saddled up on handsome horses. But they wear ball caps instead of Stetsons, and they do not think about working up a full gallop as they check on the cattle in the tight enclosure of the pens.

Paskal says it is simply wrong to blame feedlots for the water pollution, even though there are only voluntary provincial guidelines on how feedlots are to be run and how manure is to be handled. He says the larger operations like his are diligent about ensuring that manure never ends up in the waterways. He is offended that some producers are less careful.

Paskal lives in Picture Butte too, and he says he is not about to take any risks with the water. He is a member of the same community as Ed Malmberg. "I don't want my family or my neighbours being subject to poor waste management." He hints that the people who are complaining just don't like the smell that thousands of animals and their waste inevitably give off. "If people want to move out to the country for the clean air and the romance of country living, I'm telling you in the county of Lethbridge we have an intensive livestock industry. It's really in its infancy. It's an industry that is probably going to grow from here."

However, this is not a theoretical debate about the conflict between economics and the environment. The facts are clear: Picture Butte's water *was* polluted with parasites that could be traced back to livestock manure. That was confirmed by Dr. Paul Hasselback, the province's chief medical health officer for the Chinook Region. Much like the situation in Walkerton years later, Picture Butte did have a water treatment system. Hasselback's investigators found that the system in Picture Butte, like the one in Walkerton, was not operating as it should.

Hasselback has to deal with the reality that parasitic infections like listeria and campylobacter, as well as the incidence of deadly E. coli 0157:H7 contamination, often known as hamburger disease, are higher in this area than anywhere else in the country. He has been lucky in a way that on his watch people have been struck only with diarrhea, stomach upset and kidney failure; so far there have been no deaths directly tied to the water.

Hasselback is not eager to take on the industrial livestock industry, but he is clear about how he views his responsibility to people like both Ed Malmberg and Rick Paskal: "My job is to protect the health of the people that live in this region. And therefore we have to do something about it."

As I winged my way back to the city, far from the intensive livestock operations that serve our appetites, the word came: Picture Butte's water treatment system was fixed. Chlorine would vanquish the bacteria. Life would resume as it should around the coffee machine at the Red Cactus Grill.

Over the following year the province of Alberta would become more stringent about the whole question of how manure is handled, proposing new regulations and codes of practice to replace the voluntary guidelines. At the same time, two feedlot operations were charged with letting their manure lagoons drain into the Little Bow River and thus into the water irrigation system.

As the pressure builds for more intensive industrial livestock operations across the country, I can't help but wonder if cold, clean, pure water streaming from the kitchen tap is one more aspect of a vanished past.

Dave Malowski stands before his most recent attempt at diversification with a propane-powered blowtorch in hand. The Gilbert Plains, Manitoba, farmer ignites the first of a long row of big bales lined up in a field that is supposed to be seeded to oats. The bales are the stalks of the 110 acres of hemp he grew here last year. They were supposed to be worth $30 a bale, sold to produce a durable fibre that would become shirts, backpacks and rope. But the market disappeared when the company that contracted Malowski and 214 other area farmers to grow the hemp suddenly went bankrupt.

Malowski is a grain and beef farmer in the rich parklands of western Manitoba. He has already cushioned his business with a focus on both livestock and grains. But as a young bachelor coming back to take over the operations of the family farm, he was appalled at how difficult it was to make money when commodity prices were as low as they were. He was eager to believe a solution might lie at the end of the hemp rainbow.

His hope was diversification. Farmers today are instructed to get big or get out. And at the same time they are told to "diversify, diversify, diversify." Those two principles seem to be at loggerheads: one encourages specialization and the economies of scale while the other calls on farmers to try new things, to hedge their bets and produce for small, niche markets. The merit of diversification is a favourite message of both governments and agricultural economists. When Ottawa cut the support of the Crow rate benefit, it said the move would encourage diversification.

In 1999 the town of Dauphin, just down the road from Malowski's farm, was abuzz with news of a $25-million hemp processing plant that was said to be coming to town. Consolidated Growers and Processors (CGP), a two-year-old California company that boasted contacts in Europe, the U.S. and Australia, talked of giving vital new life to the hemp industry in Canada. The plant had been outlawed in Canada since the 1930s because of its connection with its cousin, marijuana. The ban came about even though industrial hemp had virtually no THC, the controversial ingredient in the drug marijuana, and even though it was accepted that the stalks could produce a good source of durable fibre and the seeds could be crushed to produce a healthy oil. Except for a brief return during the Second World War hemp had not been grown in this country for nearly sixty years. But hemp still had its promoters, and they continued to lobby the government to allow its return. In 1998 Ottawa permitted 5,930 acres of hemp to be grown, although farmers had to clear criminal checks and production was carefully regulated by Health Canada.

Enter CGP. Until its appearance on the scene, the promotion of hemp had been the purview of true enthusiasts who sold products into health food stores and other niche markets. CGP intended to change all that. It said it wanted to transform hemp into a thriving new industry. It proposed building twenty hemp processing plants across the Prairies, the first of which would be in Dauphin.

Farmers in the Dauphin area, like Dave Malowski, were quick and willing converts. "To me it looked like the pot of gold [sic] at the end of the rainbow. I thought that there would be some dollar signs. Some money. Times are tight," Malowski says, thinking back. He and his fellow farmers planted eighteen thousand acres with hemp, three times more than had been sown in all of Canada the previous year. They even overlooked what should have been warning signs. At a meeting in the spring of 1999 there were efforts to convince farmers to invest $5,000 each in the venture. Then the Manitoba Securities Commission got involved. It ruled that the money was being raised without the proper paperwork, so it seized $450,000 from a bank where it was being held and returned it to farmers.

Most farmers were focused on the pragmatic challenges of growing a new crop. And at first, hemp seemed a marvel. It could not be sprayed with any chemicals, so input costs were minimal. In late summer it grew with verve, often five centimetres a day, until it stood an impressive three metres tall. However, harvesting it was another thing. The stalks were so tough they constantly got twisted up in the combine. Malowski bought a straight-cut header for his combine that he hoped would make the work easier. It did, although he says it was still a tough slog. Along with the cost of cleaning and drying the grain, the hemp crop cost him plenty. "The cleaning was close to $900. Fuel was involved. Twine for baling. And lots of stress. You can't put a price on stress. More than enough for me not to want to grow it for a long, long time," he says, adding up the costs. Thankfully, by late fall he had $19,000 worth of hemp seeds in his bins and $2,000 worth of bales.

However, no one came to collect the grain or the fibre. Two deadlines passed, and money that was owing to Malowski never arrived. In the spring of 2000, CGP declared bankruptcy in a California court, and Malowski realized no one would be coming to pick up his seed or his bales. CGP had promised to pay farmers about $5 million for their hemp crop. Now bins in farmyards around Dauphin are bulging with hemp seed there seems to be no market for.

From his vantage point in the year 2000, Malowski can only curse himself for falling prey to the hopes that were being sold by CGP. He says he was vulnerable because the farming business is so tenuous. The chance of getting in on the ground floor of a new crop—the ultimate farm diversification—was too attractive. As he touches the torch to the first bale, he dismisses the hype on hemp as "somebody's pipe dream. Oh, it's a lot of hype. They said it's a wonder crop, it's a Cinderella crop, it's going to be the crop that saves the farm. It's not. It's got a lot of growing pains to go through. We're back to baby steps now."

As the flames lick the bales, curling in tongues of flame, it is clear Malowski's dream of successfully diversifying his farm has literally gone up in smoke.

The experience of Dave Malowski and the other would-be hemp farmers is sadly all too familiar. Agricultural producers across the country are particularly open to the sales pitch of operators who try to sell them on a dream that cannot be achieved.

Wishful thinking has motivated many small towns and farm producers. The community of Ste. Agathe, Manitoba, for example, supported plans in 1995 by an Ontario company, Canadian Agra International, to set up the country's first chemical-free cold-press plant for canola. Although the housing was up, the $55-million project was delayed and delayed until finally, in April 1999, the Manitoba assets were put into receivership. The plant never began production. The huge, hulking concrete structure stands just off the highway, a tangible reminder that what seems too good to be true often is.

Farmers across the West have strayed far from their roots. The grandchildren of the Commonwealth's best wheat farmers have experimented with all kinds of crops. Coriander, chickpeas and canary seed have all become popular as farmers attempted to diversify. Producers planted more than three million acres of field peas in 2000. However, there are limits to what diversification will allow. Farmers are dependent on their soil and climatic conditions. It was the soil and the climate that once defined the Canadian Prairies as the best wheat-growing area in the world.

Fads also come and go so fast that farmers often cannot keep up. In the mid-1990s ginseng, used in alternative medicine, offered a generous market. However, by 2000 the bottom had fallen out of that market too. There was a glut of canary seed. Even canola, once viewed as the prairie wonder crop, was falling out of favour: because of low prices farmers planted only 12.2 million acres in 2000, compared with 13.8 million the previous year.

Diversification as promoted by economists assumes that crop production is easy—that any old crop can be grown anywhere. In fact, agronomic conditions—the weather and the soil—are the key consideration. For example, durum wheat grows well in southwestern Saskatchewan; that is why Warren and Paula Jolly grow so much of it.

In 2000 they experimented for the first time with an alternate crop that was said to be well suited to their agronomic conditions. They practised diversification by planting three hundred acres of chickpeas, and so it seems did everyone else in their durum country. But the rain that fell in the early stages of the chickpeas' growth brought disease. Only farmers like the Jollys could afford the necessary fungicide. The chemical was in such demand that supplies ran out. Then a warm fall confused the plants, encouraging them to sprout again. By October what had seemed like a clever means of diversification was looking as if it might have backfired.

The finicky moods of new crops, along with fickle markets, prompted many prairie grain producers to turn to exotic livestock. The tall antlers of elk can often be seen these days beyond the high game fences of Western farms. Producers saw off the antlers of the bull elk in early summer when they are engorged with blood and ripe with velvet. Asian customers will pay a good dollar for the ground-up velvet, which they use in medicinal food supplements to improve stamina, strength and blood circulation and to fight stress and fatigue. It is a renewable resource, as the antlers naturally grow back and would fall off again in subsequent years. In 2000 the price for one pound of antlers was between $50 and $60.

Since each animal can produce about twenty-five pounds of antlers each year, proceeds are good.

But the industry is entirely at the mercy of the Asian market. When the Asian flu hit in the late 1990s, Canada's elk business was trounced. Even so, the experience of elk farmers has been an overwhelming success compared with the other exotic livestock some farmers have tried their hand at. Both ostriches and emus were originally sold with the promise that one day they would yield a low-fat, low-cholesterol meat and an exotic, valuable leather. At first, of necessity, the industry was focused entirely on developing stock; there could be no industry without it. Breeding pairs of the flightless birds became incredibly valuable, a breeding pair of ostriches costing $60,000. For a while it seemed like the ostrich and emu business was little more than a trade in breeding pairs, mirroring the pyramid schemes that bilk the hopeful.

Regardless, the enthusiasm for ostrich and emu ran high in the mid-1990s. At a meeting in the dead of the prairie winter of 1995 in Oakbluff, Manitoba, four hundred people paid $6 each to attend what amounted to an emu revival meeting, complete with an emu buffet and an emu-leather fashion show. The audience was told it would not be long before a market developed for nutritious emu meat, high-quality emu oil and beautiful emu leather.

The sales pitch was compelling. But striking it rich in ostriches and emus was anything but a sure bet. After several difficult years South African ostrich meat did find an audience, appearing in specialty stores across the West. The tough, dark meat of emus, however, never found much favour even in gourmet markets. The Australian birds are smaller than ostriches but cost just as much to keep. Emus were reported running loose in western Manitoba, apparently set free by farmers who found they could not afford to feed them with no market for their meat.

Michelle and Roland Gregoire of St. Jean-Baptiste, Manitoba, were among the first prairie farmers to try emus. They began with a couple of breeding pairs—before the prices shot up—in 1993. In subsequent years they had as many as ninety birds in the yard. But the Gregoires called it quits in 1998. Roland says their 2,200-acre grain farm was profitable compared with the emus. "Emus are definitely not the answer." The Gregoires did not manage to sell a single bird for meat during their time in the fledgling industry. Weather solidified their thoughts of liquidation. When the Red River spilled over its banks in 1997, the emu pens were flooded. The effort of trying to evacuate squawking birds built for the Australian outback convinced the Gregoires that enough was enough. The fences are down now at the Gregoire farm, no trace remaining of their brush with two-legged diversification.

Emus, ostriches, hemp, ginseng and, before them, chinchillas and hedgehogs are examples of how difficult it is to diversify prairie agriculture. Although the talk of new consumer demand sounds appealing, the fact is that many of these new endeavours have turned into complete failures.

The irony is that in the past almost all farms, small though they might have been, were diversified. In the early twentieth century just about every farm was self-sufficient, with a milk cow, some chickens and pigs, and perhaps some sheep. In 1921, 84 percent of farms had at least one milk cow, but this figure dropped steadily to 1 percent in 1996. The 1951 census showed 69 percent of farms had hens and chickens; by 1996 that number had fallen to 10 percent.

True diversification is one that helps the farm mimic nature. In ecological terms, diversity increases stability. True and valuable diversity helps build soil fertility, decreases susceptibility to weather, diseases and pest problems, and lessens the impact of price fluctuations. Farmers could achieve genuine diversity by rotating their crops regularly or considering alternative techniques like intercropping—low-tech strategies to be sure, but possibly a real route to sustainability.

The other mantra of the agriculture business these days is that farmers should get into more value-added production, that adding value to what they grow is the way out of the existing farm income crisis. "Value-added" is another term from the industrialized model of agribusiness.

Value-added refers to any and all interventions that add cost and profit to the final product, just as they would in a factory. In other words, increased economic activity is worth more than the delivery of basic food and nutrition. That message has been sent to farmers in a clear, direct way by commodity prices. There is little money to be made from bulk commodities; instead, farmers need to embrace the shift to processed and consumer-ready products.

Farmers are game to try just about anything to develop ways of further processing their products at home for niche markets. However, there are very few processing plants on the Canadian Prairies. In 1880, for example, there were more than two hundred flour mills in Manitoba and what was then the North-West. By 1891 that number had shrunk to about forty. Today, four mills in all of Canada produce 80 percent of our flour—and the biggest are located in Ontario.

They may be game, but it is not an easy task to transform men and women who have spent a lifetime of self-imposed isolation on tractors or combines into marketing and agri-food processing gurus. Just because they know how to grow a crop does not mean they know how to process or market it. But farmers are true entrepreneurs, prepared to adapt and change. In the last few years they have dusted off the prairie tradition of mutual aid that defined the early years of the last century by forming "new-generation co-operatives." The new style of co-op is designed to bring value-added processing to the Prairies and increase members' incomes by adding value to the raw farm product. Unlike the open membership of the traditional co-ops, the new-generation versions limit their membership to those who initially invest and who commit a portion of their production to the venture. Farmers own capital shares in these organizations based on how much raw product they contribute to the common enterprise. It is a modern business adaptation of the co-operative ideas of the past.

New-generation co-ops are seen as a way for farmers to band together to make their efforts at diversification work. In Dauphin, a new-generation co-op is hoping to market the hemp that farmers grew for CGP and to develop a small-scale processing operation. And the Ostrich Marketing Co-op, a new-generation venture with thirty members, is the biggest player in the ostrich business on the Prairies.

It is critical for farmers looking to expand to focus on niche markets that large agribusiness corporations either cannot or will not get involved with. Vincent D'Amanour-Boadu, the director of research at the University of Guelph's George Morris Centre, says farmers hoping to explore new processing opportunities should avoid going toe to toe with big corporations. He says they should not try to grow products for "Campbell Soup but for the small mom-and-pop operation." He recommends that farmers produce what he calls "differentiated products"—unique, convenient foods that consumers want. "If you give consumers what they are looking for, they will reward you."

He offers as an example the case of Warburtons. This is a family-owned bakery chain in the United Kingdom that successfully sells a bread that is three times the price of a typical loaf. Warburtons has been baking bread for 125 years and has drawn its wheat from the Canadian Prairies for nearly that long. The Warburtons deluxe loaf is made largely with wheat grown under contract by farmers in southwestern Manitoba and southeastern Saskatchewan. The company got special permission from the CWB to contract directly with farmers. The wheat they grow—varieties chosen by Warburtons to suit their processing—is kept separate from the wheat that ends up in the Canadian Wheat Board supply. The British company pays farmers a $20 per tonne premium for their trouble.

Drayton Grain Processors is another take on D'Amanour-Boadu's "differentiatied products." North Dakota farmers banded together several years ago with the general idea that they wanted to get some more money for the grain they grew and provide some benefits for their home community at the same time. They looked at making all sorts of products—pasta, barley products, edible bean products, even tortilla shells—before they settled on a frozen dough that is now selling very well.

However, developing value-added processing does pose some very steep challenges. First and foremost is the difficulty farmers have in raising money even from their own community in these cash-strapped times. Trying to obtain financing for a value-added venture is the perennial Catch-22. The bank will not give would-be processors a loan unless they have significant private contributions; but it is hard to convince even supportive neighbours and friends to contribute when they are short on cash themselves. The raising of funds for value-added processing is such a challenge that companies have started up for the express purpose of bringing together people or companies that are prepared to contribute venture capital in return for equity. Venture capital is the new watchword in modern agriculture.

Additionally, there are what some call "institutional blockages." That is how Warren Jolly describes the Canadian Wheat Board. He and others argue that the CWB's monopoly puts hurdles in the path of farm profit and diversification. Jolly bluntly says that value-added processing would have developed in areas encouraged by geography if the Canadian Wheat Board did not exist. Pasta production, he says, would have happened on the Prairies if the CWB did not encourage the sale of raw wheat to other countries.

The case of Prairie Pasta Producers has become the flashpoint in the debate about the CWB. About 650 Saskatchewan, Manitoba, Montana and North Dakota farmers have been trying to set up a plant to turn their durum into pasta. They spent at least a year fighting for an exemption from the Wheat Board's monopoly. Under the monopoly, farmers sell their wheat to the Board and then in turn the Board sells it to the plant. Prairie Pasta has argued that farmers could earn about 17 cents more per bushel by selling durum directly to their own pasta plant, because the plant would pay them a premium. They say producers deserve the higher price because they are going to invest in the plant. If they were required to sell their wheat to the CWB and then the plant bought it back from the Board, they would only receive the Wheat Board's lower blended price.

Prairie Pasta Producers says its member farmers deserve the higher price because they are going to invest in the plant. They say the Wheat Board offers a lot of talk about diversification but does little to further it.

Coming to the defence of the board, the National Farmers Union says any special price pool for Prairie Pasta would come at the expense of other farmers. "The cwb has a sterling track record when it comes to fostering value-added processing."

The twenty Altona farmers who started up a pasta company five years ago called Prairie Harvest Canada are watching the debate with some amazement. Instead of building a new plant, they bought one in Edmonton. Prairie Harvest Canada spokesman Les Kletke says if Prairie Pasta thinks they are having a hard time with the Wheat Board, they may be surprised by the fierce competition they can expect later from retail supermarket giants.

In the summer of 2000, Prairie Pasta put its fight with the Wheat Board on the back burner as it tried to raise money from farmers in an escrow drive.


Clearly, farming today involves much more than simply putting some seeds in the ground and waiting for them to grow. These days farmers are supposed to get big, efficient, productive and diversified, and to embrace value-added niche markets. However, Canadian farmers have already done much of what they were supposed to do. They are bigger. More efficient. More productive. More diversified. And the experience of new-generation co-ops shows they are committed to taking on more value-added processing. But still, many find it hard to make ends meet. They have been sold a prescription for their health that simply does not work. That is largely because they are confronted with circumstances beyond their control, which originate beyond the borders of their country.

*Seven*

# Go Global

*July 17, 2000*

*It is early morning on the first day of the Carman Country Fair. The dis-*
*plays are not yet open, nor is the midway, but there is a small crush of*
*people gathered around the livestock barns. More are coming in, sporting*
*plastic weekend bracelets that mark them as regulars. They congratulate*
*each other on the weather; the last fair was evidently a washout. "Wow,*
*this sure is better than last year!" The sky is indeed blazingly clear, hint-*
*ing of prairie heat to come on this, the 4-H feature day at the fair.*

*The 4-H movement is alive and well in Carman. There are four*
*barns filled with steers, calves, ponies and horses. Girls in full English*
*dressage or Western hats and checked shirts are atop impossibly tall horses*
*with perfectly brushed tails and manes. On the beef side of the fence, the*
*steers are fluffed and backcombed to show off their naturally curly hair*
*and the sweep of their long tails. The human participants in this bovine*
*beauty pageant carry a square metal-toothed comb in the back pocket of*

*their jeans for last-minute touch-ups. The boys and girls are scrubbed and neat in matching golf shirts issued by their 4-H club. They represent the future of Canadian agriculture.*

*The first competition in the beef ring is designed to show how well the kids handle their animals. It is not an easy matter to walk a 1,200-pound steer like a dog on a collar and leash. The kids use a metal stick to scratch the steer on the underbelly just behind the front legs. In theory, this is supposed to calm the animal. One young girl never gets to use her "show stick." Her steer lurches in enthusiastic bursts across the ring, pushing her into a frantic stride as she tries to keep up. He rushes the rail, then stops abruptly and will not move. The adult ring handler comes along, grabs the twitching tail and steers the animal from behind. Not an auspicious start.*

*The Wieler boys are in the intermediate group, the twelve- to fourteen-year-olds. They are tall and blond, in the maroon shirts of the Roland 4-H club. They are also jittery with nerves, unsmiling in their focused intensity. The judge is looking for children who act as if they are in control and are having fun. It does not seem as if Nicholas and Philip fit the bill. Their homegrown, non-pedigree Red Angus crosses are handsome in a bovine way, but they are fidgety too, testing their anxious masters, refusing to line up their legs in a perfect four-point stance or raise their heads in the requisite imperious manner.*

*The two boys do not make the cut of the top eight handlers. Their stoic attitude holds as they try to control their steers in the back row behind the winners, who are cut out of the pack for the appreciation of the grandparents and parents in the grandstand. But as soon as they bring their steers back to the barn, their control breaks. Nicholas cries openly, clearly frustrated by his showing. Philip, at fourteen, ties up his steer and pats him on the forelock, but muttering under his breath, he voices his frustration. "I'm never doing this again."*

*But he does, of course. Three more times during the day he and his brother guide their steers out into the ring, pretending they are leading docile little critters. One of them is guaranteed of success when the top two from each of the five clubs competing here are chosen to contend in the grand finale. Roland may be where Canada's 4-H movement started, but it now has only three members in its beef club. At least one of the Wieler boys will make the grade. Philip has calmed his nerves, and he is chosen for the finals.*

*Late in the afternoon the top two from each 4-H club, including Philip, file out again. Honed by practice, Philip stands tall, not quite smiling but certainly more confident. The steer follows his lead, stands head up, 1,300 pounds ranged over solid flanks. The competition is tough. There is a short young boy dwarfed by his massive two-toned steer but clearly self-assured and in control; and a pretty girl, almost ready for a beauty pageant of her own, is alongside a steer with locks that look as if they have been washed and set. The judge, corpulent, in a striped shirt, suspenders and big Stetson, has the youngsters circle round again and again. He weaves between the animals, patting a flank here, grabbing an ankle there. Then, with radio microphone in hand, he walks past all the pedigree-breed Herefords, Charolais and Limousins and declares Philip's mongrel steer the winner. There is the flash of an unassuming smile from the young Wieler as the purple ribbon and rosette are handed over. The photographer for the local paper takes a picture of Philip and his newly anointed champion, and the steer is led into a new stall festooned with a banner that reads "Grand Champion Steer."*

*It is a high point for Philip, and even for Gary, because he can take credit for breeding a championship steer. But there is no excess romanticism here. The steer will be sold at tomorrow's auction for $1.46 a pound—a bit of a premium for the 4-H tradition. Although he will pay his dad for feed and upkeep, Philip will take home a total of $1,730. In less than two weeks' time Philip will be invited to the Carman slaughterhouse to inspect the carcass.*

*The family revels in the reflected glory. A prize. A good sale. Even Thomas, who took Nicholas's steer out into the ring in the peewee class, earned a ribbon. (All the participants did.) Sadly, in keeping with the bittersweet mood that seems to colour farming these days, when the Wielers get home on Friday night they find a cow and two calves inexplicably dead in the pasture. There is no veterinarian available on a weekend, so the Wielers can only ruefully speculate on what happened during what should have been a triumphant couple of days.*

❧ Nothing is more intensely local than a day at the country fair. The family, the fair, Carman, Manitoba—for now these are the foci of the Wieler family. But more and more, producers like Gary Wieler are told they must keep in mind the part they play in the global agri-food system. The reality is that they are competing not with farmers down the road but with producers in Great Britain and Australia.

The headline in the *Western Producer* says much about the new global ethic on the Canadian Prairies: POOR PEA CROP IN FRANCE IS GOOD FOR CANADA. Canadian farmers are learning the modern global way: take pleasure in others' misfortune. For what happens in one corner of the world has an impact on other exporting nations. Today's unspoken truth is that people are hoping there will be a serious disaster somewhere in the world so grain prices will maybe go up.

There was a time when most food was grown locally. Just about every woman was involved in the production and processing of the family's meals. In those days women had few options. There was no way of preserving food, beyond drying or salting, and no way of transporting it long distances. Unless she was lucky enough to have hired help, a woman's place truly was in the kitchen.

Today, in the industrialized world, there is a huge distance between where food is grown and where it is consumed. It is a distance of philosophy—urban versus rural—and a very real, practical distance, one that often spans continents. Every day a complex industry based on international food agents and brokers, global shipping lines, jet transport and trucking operations sends food around the world. Wheat grown by Gary Wieler is exported all over the globe on the basis of grain prices set in Chicago and Minneapolis. Bananas, grapes and other fresh fruits and vegetables are imported into winter-locked Canada by virtue of a high-tech system. Processed food made with Canadian ingredients is assembled and manufactured in American towns and then trucked north of the border. Cargill has developed special bulk tanker ships to haul frozen orange juice concentrate from Brazil to New Jersey and Rotterdam, where it is packaged. Fish are pulled out of the ocean near Lisbon and appear on ice in markets in New York and Vancouver the next day. It is an intricate system, virtually invisible to most consumers, that somehow, mysteriously, gets food to our tables, over long distances and when the seasons would normally preclude it.

It is the global market of supply and demand that sets internationally traded commodity prices. Wheat markets are now glutted and, with a surplus supply, prices have gone down dramatically. In the past four years the world has seen four out of the five best wheat crops ever. Since 1995 the Canadian Wheat Board says wheat stocks among the five major exporters—Canada, the U.S., the European Union, Argentina and Australia—have soared by 93 percent. Between 1980 and 1999 Europe produced 42 percent more wheat, Australia's production increased 44 percent and Argentina's 26 percent.

Canada's prairie grain business was designed to be part of the global economy right from the start. John A. Macdonald's national dream demanded homesteaders for the West who were ready to grow grain to feed the East and then sell to the rest to the world. For at least two decades in the early years of the last century, Canada did just that. It was the world's number-one wheat exporter, accounting for 50 percent of the international market. The key to Canada's success were the hard red kernels of wheat that flourished in the dry grasslands.

Canada's pre-eminence on the global wheat market was soon undercut by stiff competition. By 1935, Canada had been nudged aside by the United States. In the late 1990s, Canada produced for export just 20 percent of the world's wheat. It jostled with Australia and the European Union for second place in the hierarchy of exporters. Forecasts by the Canadian Wheat Board now predict Canada's share of the global export market will slip still further. The Wheat Board anticipates our export stake will slide to third place, behind the United States, with 29 percent, and the European Union, with 18 percent. Ironically, the CWB says Canadian producers will continue to grow and export more wheat and durum in the coming decade, but they will still lose ground in the battle for market share. That is not just because of aggressive competition from the U.S. and Europe, but because countries other than the big five are expected to increase their exports. And just to rub salt into the wound, other countries have acquired improved varieties that buyers feel equal the quality of Canada's once fabled red spring number one.

The current market may be oversupplied, but the amount of actual wheat traded has remained flat. For about fifteen years demand has hovered steadily at around 100 million tonnes. In 1998, in a burst of enthusiasm, the Canadian Wheat Board talked about global trade reaching 125.5 million tonnes. However, by 2000 the Board was much more modest, and more realistic. It is now looking matter-of-factly at how politics is changing the landscape. Economic slumps in Asia, Latin America and Russia mean that demand is low. And countries that used to depend on imports are beginning to grow their own. China is now the world's biggest producer of wheat. It does not export what it grows because 13 percent of its 1.2 billion people still do not get enough to eat. India is also moving towards self-sufficiency. It is now the third-largest wheat producer in the world.

Canada's dream of being a lead export player in the global wheat economy once again seems overly optimistic. Even the European-based Organization for Economic Co-operation and Development predicts the industrialized world will have to take a back seat to developing countries on the food front in the future. Although the OECD forecasts world agricultural production will grow by an average rate of 1.8 percent a year through to 2010, most of that growth will happen in developing countries as they move more towards industrialized systems. OECD countries will contribute only "marginally."

Brian White is the vice-president of market analysis at the Canadian Wheat Board and the man responsible for forecasting what will happen to global wheat markets. His office is decorated with a simple diagram of a kernel of wheat—more functional than aesthetic—and a series of Russian nesting dolls is lined up on the credenza. Stacks of paper litter the floor in the filing system of the busy office. He swears he can put his hand on just about any document at a moment's notice. But with an easy smile he admits that it is a bit more difficult to predict world events.

As a young man, White lived in the Soviet Union for a year and acquired the language fluency that made him attractive to the CWB. He was the Board's lead man on the Soviet file through much of the 1980s, when the U.S.S.R. was Canada's primary customer for wheat exports. He had no sense then that the days of the Soviet empire were numbered. After he attended a conference on Soviet relations in November 1990, he reported in a routine memo that there had been talk of an overthrow. Within six months the Communist republic disappeared, and so did its single buying desk. Canadian wheat sales dried up as the new market-oriented countries found themselves without money for imports.

Political events conspired to make the early 1990s a challenging time for the wheat business. When the Berlin Wall came down, CWB sales to what had been East Germany dried up. The largest importer in the Middle East used to be Iraq. Who would have anticipated the 1991 Gulf War that placed embargoes on Iraq and made Iran the big market? "Food is a political business," says White with obvious relish.

It is a lesson for Canadian farmers. These days Russia, Ukraine and other Eastern European countries are struggling to get their own agricultural houses in order and produce their own wheat. Brazil is now the world's biggest importer. The fallout from political upheaval is reflected in the international food trade. What happens in Russia has an impact on Gary Wieler's farm, 8 kilometres northwest of Kane, Manitoba.

The current federal government's national dream is all about securing Canada's place in a free-trade-based global economy. Its energies are directed to international trade negotiations, to the furthering of liberalized trade policies and to its own domestic efforts to score trade surpluses. Ottawa's agriculture policy is dominated by trade concerns to the point where export considerations set the policy for domestic agriculture. In many ways we do not have an agricultural policy; we have a trade policy. In December 1998 the National Farmers Union held a convention pointedly called "Trade, as if farmers mattered."

The Agriculture and Agri-Food Canada Web site reflects Ottawa's aspirations. It says Canada is using the World Trade Organization, the North American Free Trade Agreement and other forums to "improve access for producers and agribusinesses in markets as diverse as the United States, Mexico, Europe, Puerto Rico, Korea and South Africa." That is small consolation for producers who cannot seem to keep the farm afloat.

The federal government takes pride in saying it has long maintained a trade surplus. Canada's overall exports have increased from 25 percent of the GDP ten years ago to 43 percent in 1999. Pierre Pettigrew, the minister for international trade, points out that one in three jobs in Canada are related to trade.

Agriculture is an important component of our trade. More than 70 percent of the value of all Canadian agricultural production—about $21 billion—is sent out of the country. That represents a trade surplus of $6.7 billion, or 16.7 percent of Canada's overall trade surplus. However, the food portion of Canadian merchandise exports has been dropping, down to 7 percent in 1998 from more than 8 percent in 1992. And our primary market is increasingly the United States. Canada sent about 52 percent of its exports south of the border in the years from 1994 to 1998; in 1999 that leapfrogged up to 61 percent.

Exports are a natural consequence of Canada's circumstances. The country simply does not have the population to consume its natural resources and productivity. At 43 percent, exports as a proportion of Canada's GDP are currently among the highest in the industrialized world. Canada is the third-largest exporter in the world and the fifth-largest importer.

In 1993 provincial and federal agriculture ministers were so enamoured of trade that they set a target of $20 billion in agri-food exports by the year 2000. Canada reached that target ahead of schedule, as exports doubled between 1989 and 1997. In 1998 ministers decided to better themselves: they set a new goal of $40 billion in exports by 2005. The federal government hopes Canada can realize 4 percent of total global agricultural trade by 2005; our share currently stands at 3 percent. In doing so, Ottawa imagines untold economic wealth will accrue to Canada; the Conference Board of Canada has suggested between 220,000 and 447,000 jobs might be created if the industry reaches this export target.

Most of Canada's agri-food exports involve bulk grain (such as wheat), meat and meat by-products. About 80 percent of the milling wheat grown in Canada is exported rather than milled here. While politicians are focused on export volumes, they pay little attention to imports. In fact, imports have largely kept pace with rising exports. That means our net exports remain at about $5 billion a year, much as they have for fifteen years. So although there is grand talk about how we are capturing new foreign markets, we are losing Canadian domestic markets to imports at about the same rate. In essence, we are replacing stable Canadian markets with more volatile offshore ones.

Of course, we have to import fresh fruits and vegetables when the country has sunk into the grip of winter. However, Canada continues to import more processed food than we export—food that could easily be processed here. In 1997 we shipped out a commendable $9.8 billion worth of processed food. However, in the same year we imported $10.9 billion worth of convenience and processed foods to satisfy the appetites of the consuming public. That trade imbalance was aggravated in 1999 when overall agri-food exports fell for the first time in years, and imports increased. That reversed what many officials had seen as a trend to larger, consistent food trade surpluses. Agriculture Canada officials insisted the statistics represented a one-year blip caused by low prices and sharply reduced sales to Asian and European markets. "We do not judge this year to year so much," Gilles Lavoie, a director general within the department's market and industry services branch told the Commons agriculture committee. "What is important is the trend, and over the past few years the trend is up."

No matter what the future holds, Canadian governments, regardless of their political stripe, are committed to pursuing free trade policies and the push for increased agri-food exports. The country's largest agricultural organization, the Canadian Federation of Agriculture, wholeheartedly endorses Ottawa's approach to trade. Its trade policy statement acknowledges that the world is undergoing what it describes as inevitable globalization. "The increasing interdependence of national economies and the growing and competitive global marketplace have reinforced the importance of export market opportunities and the importance of fair and effective trade rules." In what almost seems like an afterthought, the CFA's policy on trade acknowledges that free trade should "respect the domestic interests of Canadian farmers."

The domestic interests of Canadian farmers have not been well served by Canada's myopic focus on global trade. Our trade may be increasing, but farm incomes continue to fall. Canada's agri-food exports doubled between 1989 and 1997, yet net farm income over the same period remained stagnant. The benefits of growth are not being shared by all sectors. In the past the rule was to feed your family and trade the leftovers. Now the advice seems to be: trade all you can and hope there will be something left over for your family.

Consumers are not benefiting either from Canada's trade-oriented agricultural policies. You would think that lower retail prices would be an inevitable result of vigorous international trade. However, the price of bread or a pork chop has not gone down as internationally traded wheat and pork prices plummeted. The Statistics Canada consumer price index for food items has tripled over the twenty-five years from 1974 to 1999.

And what about indigenous farmers in other countries? By promoting a global trade policy Canada is fostering an international food system that depends on money, not local initiative. When Canadian farmers "find" new Asian markets, they are displacing products that were often grown by local farmers. When cheap grain was imported to Costa Rica, there were reports of massive dislocation. In the proceedings of a forum held in Manila in August 1998, it was reported: "A flood of cheap imported grain drove local farmers out of business as the number growing corn, beans, and rice, the staples of the local diet, fell from 70,000 to 27,700." The Philippines told the same conference how their economy was shifting to an import-based, cash-based food distribution system even though a third of the population cannot afford the new globalization. That hardly seems to fit with the much-ballyhooed objective of producing enough food through increased productivity and trade to feed a hungry world.

So if farmers do not benefit from increased trade, or consumers, or peasant farmers in other countries—who does? Well, the benefits of increased trade and trade liberalization go to Canada's food-processing sector. That sector in turn is not controlled by homegrown Canadian business operators but by the foreign transnational corporations that play on an international stage without much limitation from irritating national boundaries.

For many there is no doubt that the winners in the era of international agri-food trade and the globalization of our food system are transnational corporations. Our global economy is, after all, increasingly dominated by powerful corporations. Of the world's hundred largest economies, fifty-two are corporations. One of the top ten is Wal-Mart, the biggest retailer in the world. On the food front, the National Farmers Union says Archer Daniels Midland's revenues have doubled since 1990; ConAgra's have doubled since 1989; Philip Morris's have tripled since 1987.

In the last two years there has been a groundswell of protest against the globalization that is defining so much of modern life. Most of it has coalesced around the organizations that are intent on liberalizing international trade. The key agency in this regard is the World Trade

Organization, arguably the most powerful international institution in the world. It was established through the Marrakesh Agreement of 1994, which concluded the multilateral trade negotiations of the Uruguay Round of the General Agreement on Tariffs and Trade (GATT). The WTO enforces several sets of trade rules: the GATT, the mandate of which was to eliminate all remaining tariff and non-tariff barriers to the free movement of goods and capital between countries; regulations on services; conventions on patents, copyrights and trademarks; government jurisdiction on food safety; and the Agreement on Agriculture, which sets rules for the international food trade and restricts domestic agricultural policy.

What makes the WTO different from other global institutions is its legislative and judicial power to challenge the laws, policies and programs of countries that are found to be in violation. WTO cases are decided in secret by a panel of three trade bureaucrats. Once a ruling is made, worldwide conformity is demanded and countries must harmonize their laws or face the prospect of trade sanctions or fines. Governments have less capacity to influence the behaviour of transnational corporations under this new world order. As corporations move their operations around the world, they can pit workers, communities and entire countries against one another to see who will provide the lowest wages and the least environmental protections.

Opponents of globalization believe it represents the diversion of power away from citizens and their democratic institutions to private corporations and trade treaties. The WTO's free trade policies have been described as the most direct threat to democracy and sovereignty since the rise of the corporate state under National Socialism in Germany in the 1930s.

The Council of Canadians, which provides Canada's most structured opposition to the WTO, says the organization upholds no minimum standards to protect the environment, labour rights, social programs or cultural diversity. The Council says the WTO has already been used to strike down a number of key national laws on the environment, food safety and human rights. "In less than five years, it has become the most powerful tool of transnational corporations working with trade bureaucrats in Geneva, Washington and Tokyo (as well as Ottawa) to establish what is essentially a system of corporate world government," the Council declares in an information package.

Topping the Council's "hit list" of concerns are food security and food safety. In the first case the group fears that pressure from exporting nations at the World Trade Organization to complete the task of opening up world markets will undercut government support and regulation of agriculture around the world. In Canada, it says the Canadian Wheat Board and the country's marketing boards may become targets. Under the heading of food safety the Council lists the United States' efforts to put genetically engineered food products on the WTO agenda. Both the U.S. and Canada would like to guarantee market access for the biotechnology industry to Europe, Japan and the developing world, where resistance to GMOs runs high.

The Council of Canadians is working with a number of international non-governmental organizations (NGOs) that view the WTO and other free trade agreements as a way for transnational corporations to crush the independent aspirations of developing countries. Ironically, the NGO opposition is effectively using the powers of globalization to its own advantage. The Internet is proving to be the opposition's most powerful tool. Web sites maintained by groups like the Third World Network are filled with articles on the evils of globalization. And e-mail technology allows protestors around the world to contact one another quickly and easily.

That was how fifty thousand people came together in Seattle in December 1999 when the World Trade Organization was attempting to set the timetable for resumed talks. The Uruguay Round had called for a resumption of negotiations in at least two areas, agriculture and services, by no later than January 1, 2000. These new negotiations were to be started at the third WTO ministerial conference meeting in Seattle. Intractable differences between Europe and North America, along with the clamour outside, short-circuited the talks within four days.

Similar protests were to erupt at the Biodiversity Protocol in Montreal in early 2000, the April 2000 meeting of the World Bank and International Monetary Fund (IMF) in Washington, the Organization of American States meeting in Windsor in June, and the World Bank and IMF meetings in Prague in September. Demonstrations are becoming routine whenever international trade meetings of any sort are called. At these meetings the global elites—the trade negotiators—are now forced to huddle behind closed doors as the demonstrations rage outside.

It may be tempting to dismiss the demonstrations as a misguided display by young protestors shouting slogans, disrupting meetings and dodging pepper spray. The *Globe and Mail* denigrated them as "the young and the witless." But in fact the protests, beginning with Seattle, have brought together people from across the generations with a wide range of concerns. Some complain about the effects of genetically modified foods; others decry cuts in social spending; still others demand an end to clear-cut logging in some of the world's most fragile ancient forests. In his 1996 book *The Decline of Deference*, Neil Nevitte makes it clear that the broad coalition of activists represents a fundamental social and cultural shift, not the passing fancy of a few overenergized youth.

Canada's minister for international trade, Pierre Pettigrew, has a lot of experience in the field of global relations. He was a director of NATO's political committee, foreign policy adviser to Pierre Trudeau and author of a book on globalization called *The New Politics of Confidence*. He says we should see globalization as more "inspiring than alarming" because open markets are still the best system for creating prosperity. According to Pettigrew, the WTO is not really an agent of globalization anyway; rather, he says, it is a mechanism that furthers internationalism because it demands negotiations between countries.

Whatever the role of the WTO, there is a growing sense that transnational corporations are using trade organizations for their own purposes. Liberalized trade was first sold to farmers around the world as being advantageous to them. But farmers in industrialized countries like France, Germany and the United States are frustrated with low prices and unstable markets; and farmers in developing countries are being squeezed by imports. Now it is beginning to seem as if farmers in both industrialized and developing countries are losing. And there is widespread disenchantment with the whole idea of agricultural free trade and globalization.

A sheep farmer from southern France has become the poster boy of the international anti-globalization movement. José Bové, forty-six years old, wiry, with a distinctive walrus moustache, catapulted to international fame by taking on the local McDonald's. Now he is carrying the crusade against "la mal bouffe"—bad food—by targeting the monster multinationals he says are lurking behind international trade agreements. He has become a symbol for many Europeans who feel American-dominated globalization threatens their culture and national identity.

Bové's rise to fame started in August 1999 when he and a band of cohorts tore down half the roof of a McDonald's that was going up in the tiny, picturesque town of Millau. They caused $120,000 worth of damage. Bové said McDonald's "provoked" him into action by opening an outlet in the village. "Our struggle is not against America but against uncontrolled globalization," he told *Time* magazine in December 1999. "McDonald's is a symbol of industrial food production. Whether such producers are American or French, the effect is the same: the destruction of traditional farming, different cultures and ways of life."

Bové and his wife embraced the farming way of life when they moved to the tiny hamlet of Montredon in the Larzac region of France in 1975. The view from their five-hundred-year-old stone house shows the five other houses in the community and the hundreds of sheep on the rocky, windswept hills around it. It sounds like the ideal place for a sleepy retirement. But Bové is a rabble-rouser at heart. He started up a movement that would eventually launch commando actions in support of traditional French agriculture. When the U.S. decided to clamp 100 percent tariffs on Roquefort cheese and other luxury French food imports, he retaliated with the attack on the local McDonald's.

Globalization went on trial alongside Bové and the other McDonald's vandals in Millau in July 2000. The two-day trial turned into a carnival as thrill-seekers converged on the small town from all corners of France and the world. Extra trains were made available to transport everyone who wanted to attend the "happening." An anti-globalization concert attracted forty-five thousand people. It seemed everyone was sporting T-shirts with slogans saying "Le monde n'est pas une marchandise" ("The world is not merchandise").

France fell under the spell of Bovémania. He was likened to Joan of Arc and Gandhi. Even the government seemed taken with him: Prime Minister Lionel Jospin said, "Here is a strong, vigorous personality." President Jacques Chirac declared that he, too, detested McDonald's food.

Although Bové's trial prosecutors recommended a slap on the wrist, the magistate wanted to be firm. She sentenced him to three months in jail. Bové refused to be released on bail. After spending twenty days in prison, he emerged as one of France's most popular heroes.

In Canada the impact of globalization on food has not generated anywhere near that kind of interest. The issue has been left to the National Farmers Union, which in turn has built connections with farm groups in other countries. The international movement called the Via Campesina, representing farmers from thirty-seven countries, says the WTO regime leaves countries defenceless in the world market. At its 1998 meeting in Geneva, Via Campesina made the following declaration: "The loss of national food sovereignty within the WTO is dangerous and unacceptable. Via Campesina strongly objects to the conduct of negotiations in agriculture under the terms of the World Trade Organization. The WTO policy is above all organized in the interests of multinational companies that dominate international trade, destroying our capacity of food production, our communities, and our natural environments."

The NFU says the government of Canada should take a "pro-farmer" position in future rounds of WTO negotiations and align itself with nations that are working to change the focus of the trade talks. Canadian producers may like to think they have little in common with peasant farmers in developing countries. Indeed, as a nation we enjoy untold wealth, and food security has not been, and is not now, an issue for

Canada. But it does seem as if Canadian farmers work harder and harder to export their goods, yet they are paid as if they were the peasants of the industrialized world.

The Canadian Wheat Board is one of the institutions under attack in the name of trade liberalization. Brian White feels vulnerable even on the sixth floor of the sturdy, fortress-like CWB headquarters on Main Street in Winnipeg. He would like to get on with the business of developing international wheat sales, but he and other Wheat Board employees are distracted by the determined efforts on the part of the United States to bring down the Board.

American farm organizations have tried to undercut the CWB through international trade negotiations and laws. In 1998 there was even an investigation into whether Canada was underhandedly dumping grain— disguised as cattle—into the American market. Despite these persistent claims that Canada markets its grain unfairly, international investigations have now dismissed these allegations eight times between 1989 and 2000.

The North Dakota Wheat Commission launched attempt number nine early in 2000 by filing a petition with the U.S. trade representative to restrict the amount of Canadian wheat and durum allowed south of the border. It claimed the Canadian Wheat Board is driving down wheat prices by at least 8 percent through its "inappropriate state-owned enterprise activities." It chose to use a controversial piece of U.S. trade legislation called a Section 301 petition to push for elimination of the Wheat Board's monopoly. The Americans tried to use Section 301 during the softwood lumber dispute, but it was overruled by a GATT panel.

The logic the Americans have used in all of their challenges over the past decade is that Canadian grain is too clean, that the Board routinely gives its customers better quality and service than the competition, and that it charges customers different prices based on local markets. In any other sector this would be described as good business, but in the wheat industry the Americans call it unfair. It may seem like a silly irritant, but the CWB has to spend considerable time and money fending off these challenges from a protectionist nation that proclaims its free trade philosophy while shielding its own producers.

White knows that as an organization the CWB is out of step in a time that celebrates free trade. "Monopolies are not popular today. But I would note that monopolies are good for sellers. And that is what we are," he says. The Americans have also been pushing for "harmonization" of wheat selling under the spirit of trade liberalization. "But the subtext is 'harmonization, our way.' No one talks about the North American Wheat Board."

It has been doubly irritating for White and others at the CWB that the American efforts to undercut the Wheat Board are supported by some farmers on the Canadian side of the border. The Wheat Board was first formed nearly seventy years ago to respond to farmers' efforts to gain greater control of the marketing system. It is a measure of how much things have changed when you hear Canadian farmers calling for increased competition in the marketing system. The domestic demands for an end to the CWB monopoly hit a high point in the 1990s when the Farmers for Justice counselled civil disobedience. The pressure did prompt the Wheat Board to adjust to the times: in 1998 it replaced a slate of government-appointed commissioners with ten farmers democratically elected by the farming community.

In no way does Brian White seem like one of the stuffy bureaucrats the critics used to complain about, but he is an ardent defender of the Wheat Board system. He says if the Americans or the dual market promoters succeed in stripping the CWB of its monopoly, farmers will lose. Although prices hardly seem good now, they do reflect a CWB premium. The Board's internal research tells it most farmers like the pooling system and the fact that the federal government will back up any deals that go bad. White says the CWB is the least Canada can offer farmers who have to compete with farmers in the U.S. and the European Union who benefit from subsidy support. "We are added value to the wheat commodities."

White's position is backed up in a report released in January 1996 by three eminent prairie agricultural economists. Hartley Furtan, Daryl Kraft and Ed Tyrchniewicz examined fourteen years' worth of sales data and concluded that the CWB's monopoly put $265 million extra into farmers' pockets each year that they would not see in a competitive environment.

World trade has increased elevenfold since 1950, yet poverty, unemployment, environmental destruction and social disintegration have grown at the same time. There have been few beneficiaries in the relentless pursuit of growth through globalization. Instead, the gap between the rich and the poor continues to widen. According to the 1999 *UN Human Development Report*, eighty-nine countries are worse off now than they were ten years ago. Meanwhile, the world's two hundred richest people doubled their wealth between 1994 and 1998.

Back in the 1970s there were calls for people to "Buy Canadian." Purchasing products that were made in Canada was beneficial to the country, those voices said. Money and jobs stayed in the domestic economy instead of being exported beyond Canada's borders. You do not hear the "Buy Canadian" slogan very often these days. It has faded away in the last ten years, drowned out by the clarion call for global competitiveness. According to the new economic logic, Canada must now trade on a worldwide scale.

Canada's "go global" policies are more attentive to the needs of corporate food processors—many of them headquartered in other countries— than to the farmers who grow our food. Canadian farmers have been allowed to slip through the cracks. Other countries, as we will see, have acted more definitively and compassionately to soften the brutal effects the global economy has had on the stewards of their land.

# Eight

## Endangered Species Support

*July 26, 2000*

*The prairie shimmers in pulsating heat waves along the horizon. You can almost hear the crops growing, stretching for the sun. At the Wielers', Thomas, Nicholas and the pup Daphne are trying to cool down in the plastic wading pool. They have designated the dugout off-limits since they found salamanders in the slimy growth on the bottom.*

*Along the gently sloping bank of Tobacco Creek across the road from the Wielers' yard, Gary and Philip are collecting hay bales for their cattle. The bales look like big, round, rolled loaves of bread scattered on a newly cut lawn. Gary spears one with the fork hooked on to the front of the open tractor, trundles over to the oversized hay wagon with the bale suspended precariously in the air, and piles it on top of the others heaped on the wagon. Philip gingerly pilots the precarious pyramid to the back of the yard where other giant hay bales are already stacked. Then the procedure is repeated, in reverse order. Gary forks each bale and adds it to the pile growing on the ground. Philip watches from the hay wagon with a teenager's practised nonchalance. His left arm is in a cast—fractured in exuberant but perhaps ill-advised mud wrestling with friends last Friday.*

*It is difficult to think of winter when the summer sun is this hot, but the Wielers know they have to collect enough hay to feed their cattle when snow blankets the pasture. They collect hay from the ditches around their fields, and they pay a nominal lease fee to pull hay off some neighbouring pastureland.*

*Gary Wieler and a fellow farmer about 11 kilometres away share the baler, hay wagon and cattle truck. Although Gary has to spend time on the phone organizing the whereabouts of the equipment, he generally gives the co-operative arrangement high marks. When Gary is out cutting hay with the crimper he owns, his partner is out with the baler. And vice versa.*

*This kind of co-operation saves money. It is something that Gary would like to do more of. He knows of one farmer who teams up with another, each having sold their own small combine, to lease one large one. Gary suspects this is the only way he is going to get the new, sophisticated equipment he covets but cannot afford. "I'd be happy to go into debt if I thought I could pay it back," he says wistfully. This is beginning to look like another year when the Wielers will not be able to consider buying any new machinery.*

*As if on ironic cue, a hose blows on the 1960-vintage open tractor. Lorna is dispatched to Carman to get a replacement hose cut. When she brings it back, Gary wields his wrenches with a mechanic's skill and a farmer's confidence. In five minutes the hose is in place. In that time the wrenches have begun to bake in the relentless sun. Thomas is handed a rag so he can transport them back to the shop without burning his hands.*

*The heat drapes the countryside, casting every human and animal with a palpable lethargy. Gary says there is nothing more he can do to improve the crops; now it is all up to the weather. Today's sun may not be enough to offset the impact of the long wet period that threatened to flood the crops in early summer. Already there are signs of trouble. Disease is showing up in the canola. And although it is Roundup Ready canola, Gary can see weeds spotting the entire field. "We should have sprayed it one week earlier," he says.*

*The view of the field of peas from the open window of the half-ton truck is "pretty dirty." That indictment from Gary refers to the wild oats and wild mustard that have made their home in the field, particularly along the road.*

*The Wielers' wheat stands tall, but the heads of the plants are ghostly pale rather than the robust red Gary would like to see. Fusarium, a fungal disease encouraged by the rain, seems to have struck. When it was first discovered on the Canadian Prairies several years ago, farmers wore masks when handling it for fear that the fungi spores might be infectious. Now they are almost blasé about the fact that one more of life's mishaps has beset them.*

*It is a classic midsummer day on the Prairies. For any urban dweller it is a perfect day to hit the beach or enjoy a barbecue. On the farm, even under the summer sun, the crops are not offering the Wielers what they were counting on for the future. They do not look like the exceptional crops Gary Wieler needs for his farm to compete in the new global, industrialized marketplace.*

&. A Canadian travelling through the countryside of Western Europe will see a landscape that is truly foreign. Every turn in the country road reveals the spire of another church, the heart of yet another town. Stone hedgerows prettily edge the fields. The rural cemeteries of polished granite are carefully tended with flowers. Silos and barns, freshly painted a jolly red, silhouette the many small, prosperous farms that dot the landscape. It is a scenic vista, but one that also speaks of an economic reality. Farming is thriving here; as are the communities it supports. Europe props up its agriculture with policies and dollars—unlike Canada, which seems to have turned its back on its farmers.

The difference between the Canadian and European philosophies was underscored at the WTO meetings in Seattle in late 1999. The Europeans talked about families and communities; the Canadians and Americans talked about markets. The meetings collapsed, differences encouraged by the sound of protestors who had gathered in the streets of Seattle from around the world.

Why does Europe care about its farmers? For starters, in the European psyche, its seven and a half million farmers stand between the consumer and hunger. Europeans understand what it is like to go without food. After all, Europe was the battlefield for two world wars; during and after the war years, food was strictly rationed. In the post–Second World War period European nations were focused on becoming self-sufficient in food production. The hunger of the war years had convinced them never to let it happen again. Farmers were given government subsidies so they would grow more. Their productivity increased with remarkable success. One British farmer, Chris Skinner in the county of Norfolk, told CBC-TV in the early 1990s that he got four tonnes of wheat from one acre. That is four times more than his father was able to harvest on the same land twenty years earlier, and four times more than the yield experienced by the typical Canadian farmer. With the advantage of a favourable climate and intensive chemical use, production tripled between 1970 and 1991. Chris Skinner's wife, Maurie, was direct about their good fortune: "You could say we got fat on the good living in the seventies and eighties."

Today, Europe is still the world's biggest importer of food products, like fresh fruits and vegetables and luxury items. At the same time Europe can claim to be almost entirely self-sufficient in the essentials. In fact, the massive productivity gains enjoyed by its farmers have made Europe the world's second-biggest exporter. For most, hunger is a distant memory.

There is also an appreciation for food in Europe that cannot be replicated in North America. In Europe the focus is on the quality of food, not its quantity. A German family will debate the merits of various potato varieties with endless enthusiasm at the dinner table. A French shopper will sniff a tomato carefully before selecting it, no doubt imagining the burst of flavour that will spurt with the first bite. European consumers would be horrified at the homogenized quality of food products in the typical North American supermarket. Europeans demand quality and variety. And they matter-of-factly pay for it, too.

The European pleasure in food has translated into an activism Canadians of the baby boom generation might vaguely remember from the 1960s. The opposition in Europe to genetically engineered food has brought grandmothers and young families to scientific test plots across Britain to mow down what has been described as Frankenstein efforts to "tamper with food." In the summer of 2000, forty-five thousand people descended on the small town of Millau in southern France to support the men who trashed a McDonald's restaurant in protest against the globalization of food.

Another marked difference between Europe and Canada is the density of the population. Huge numbers of Europeans are packed into a small space with very little elbow room. Saskatchewan, for example, is the size of France, but only 1 million people live in the desolate stretches of that Canadian province, 56 million in France. Environmental damage was an inevitable outcome of such a press of people. In Europe pollution has already soured the Danube, killed the trees in the last remaining forests and sullied the North Sea beaches. Europeans are now much more concerned about maintaining their environment. And as urban dwellers live right next door to rural Europeans, they are not about to turn a blind eye to environmentally suspect agricultural practices.

Although there are a lot of people living in Europe, they do not all live in cities. There are 7.4 million farmers in Europe, compared to fewer than 270,000 in Canada. It seems that every inch is cultivated. Agriculture uses up 331 million acres of European land, and just 168 million acres in Canada.

The universal appreciation of the value of agriculture in Europe has led the fifteen members of the European Union to share their farm policies. The Common Agricultural Policy (CAP) is the backbone of the EU structure; 48 percent of the EU's budget is spent on CAP. The spending is surprisingly generous when you consider that the farm sector accounts for only 3 percent of the EU's income. Like Canada, Europe has seen a sharp decline in the number of farms and the number of people working on them. Farming now employs only 5.5 percent of the population; only a few regions are defiantly agricultural, with employment climbing to 20 percent.

But Europe has a sensible loyalty to its farmers. Farmers are seen not only as the producers of agricultural commodities: they are stewards of the social, cultural and environmental facets of rural life. They are viewed as essential to the public good. There is a palpable fear that any move towards a more market-driven agricultural policy will strip the rural landscape. That was abundantly clear when forty thousand protestors gathered in the streets of Brussels in February 1999 as EU ministers met to consider reform to the Common Agricultural Policy. Farmers carried a blunt message on their protest banners: "We will never accept American style agriculture in Europe."

The Common Agricultural Policy was established in 1962 with the aim of encouraging production. It was the agent of the post-war years. At times, especially in the late 1980s, the subsidies generated substantial surpluses. Other countries, like Canada, became increasingly irritated with what they described as an unfair advantage for European farms in the international marketplace. In the 1990s Europe acknowledged it should become more competitive, but not at the expense of a "reasonable living for farm families." The EU agriculture ministers agreed to reform CAP in 1992 and again in 1999, when member countries hammered out Agenda 2000 to define agricultural policy from 2000 to 2006.

Agenda 2000 was a compromise, designed on the one hand to cut costs for a union that would soon have to welcome new, less advantaged member states from Eastern and Central Europe, and on the other to maintain some critical level of support for farmers. The EU stabilized agricultural expenditures at about US $43 billion, putting a ceiling on support. From a European perspective this represented a significant limit on agricultural spending. Nevertheless, according to the OECD, European countries spent

$114.5 billion through CAP and individual national support for farmers in 1999. That amounted to about $7 of aid per bushel of grain, or the equivalent of 49 percent of gross farm revenue. It solidified Europe's reputation as the world's biggest subsidizer. Canada is convinced that generosity has skewed the marketplace and left Canadian producers in trouble.

Under the reform of CAP, the EU embraced a shift in subsidies that would satisfy the clamour of the free traders and still support its farmers. So the EU decreased commodity support prices and increased direct aid to farmers, technically shifting money from price supports and supply control to a more targeted and less distorting mechanism. In the 1960s the typical European farmer was encouraged to get big and rely on chemicals to boost production. Today that farmer is rewarded for reducing chemical usage, if not going organic altogether. Twenty years ago there were grants to take out hedgerows and plough the meadows; now there are grants to save them.

The heart of Agenda 2000 was the introduction of "multifunctionality." This concept was first recognized in 1992 when world governments at the Rio Earth Summit addressed in Agenda 21 the "multifunctional aspect of agriculture, particularly with regard to food security and sustainable development in tribute to broader aims." Europe's interpretation of this concept was more direct: the public is indebted to farmers because farming offers people more than just steaks or fresh vegetables. Europe argues that farming plays an important role in preserving the environment, protecting rural communities from depopulation and cushioning the state against the costs of increased urbanization.

The EU's multifunctional policies are built around five basic principles: there must be a continued commitment to a fair standard of living for the agricultural community; environmental concerns are best addressed by family farmers; the rural infrastructure must be maintained; a competitive agricultural sector must be able to participate on the world market without being oversubsidized; and there have to be simpler, more understandable agricultural and rural development systems. It is a complicated way of saying that farmers are eligible for grants when they enhance rural landscapes, ensure the viability of rural areas, and guarantee food security, quality and safety.

Reform under Agenda 2000 affects three sectors of European agriculture: cereals, beef and dairy. For example, grain support prices were to fall by 7.5 percent on July 1, 2000, and by a further 7.5 percent in 2001. According to the "multifunctional" interpretation, instead of trade-distorting supports, Europe is paying its farmers to undertake very specific multifunctional responsibilities. Cereal farmers, for example, are obliged to leave 10 percent of their land fallow until 2006—and of course they are paid for their inactivity. France offers its farmers five-year contracts worth more than $40,000 for their environmental and social contributions.

For most Canadians it hardly matters how you define it: aid is aid. But under the WTO the Europeans have been able to argue successfully that their multifunctionality does not violate fair trading rules. Europe insists this is the only way to preserve a natural and socio-economic heritage that has developed over centuries. European farmers have been assigned the broad responsibilities of producing food, maintaining the land and preserving the region's heritage.

Franz Fischler is the Commissioner of Agriculture and Rural Development for the EU and in many ways the chief architect of European farm policy. He agreed to speak to 250 farm leaders from around the world who gathered at the Westin Hotel in Seattle for the Family Farmers Summit on Agricultural Trade just before the WTO debacle. He clearly felt at home at this conference, noting that he grew up on a farm and remained "a family farmer at heart." It was with some frustration that he said he is often misunderstood when he speaks to audiences outside Europe. "I feel sometimes that there is a perception that the CAP is designed as a great farmers' gravy train, pumping huge amounts of money into farmers' pockets, encouraging them to produce massive surpluses which are then dumped onto the world market at giveaway prices while a giant barrier prevents imports into the EU." Fischler described this as "Euro bashing"—well timed, he noted, to coincide with the U.S. presidential election.

Fischler offered some political advice when he told the audience that Europe believes depopulation ends up costing governments more when they allow it to continue as it has in Montana or Saskatchewan. From Fischler's perspective, governments incur the costs of improving failing urban infrastructure when more and more farmers move to the city. "Essentially we have taken the view that there is a social, economic and environmental cost to urbanization and rural depopulation."

Fischler was clearly annoyed that the EU is routinely depicted in North America as refusing to cut its subsidies. He said subsidies under the CAP have steadily decreased through the reforms of 1992 and 1999—45 percent less in cereal price supports and 35 percent less in beef price supports. With an ironic dose of foreshadowing he urged trade negotiators from outside the EU to approach the upcoming WTO talks "with a serious degree of realism." He said Europe would not back down from its position. "To treat agriculture like any other trading sector is not an option. It would spell the end of most family farming."

Despite generous supports and the cushion of multifunctionality, farmers across the European Union talk about a "farm crisis" and the "end of family farming" in the same way we do in Canada. Although they are still very comfortable compared with the Gary Wielers on this side of the Atlantic, individual European farmers have had to deal with their own structural change.

The statistics bear out their concerns. European farmers complain that their numbers are shrinking and at the same time the size of farms is swelling. The U.K. has the most industrialized system of all the European nations and is undergoing the most severe structural adjustments. A single farm holding that currently supports one family used to be home to thirty people just a generation ago. The number of working farms in Britain has decreased by a third, from 357,000 in 1966 to 244,000 in 1994. Much like in Canada, the average farm size has also increased, in this case by 58 percent. In 1939 the average size was 103 acres; by 1989 that had risen to 163 acres. British farms are still tiny by Canadian standards, but the repercussions of adjustment are nevertheless harsh. In the past decade 88,000 jobs were lost in farming in the U.K.

Scotland's farmers are among those who have seen their world change, and who fear even more change to come. Like Canadian grain farmers who saw cereal prices slide to record lows, highland farmers watched sheep prices collapse by nearly 40 percent in early 2000. And because of the export ban on British beef and the continuing fragile consumer confidence caused by mad cow disease, beef prices have also bottomed out. At the same time, the government has declared it cannot afford to continue supporting production. In the brash twenty-first-century spirit of free trade and open competition, it has warned farmers that the production-based subsidies they now depend on will gradually disappear. Despite the unyielding rhetoric, however, in 1999 the supports were still generous. Scottish taxpayers paid £500 million a year in aid to farmers. Thousands of farmers get more in subsidies than they earn from actual farming.

Bert Leitch is a twenty-six-year veteran of the sheep-farming way of life on the verdant hills of the island of Mull, off the west coast of Scotland. A flat wool cap replaces the baseball cap of Canadian farm fashion, and Leitch speaks in a roiling brogue rather than the flat, open inflections of prairie English. But he has that same sardonic humour that many Canadian farmers use when faced with grim news. "If I didnae laugh, I would cry," he explained to a BBC television crew in early 2000 about falling commodity prices and the threat of reduced subsidies.

In 1999 Leitch earned less than £10,000 by raising cattle and sheep on the hills of Mull. In 2000, in addition to a significant drop in cattle prices, Leitch knew he would earn only one-half of the previous year's price for each lamb he sold. He braced himself for a poor year. He figured his income in 2000 would drop to £2,000.

In Canada that kind of accounting would sound the death knell for the farm. This clearly is not a sustainable operation. But then subsidies gallop to the rescue. Much to his relief Leitch gets £26,000 a year in government support. Without subsidies Leitch says there would be no hope for him. It would be cheaper for the U.K. to import lamb, yet CAP pays Bert Leitch to graze his sheep in the picturesque green Highlands of Scotland.

Leitch seems slightly embarrassed when asked how big his subsidies are, but he gathers himself and then speaks in defence of the system: "We're going to be unable to farm in areas like this without subsidies. There's no two doubts about it. We just couldn't compete." He notes that the money he gets from the government percolates through the entire community. He pays local folks to haul his livestock, to build his fences. "If we go, well, places like this will just turn into scrub." He offers what is surely a familiar refrain to many Canadian farmers. "Anyone that comes in to hill farming expecting to make a lot of money, no. But it is a way of life." The way-of-life argument may carry extra weight in a country where shipbuilding has virtually disappeared and thousands of men lost their jobs when coal mines were shut down in the late 1980s and early 1990s.

Subsidies specifically directed at production are falling. However, the principles of multifunctionality mean Leitch will be compensated for whatever he does to improve the environment. Already, he is paid £7,500 not to produce sheep but to let one remote corner of his farm revert to its natural state. He has planted a few trees, some flowers; but essentially he is simply allowing this field to run wild. He views it as recompense for looking after a small piece of the countryside. He knows the general public will appreciate his efforts to grow nature perhaps even more than his efforts to grow beef and lamb. The pragmatism born of several decades in farming surfaces: "I would rather farm, mind you. I would rather have my stock and I suppose a hell of a lot of other boys would do the same, but we've got to look to whatever way we can get that money."

Times are changing, even in the distant stretches of the Scottish Highlands. Leitch's dreams of a family dynasty have already faded. He is adjusting to the thought that he may become a custodian of the environment rather than a farmer who produces the essentials of life. And he is adjusting to the realization that farming, even with European-style subsidies, may not be attractive to the next generation. His son Robert is likely going to get a real job, not take over the farm. "It's a very enjoyable way of life and Robert appreciates that too, but you have to have money to live," says Leitch with the resignation of farmers everywhere.

Europe is always held up as the bad guy whenever free traders gather. According to the logic of the open market, the subsidies—whether linked to production or to environmental or socio-economic concerns—skew the competitive marketplace. The United States is one of the biggest promoters of this point of view. At the same time, though, the U.S. is the second-most highly subsidized country in the world. Although it has polished its "free trade" line over the years, it spent $54 billion on farm subsidies in 1999, or 24 percent of gross farm revenue. That adds up to $2.50 of support per bushel.

Europe is a distant adversary for most Canadians, and "multifunctionality" an unfamiliar concept. But many Canadian producers see all too clearly how farmers not that far away—albeit across an international boundary—benefit from government assistance. Think how frustrating it must have been for western Manitoba farmers who were flooded by unforgiving rains in 1999 that prevented seeding. Just kilometres away, across the forty-ninth parallel, the same rains soaked their American neighbours, yet they were able to collect unemployment insurance to compensate them for not being able to get out in the fields.

The U.S. government's stated position is that it favours a competitive, unsubsidized market. However, through much of its history it supported a system that bankrolled quite the contrary by setting federal price supports. Under presidents Ford, Carter and Reagan, U.S. governments became steadily more involved in subsidizing and controlling agriculture. The U.S. subsidy system has had little to do with ideology. Ronald Reagan, who campaigned for a market-driven agriculture, created the largest and most expensive program in history to pay farmers for not producing.

Americans talk a lot about the free market environment but continue to act in a very protectionist manner. U.S. politicians and farm groups have to date launched a total of nine efforts to force Canada to strip the Canadian Wheat Board of its power. And the U.S. has also been behind attempts to undercut Canadian supply management boards. It justifies its position by arguing that it would like to see an end to domestic supports that help farmers export cheaply.

In the spirit of open competition and free trade, the United States seemed prepared at one point to change its ways. In 1996 the Republican-controlled Congress set a policy for seven years that was going to revolutionize the support structure. Freedom to Farm was supposed to inject the free market into the agricultural sector and put an end to ad hoc bailouts for farmers. It was going to be the model for other heavily subsidized sectors of the economy. President Bill Clinton, a Democrat, signed the act under protest, promising to try to revive failed programs and policies as soon as possible. The *Wall Street Journal* was more complimentary, declaring, "this is the kind of change the 1984 election was supposed to be about."

But if the expectation was that price subsidies would be eliminated, there was disappointment over what happened next. Freedom to Farm offered farmers a complicated system of "market transition payments" to help cushion the impact of reduced price subsidies. The old law had been tied to prices: when prices rose, farm subsidies fell. But in 1996 crop prices hit a high, so subsidies would have been low under normal circumstances. Instead, Freedom to Farm paid out three times as much cash in 1996 and 1997 as would have been paid under the previous farm bill. Wheat farmers got fifty times more in subsidies for their 1996 crop than the previous law would have offered.

When commodity prices fell in 1998, Freedom to Farm ensured there would still be supports for farmers struck by collapsing markets. Then the government sweetened the pot still more by providing additional money to assist with weather disasters. Just before the November 1998 election Congress approved $500 million in disaster payments, plus an early payout of $5 billion. The next fall there was another mad rush; this time farmers got an extra $4 billion—$2 billion for "disaster relief" and

$2 billion in direct handouts. In 1999 the U.S. aid package topped a record $28 billion.

This was too much political fodder for Franz Fischler to resist. The EU agriculture commissioner accused the U.S. in June 2000 of increasing its support to farmers by 700 percent since 1996. The U.S. testily replied that everyone who followed trade issues knew U.S. assistance was only one-half that of the EU; and besides, it was not fair to use 1996 as a benchmark, as commodity prices were high then and subsidies low.

The U.S. has acknowledged there are weaknesses in its 1996 farm bill, and it says it intends to fix them without resorting to trade-distorting options. Although it does not say so explicitly, the U.S. follows some of the same principles as European multifunctionality. For example, the Conservation Reserve Program compensates farmers for letting some of their land lie idle, in essence protecting the environment. But however the subsidies are framed, the bottom line is that American farmers benefit.

Lee Cook is a big, burly type who straddles both sides of the Canada–U.S. border. He farms 1,500 acres in Montana, 2,280 in Saskatchewan. About 750 acres on the U.S. side is grass subsidized by the Conservation Reserve Program. The land in Saskatchewan is largely dedicated to forage crops to help sustain Cook's cattle in the winter.

The Cooks began farming just south of the border, in Montana. In 1973 Lee Cook's father was looking to expand, but land in the U.S. was going for $350 an acre. Just 40 kilometres north of the border, near Bengough, Saskatchewan, it could be had for $75 an acre. Today, Lee Cook lives six months of the year in each country. He offers a textbook example of how different the Canadian and American systems are. In the U.S. in 1999 he earned $10,000—on less land. In Canada, where support is non-existent, he says he lost $20,000. (His wife works double duty as a book-keeper and substitute teacher, and once he puts on a fake white beard, he gets lots of work as Santa Claus.) "Without payments I couldn't survive," he says frankly.

He knows he needs the subsidies to carry on, but he is also critical of how the U.S. administers its programs: Cook says 30 percent of farmers receive 70 percent of the subsidies. So he has made it a calling to convince the Canadian government to offer its farmers increased support— but to do it the right way. He came to Winnipeg in early 2000 to speak to hearings of the net income advisory committee, a non-partisan group that was supposed to come up with recommendations on how to develop income supports.

He may work as a Santa Claus, but with his black shirt, black vest, overgrown beard, staccato speaking style and endless array of overhead slides, Lee Cook is intense, almost intimidating. He wants Canada, and other trading countries, to set up an international market price for commodities that would eliminate global competitiveness and guarantee farmers what amounts to a minimum wage. Lee does not think there is much point in Canadian and American farmers fighting with one another, particularly over who gets what support. Even European farmers are not the problem. "We've given this free market thing a good chance and it's been a huge failure. We have to compete with people who live in mud huts, with kids who don't go to school."

It has become conventional wisdom that subsidies are the reason for Canadian farmers' income crisis. The irony is that although more and more countries are presenting a free trade face to the world, subsidies continue to rise. In a report released in June 2000 the OECD noted that although subsidies fell for a time in the 1990s, they seem to have rebounded to the high levels of the mid-1980s. In 1999 government support around the world totalled 40 percent of producers' gross receipts. "The main policy developments of the past two years were inconsistent with the shared goals and policy principles adopted by OECD Agriculture Ministers in March 1998," said the report. The OECD ministers had called for greater responsiveness of agriculture to the market through reduced support to farmers and lowered trade barriers. At the same time, though, governments had given themselves a way out by agreeing to address domestic interests related to environmental sustainability, food safety, security and rural development in ways that did not distort production and trade.

Despite what may be happening south of the border, Canada's focus is on European subsidies. The Canadian government wants to use WTO talks to force the EU to cut its agricultural support. The EU, however, remains adamant that it will not abandon its farmers to the defective markets it says have devastated farmers in Canada and around the world.

In July 2000 the European Commission issued a blistering defence to the WTO of its approach to agricultural trade. But from the perspective of Canadian trade negotiators the EU does not have a good track record in supporting open agricultural trade. Sceptics suggest multifunctionality might be more about preventing international competition than creating a public good. In Canadian trade circles there is an unspoken suspicion that multifunctionality is merely an excuse for defending current protectionist agricultural policies.

WTO rules say subsidies must not encourage farmers to plant crops already in such oversupply that prices are falling. Both the EU and the U.S. have fashioned their aid in ways they say does not affect production.

Plans for a new "millennium round" of ministerial WTO talks were put on hold when the "Battle in Seattle" erupted. However, the negotiations on the liberalization of trade are already back in full swing on the basis of Article 20 of the Agreement on Agriculture. The built-in schedule means agricultural talks are going ahead on a bureaucratic level without the unwanted attention that was focused on Seattle. At the talks in Geneva, Canada is finding itself on the defensive about the Canadian Wheat Board. American negotiators are listening to the complaints from the North Dakota Wheat Commission, listing the Wheat Board as one of their priorities at the talks.

Canada has aligned itself with the Cairns Group in order to press more successfully for reduced subsidies. The Cairns Group includes eighteen countries, among them Australia, New Zealand, Brazil and Argentina, all major exporters of agricultural products. The group held meetings in

October 2000 in Banff, where Agriculture and Agri-Food minister Lyle Vanclief had a chance to sit down with Franz Fischler from the European Union. After the meeting Vanclief proudly told reporters he had informed Fischler that Canada will aggressively pursue the reduction and elimination of agricultural export and other trade-distorting subsidies that are hurting Canadian farmers. Reports are that Fischler was neither surprised nor shaken by Vanclief's warning.

Canada's trade negotiators truly believe they can change the world. At the Canadian Federation of Agriculture annual meeting in February 2000, Mike Gifford, the director general of the trade policy department, appeared to thundering applause. He was about to retire after thirty-five years of service, and the audience appreciated his tenure. He in turn rewarded them with a dose of optimism: "Very soon they will go along with the elimination of export subsidies." Unfortunately, the language of trade talks was beyond most people in the room.

Another negotiator appeared to assure farmers "we are trying to pry open opportunities for you." According to his assessment, they had done "a pretty good job in Seattle." He wryly commented that developing nations did not feel increased trade would solve their social and economic problems. It is evident how he feels about developing nations' reluctance to embrace free trade; what he thinks open markets have done for Canadian farmers is not so clear.

The belief in many Canadian circles is that agriculture should be treated like any other industrial product—that it does not deserve any special treatment in trade policy. The left-leaning NFU is one of the few public sceptics about Canada's strategy. A recent report by the National Farmers Union shows subsidies in Europe and the U.S. were not solely responsible for the surplus production that has forced down prices. From 1980 to 1999 wheat production also rose significantly in other, relatively unsubsidized countries—by 44 percent in Australia and 26 percent in Argentina. The NFU says the government's obsession with trying to eliminate subsidies is misguided. "If you took subsidies away, all you would have is fewer farmers," says NFU vice-president Fred Tait.

In much of the world, food production is not just a commercial activity, defined by rules of production and trade. In the EU, government policy recognizes that agriculture affects other aspects of life. Agriculture can support the vitality of rural communities by maintaining family farming, rural employment and cultural heritage. It can also make positive contributions to biological diversity, recreation and tourism, soil and water systems, bioenergy, landscape, food quality and safety, and the welfare of animals.

In Canada, meanwhile, a polarizing debate about "free trade" versus "protectionism" dominates the whole question of what kind of public support should be offered our farmers. The countries of the EU and others pay tribute to what their farmers do for the public good. In Canada, it seems, the goal is simply to produce agri-food worthy of export, even as our farmers go broke.

*Nine*

## House Rules

August 17, 2000

*The winds and rains came on Friday. Lashing the landscape in angry squalls. Hail and sleet travelling on their coattails. In the city the gales turned umbrellas inside out, lopped off the boughs of the sickliest elms. In the country the winds whipped through the ripened crops. The heads of the Wielers' seasoned wheat were bent and twisted.*

*It is Thursday now. Nearly one week of relative calm. And the Wielers are feeling grateful. When they drove to Altona yesterday in search of a part for some ailing equipment, they saw the band of destruction the wind, rain and hail had cut through nearby fields. They realized they were lucky their damage was limited to one field of wheat. But they also saw combines in nearly every field, as the farmers of southern Manitoba scrambled to begin the harvest.*

*Thanks to early spring seeding, the harvest too is early this year. Caught in the neighbourly competitiveness of prairie grain farming,*

*Gary cannot help but note he is two days behind the pack. Weather has slowed Gary and Lorna down, as have equipment problems. Gary spent two days trying to fix the header on the combine. Yesterday, he says, counting off the hours on impatient fingers, he lost another four hours when he could not fix a second problem with the combine. He eventually had to admit mechanical defeat and drive to Altona for a part.*

*The cattle are also taking up precious time Gary would prefer to spend in the field. One calf was discovered last week with a huge infected gouge on its neck. Another cow has hoof rot. Together, they demand the Wielers begin each morning by wrestling a bellowing bovine into a cattle chute for her medication.*

*Despite the wind and rainstorms the Wielers have managed to spend some time in the fields. They have mowed their canola and their peas. Both crops are now drying in fluffy swathes on the field. If it stays dry, either Gary or Lorna will take the combine through in about ten days.*

*The weather is co-operating now, albeit in a tentative and uncommitted way. The sky is absolutely clear, though an insipid blue. The thermometer will rise to twenty-three degrees today, but it has been so cool overnight that morning dew will dampen the field until eleven o'clock in the morning or later. The days are still long, but when the sun goes down, it really starts to cool off. It feels more like September than August.*

*In mid-afternoon Gary is piloting the combine—a 1986 model with 2,700 hours of service—through a wheat field of pale gold. Gary has a full picture-window view in front of him, right down to his toes. He is bent over the steering wheel, looking intently past his feet to the ground, raising and lowering the blades of the swather with the dips and rises in the field. In places the wheat hugs the ground, the stalks mangled or bent by Friday's wind. It takes a gentle touch to scoop the heads of the wheat without burying the blades in the mud. Gary makes it look easy.*

*The combine kicks a shower of golden kernels into the bin behind the cab. When the bin is full, Lorna, who is on truck duty, pulls the grain truck alongside the combine. She keeps pace; to stop would be an unnecessary interruption. Gary and Lorna speak in the hand gestures of harvest, a language honed by practice. "Hurry up," his waving hand says through the window of the combine as she cranes her head to see. "Slow down," says his hand. An auger sucks the kernels out of the combine and spills them into the grain truck. The combine and the grain truck go bumping down the field, the auger bobbing like an umbilical cord between them*

*Two turns of the field with the truck and combine, and the truck is full. Lorna winches the tarp over the hold and lumbers the truck over the field and down the lumpy gravel roads, home to the bins. There, Nicholas is standing by with another auger. Philip is spared this job; he is off harrowing the wheat stubble in another field. Lorna negotiates the grain truck over to the auger, its ancient gears squalling in protest. The wheat spills from the tipped truck into the vacuum of the auger, then is sucked with a satisfying plop into the grain bin.*

*The family is working together in complete synchronization. The bins are beginning to swell with this year's harvest. But the flush of accomplishment at harvest time seems misplaced. Wheat prices stand at about $5 a bushel—no higher than they were last year. Yields appear to be good—more than forty bushels per acre. In fact, the initial forecast is for a bumper harvest for Manitoba. But many of the kernels of the Wielers' wheat do not meet the full, red and crunchy ideal. Instead they are pale and hollow, struck by the fungal disease fusarium. It is unlikely this wheat will earn the top-quality grade the Wielers need for a comfortable return. And they can expect no extra help from the government. The much-vaunted Agricultural Income Disaster Assistance program does not apply to them. They have not seen their income drop enough to qualify. Gary says it "sure was nice" years ago getting those "subsidy cheques." It may have been nice, but he wraps his mouth around the words with distaste, as if he was saying "welfare cheques." This is not a man who likes to live with his hand outstretched.*

*Without those "nice" cheques, and given the fickle weather this season, it will take concentrated positive thinking to pretend the frantic pace of the harvest is all worthwhile. Luckily, when the Wielers are this busy, there is no time for idle musing. "We do what we have to do," says Lorna, thoughtfully thumbing a handful of empty kernels.*

*At eight years of age Thomas is the only one spared the anxious tempo of the harvest work. Like other boys across Canada, he is sitting cross-legged on the carpeted floor in front of the TV. His eyes are huge and focused on one thing only. The two older boys have spent their earnings from their 4-H steers to buy a Nintendo 64 unit. But they could afford only one game. Under Thomas's concentrated gaze the Mario Brothers slip here and there through booby-trapped castles and forests to escape the bad guy, Bowser. Outside, under the uncertain harvest skies, Thomas's parents will battle their own bad guys until well after midnight tonight.*

&. Canada has earned a reputation as the Boy Scout of international grain trading. It goes to trade talks armed with good intentions and little else. It has chosen to play by the new rules that call for no subsidies—rules that no one else seems to follow. While Europe and the U.S. continue their supports, finding various loopholes, Canada sticks to the letter of the law.

The Organization for Economic Co-operation and Development reports that Canada has been nearly alone among OECD countries in making dramatic cuts to farm subsidies. While government spending is falling in some industrialized countries, like Australia, the cuts are tiny in comparison with Canada's. The OECD's assessment is that for every dollar in income from the sale of wheat in the European Union, 56 cents comes from subsidies. In the U.S., it is 45 cents. In Canada, just 9 cents.

Today, Canada's spending on agriculture has fallen to half the level it was at ten years ago. In 1991–92, the peak year of public generosity, provincial and federal governments spent $6.1 billion on agriculture and the agri-food industry. That included spending for research, food inspection and grants to manufacturers of farm inputs—what most would call routine government business. In 1999–2000, Agriculture and Agri-Food Canada's *Farm Income, Financial Conditions, and Government Assistance* data book said federal and provincial governments spent $2.9 billion on the farming business. Just $600 million of that was in the form of direct payments to farmers.

There is quibbling about what exactly constitutes support. The broadest interpretation includes supply-managed sectors, the Canadian Wheat Board, crop insurance programs, the Net Income Stabilization Program (NISA)—a voluntary self-help initiative funded by farmers and matching contributions from governments—and the $1.7-billion AIDA disaster assistance program earmarked for farmers in deep trouble. AIDA represents the only direct payout to producers—and because of onerous eligibility guidelines and a clogged bureaucracy, only 41 percent of the money had been spent by late 2000.

Canada says it wants to create a level playing field, not by increasing supports for its farmers but by weaning the rest of the world off subsidies. So far neither the EU nor the Americans are paying much attention to our complaints.

University of Manitoba agricultural economist Daryl Kraft says Ottawa could opt for an easier way to even the field—with the stroke of a pen on a cheque. Kraft says Ottawa has chosen to reduce its support to farmers below the subsidy levels agreed to at the World Trade Organization. In 1994, at the last round of the GATT talks (the precursor to the WTO) a deal was signed to reduce subsidies in an effort to break a deadlock. Europe subsequently refused to make cuts, instead reclassifying its subsidies as exempt from the deal. The United States also found ways around the agreement. It introduced "emergency aid" programs that it also declared exempt from the deal's requirements.

Canada, on the other hand, decided to go further than the drop of 20 percent called for in the WTO deal. Under the terms of the agreement Canada could have spent about $4 billion a year on its farmers. Instead, it voluntarily made dramatic cuts, most notably ending the hundred-year-old, $500-million-a-year Crow benefit that subsidized the cost of transporting grain. Before the cuts, in the mid-1980s, Canada's support for wheat producers was comparable to that paid out by the EU and the U.S: 45 percent compared to 54 percent and 50 percent respectively.

It has not been totally clear whether the cuts were made as a result of free-market ideology or simply in an attempt to cut federal spending. Either way, according to a June 2000 report by the NFU, "The result has been a policy error in Canada that echoes the errors made at the beginning of the Great Depression and that has had similar results." Rather than stabilizing the farm economy by increasing supports during downturns and decreasing aid when markets thrive, the NFU says the government chose to cut farm spending just at the time when commodity prices collapsed.

The cuts came at a time when the federal government had money to spend. Finance Minister Paul Martin posted a whopping $12.3-billion surplus for 1999–2000. In February 2000 his budget put forward $58 billion in tax breaks over five years. However, there was no mention of extra funding for Canadian farmers. His pre-election budget update in October 2000 explained the omission this way: "Canada has been at the forefront in condemning the policies of countries that provide massive, trade-distorting subsidies to their producers. We will continue to do so. Looking ahead, the Government will take into account and carefully monitor the impact of international developments on the economic prospects for Canada's farmers."

The government's trade policy once earned respect from farm groups. Now most of them are impatient with the Chrétien administration's blinkered insistence that it can find a way of lowering subsidies in other countries. Even the Canadian Federation of Agriculture has begun to say Canada cannot wait for its trade negotiators to force down subsidies in the international arena. Although the CFA had been supportive of Canada's free trade stance, within a few weeks of the collapse of the WTO talks in Seattle, president Bob Friesen called on the Canadian government to increase its subsidies to the level of American support. He said individual farmers are paying too big a price for the government's budget cuts.

But federal agriculture minister Lyle Vanclief says Canada does not have deep enough pockets to match what other countries give their producers. He says it would cost about $10 billion for Canada to achieve parity with the U.S. government. In other words poverty, not ideology, is behind the government's position; with all the other demands for support, there just is not enough money to bail out Canada's farmers. "I've pointed out to [then U.S. secretary of agriculture] Dan Glickman that farmers in the United States are farming the mailbox and not the marketplace, and they're making decisions on [the basis of] government support rather than on the marketplace. In Canada, we don't have those kinds of resources, so we're trying to target them to those who need the support," he told the *Western Producer* in November 1999.

In that spirit the Liberal government has vowed there will be no more broad-based support programs for farmers like the Crow rate or the Crow benefit. It explained its disaster assistance program by saying it was one-time help and one time only.


There have been lots of government support programs over the past two decades, some of them expressly designed to help grain farmers when international prices collapsed. All have been eliminated.

Here is a sampling. The Feed Freight Assistance Program was cut in 1995. It covered a major portion of the cost of shipping feed grains to the Maritimes and B.C. The Tripartite Stabilization Program, which stabilized the price of hogs, cattle and other livestock, honey and some beans, was terminated in 1994 after a decade of service. The Special Canadian Grains Program lasted only two years. Designed to shield Canadian producers from low prices caused by a U.S.–EU trade war, it was cut in 1988. The Western Grain Stabilization Program calmed volatile grain prices for Western farmers. Between 1976 and 1991, when it was cancelled, it paid out $3.4 billion. And the Gross Revenue Insurance Program (GRIP), designed to stabilize grain prices and yields at a percentage of historic averages, was introduced in 1991 and phased out by 1996.

Undoubtedly the single biggest blow to Western farmers was the loss in 1995 of the system that underwrote the shipment of grain from farm to port, for export. The agriculture minister at the time, Ralph Goodale, said the change in the government's policy would diversify prairie agriculture, boost value-added sectors and bring Canada into compliance with international trade rules; he made no reference to the money it would save. There was a one-time payout to farmers of $1.6 billion in 1996 to compensate for the loss of the Crow benefit, but it has been estimated that the cancellation has cost Western farmers $2.5 billion in just five years. Since Ottawa first began the process of deregulating grain transportation in 1984, farmers' freight rates have risen 700 percent. Farmers now pay the entire cost of shipping their produce to distant ports. At the same time, farmers have had to deal with a major structural reshaping of the grain-handling system. They have been forced to stand by in futile frustration as local grain elevators were knocked down to be replaced by distant concrete high-throughput facilities.

The federal government now seems to recognize that its grain-handling deregulation has put a heavy burden on Western farmers. In June 2000 it passed a grain transportation reform program that would clear the way for a freight rate reduction for most farmers on August 1 as a new cap on railway grain revenues took effect. The initiative was designed to reduce hauling charges for the typical 30-million-tonne prairie harvest by $178 million. That was to add up to savings to the average farmer of 18 percent, or $5.92 per metric tonne on a freight rate at $32.92.

"This is the best outcome for the greatest number of producers," said Agriculture and Agri-Food Minister Lyle Vanclief. "This will result in a reduction of an estimated $178 million a year in grain transportation costs, and will build on our continuing efforts to create a more secure future for farmers." As well as reducing freight rates, the government said the reforms would create a more efficient, accountable and competitive grain-handling system, much as prescribed by Justice Willard Estey in his review in 1998. Further changes to that system were sure to happen as the Canadian Transportation Agency was charged with undertaking additional evaluation.

The government's reform has been hailed as a step in the right direction. But many farmers took issue with the application of a "revenue cap" on CN and CP as opposed to a "rate cap" on what the railways were able to charge. The "revenue cap" granted the railways the flexibility to charge higher rates on less-travelled lines. By replacing the old maximum freight rate scale, the revenue cap allowed the railways to discriminate against elevators on branch lines or against certain kinds of crops.

"Where is my six dollars?" asks Alberta farmer Ken Larsen in a sarcastic indictment of the government's grain-handling reforms. He says he has not seen any lessening in the burden that was foisted on him and other grain farmers when the government dropped the Crow benefit in 1995. Larsen, forty-eight, runs a mixed barley and cattle farm near Benalto, in western Alberta. The total bill for a two-thousand-acre farm delivering grain from nearby Eckville stands at about $56,000.

In the early 1980s, before Ottawa began its process of freight rate deregulation with the withdrawal of the Crowsnest Pass rate, the Larsen family spent 5 percent of the money they received from growing grain on freight. After combining his grain, Ken Larsen would either store it in the bins on his farm or transport it in his grain truck to the nearly elevator in Benalto; and when that elevator was closed, he made the trip to the Agricore elevator in Eckville. Now, 32 percent of his grain cheque goes to shipping the crop by rail to port. What used to cost him $3.50 a metric tonne to transport now costs $28. A farmer in Saskatchewan will have seen his charges rise even more, because freight rates are higher for those farther from port.

Larsen is anticipating still-higher costs. The elevator in Eckville is expected to close when Agricore builds a planned high-throughput facility in Lacombe. When that happens, the distance will impose additional costs on him, beyond the rising freight rates. Because the new elevator will not be able to store much grain, Larsen will have to buy more grain bins to hold all of his grain on the farm until he gets a call to deliver. Even now, peculiar mounds of grain have begun to appear in farmyards across the Prairies, as farmers find they cannot afford to buy additional bins for on-farm storage.

Lacombe is too far away for Larsen to shuttle the grain himself. So he will have to hire a commercial hauling company to pick up his grain and get it from the farm to the elevator. He suspects he will have to make improvements to his driveway and loading equipment to accommodate the larger trucks. All in all, it means even more expense and trouble. The government's more efficient, accountable and competitive grain-handling system will cost Ken Larsen more and more.

Of all the cutbacks in support that have befallen Canadian farmers in the past decade, Larsen says the deregulation in freight rates has been the most difficult. Farmers were encouraged right from the beginnings of prairie agriculture to grow for export. Part of that encouragement was the government's agreement to underwrite the cost of getting grain from prairie farms to coastal ports. Larsen says farmers have fulfilled their end of the bargain: 80 percent of the grain he and other producers grow is exported. However, the government has reneged on what it promised to do.

He bristles at the suggestion that the Crowsnest Pass rate was a subsidy. "It was a business arrangement," he says curtly. The grain and hay farmer says the government's assault on legitimate supports for freight rates over the past fifteen years has been nothing short of a "swindle."


The federal government's Agricultural Income Disaster Assistance program was supposed to be the salvation for farmers ravaged by low commodity prices, reduced government subsidies and an industrial system increasingly dominated by transnational corporations. But there were complaints as soon as the details of the program were announced. Farmers said the eligibility requirement of a 70 percent drop in income from the previous year's average disqualified many producers. They demanded that "negative margins" or losses be allowed. One year into the program, the government did change the income averaging formula and allowed farmers to file claims even if they had losses. Nevertheless, the program had limited scope. By mid-December 2000, AIDA had paid out just $705 million of the available $1.7 billion to farmers across Canada.

AIDA has a bad reputation in the farming community. Farmers have found they have to ask their accountants to assess whether or not they would qualify, often for no return. Before Gail and Murray Forbes gave up farming in 1999, she says they had their accountant check into whether AIDA might give them a little breathing room. "I was devastated when our accountant informed us that we would not see one nickel of farm aid. Tears rolled down my cheeks, and I said this doesn't make sense. We have only five out of fifteen bins filled with grain and we cannot make all of our payments this year," says Gail.

Lawrence Solomon strides confidently into what he might see as the lion's den on a frosty Friday morning in October 2000. It is unfamiliar ground, this hall in Brandon, the heart of the agricultural Prairies. About 250 farmers are waiting to hear what the upstart from Toronto has to say. Solomon, a self-described market-oriented environmentalist, has made headlines by arguing there are too many farms and too many farmers in Canada; and that farmers still earn too much in government subsidies.

That kind of message from the director of Toronto's Urban Renaissance Institute is sure to irritate many on the Canadian Prairies. It even goes too far for Mike Byfield, from a family well known in Alberta for its right-wing politics. "The Urban Renaissance Institute, by concentrating its purist venom so categorically against the resource sector, helps to project an image of rural folk as wasteful, ecological wreckers in the minds of the city dwellers who dominate most elections," Byfield wrote in *Report: Alberta Edition* in May 2000.

Seemingly immune to critical reviews, Solomon has the self-assurance of a poised Daniel as he speaks in Brandon at the Recapturing Wealth on the Canadian Prairies conference. He pulls no punches in deference to his audience. He tells the farmers they seem to be confused as to whether governments or consumers are their customers. "You will wilt on the vine with government. But throw government off your back, get close to your customers—in other words, back to your roots—and you will thrive."

From his perspective there are still lots of subsidies for Canadian farmers. Solomon says that, despite the complaining, farmers still earn subsidies through programs like Crop Insurance, to which the federal government contributes 30 percent of costs, the Net Income Stabilization Program, under which the government matches farmer contributions, and support for manufacturers of inputs like chemicals and fertilizers. A study by his Urban Renaissance Institute says that for every dollar Canadian farmers earned in profit in the 1990s, federal and provincial governments provided an average of $3.55 in support. He calls this basic spending on agriculture "subsidies." According to his research, Newfoundland producers were the most heavily subsidized in the country, with $6.57 in support for every dollar earned. Ontario farmers were the next luckiest, receiving $6.20. Solomon concedes that supports are lower on the Prairies: for every dollar a Saskatchewan farmer earned from 1991 to 1999, federal and provincial governments provided just $3.04. But even that is too much, Solomon tells the farm audience. "No one should need encouragement to farm or do anything else."

Solomon suggests farmers will be in real trouble once consumers realize their hard-earned tax dollars are going to farming systems that affect the environment. He says most taxpayers do not understand that modern livestock production happens on factory farms or that today's farmers make intensive use of pesticides. He said farmers have been relatively immune to consumer attention, but that is likely to change in the future. He says, for example, the town of Walkerton's experience with the deadly E. coli bacteria in its water may be the start of a new, unpleasant focus on farming.

Solomon says Canada could learn from New Zealand's example. That country totally eliminated its agricultural supports in 1985, when the country's economic structure imploded. In 1984 New Zealand farmers earned 40 percent of their income from subsidies; in 1985, nothing. Solomon says that with subsidies, farming was simply not sustainable. About 10 percent of the soil suffered from extreme erosion, caused by the overuse of fertilizers because they were subsidized.

Today, without subsidies, nearly five million acres of land have reverted to forest. At the same time, he says, productivity has increased by 6 percent a year as farms diversify or opt for organic production.

He admits there were human costs as the savage cuts took effect. About eight hundred farms failed when subsidies disappeared. Ever the pragmatist, though, Solomon figures a 10 percent loss in the farm population is one that can be tolerated. Besides, he says, as farmers left the land, urban dwellers moved back to the country, bolstering the rural population in small communities. (This is hard to imagine in the West.)

Solomon lays out his argument clearly and articulately. The farmer-lions seem lulled by the logic of his case. But then he stumbles, suggesting that one of the most successful agricultural areas in the country is the ring right around Toronto. And you can hear the sharpening of teeth when he blithely proposes it would be best for all if more of the Prairies was allowed to revert to its natural state—forest.


While the government has terminated most of its subsidies, stabilization programs and price supports on grains, oilseeds, hogs and cattle, the supply management sectors—milk, eggs and poultry—have remained untouched. But the good times may be numbered. Canadian dairy, egg and poultry farmers have to contend with an increasingly hostile world environment. The cushion of supply management may not survive.

Recent WTO decisions have upped the international trade pressure on Canada's supply management systems. Supply management is not a subsidy in the strictest sense, but it can be viewed as a form of government support because it exists by government fiat. The system gives consumers a stable source of eggs, milk and poultry and farmers secure markets and prices. It is a system whereby Canadian production of eggs, milk, chickens and turkeys is matched to consumption through a quota system administered by provincial marketing boards. Farmers are allowed to produce only as much as their quota allows. In return they are paid an average cost of production.

Supply management came into being in the 1970s to bring some stability to a volatile industry facing growing concentration and vertical integration. Bud Olson, agriculture minister at the time, pushed the National Farm Products Marketing Act through Parliament against the vehement opposition of the Conservatives.

Under the dairy system, farmers buy "quota"—about $18,000 a cow—which determines how much milk they can produce. The price for quota milk is set at a high, stable price. Anything the farmer produces above quota must be sold on the world market, which offers a much lower price. In late 2000 the quota price paid to farmers for milk was 55.7 cents per litre; the world price was 22.4 cents. Not surprisingly, there is little above-quota production; only 5 percent of the milk produced on Canadian farms is exported.

In order to have a supply management system that matches production to consumption, a country must have a way of preventing products from other nations entering the domestic market. Before 1994 Canada did this with a system of import controls. But the Uruguay Round of the GATT talks eliminated Article 11, which allowed those import controls. Canada was forced to replace the controls with tariffs to be imposed on imports—tariffs that are being reduced with each passing year. The very high tariffs within North America may be reduced soon after the year 2001.

The government had vowed to protect Article 11, but it found itself isolated during the tough negotiations towards a comprehensive trade deal in 1993 and finally conceded defeat. The loss of Article 11, which allowed import-restrictive supply management to be created, was viewed as the death knell for the system. The tariffs gave supply management a decade or two of breathing space, until the border opens. The industries themselves were sure the whole system would collapse. It did not, although there is still ample speculation that the system is in decline, if not dying.

Now the pressure is focused on exports. First up is the dairy industry's two-price system. Acting on a complaint from the U.S. and New Zealand, the WTO ruled in 1999 that marketing boards are government agencies, which subsidize milk exports by paying farmers higher prices for domestic sales; in essence, an illegal export subsidy. The marketing boards responded by cutting their ties to export sales as of August 1, 2000. Whereas they used to arrange contracts for farmers, the boards now require farmers to make their own export deals.

The marketing boards hoped the move would eliminate the taint of subsidy from the transaction and put the U.S. and New Zealand off the scent. Instead, the U.S. has served notice that it plans to launch a WTO challenge to Canada's new dairy export policy—not, according to American trade negotiators, because of some hidden agenda to destroy Canada's supply management but because Canada is trying to move beyond supply management while keeping its domestic protections.

Federal minister Vanclief has vowed to defend supply management at the WTO talks. He says the boards are a domestic policy and therefore outside WTO jurisdiction. But sceptics remember that the government promised to defend supply management with Article 11 back in 1993—to no avail.

The Dairy Farmers of Canada, the national umbrella group that represents all the provincial milk marketing boards, is not prepared to leave its defence to the government. It has amassed a $2-million war chest to send dairy farmers on trade missions around the world in an attempt to find allies for Canada's position. The extraordinary steps are being taken because of fears that supply management may go the way of Canada's other farm supports.

There is no doubt that multinational corporations will offer their advice. In the U.S., where there is no supply management, a handful of large corporations, like Tyson Foods, dominate the poultry business, contracting production to farmers but otherwise controlling every aspect of production and marketing. The same trends exist in the dairy sector. California, with massive farms of thousands of cows, is now the largest milk-producing state in the country—a position it has attained only by relying on an unsustainable water supply.

•　•　•

If supply management is viewed as a subsidy, then the Canadian Wheat Board will surely be assessed in the same way. By virtue of its monopoly on wheat and barley sales it is one of the key players in the international grain trade, responsible for 20 percent of the world's wheat exports. That puts it on a par with some of the largest U.S. grain companies, like Archer Daniels Midland and Cargill. Its size gives it clout that has allowed it to win contracts, much to the annoyance of U.S. farmers and companies. Its clout, in turn, has made the cwb a target at international trade negotiations.

There have been a total of nine trade-law investigations of the Board by the U.S., culminating in the most recent effort by the North Dakota Wheat Commission, which says the Canadian Wheat Board is driving down domestic American prices. Investigations of the eight previous challenges all concluded that the cwb's activities met the terms of the North American Free Trade Agreement. This time the ndwc is using a controversial piece of U.S. trade legislation, called a Section 301 petition, to undercut the Wheat Board.

The Wheat Board is not a subsidy by the wto's definition, but it does give farmers the benefit of several "add-ons." For example, the federal government guarantees the initial payment to farmers. That became very important in 1990–91, when the Gulf War would have interrupted payments of $744 million. Ottawa also underwrites credit sales—which proved beneficial when Poland was unable to pay its bills. And when the cwb has to borrow about $6 billion a year, it has the advantage of paying the government rate on those loans.

Brian White, vice-president of market analysis, says in the late 1930s the cwb was used to transfer payments to farmers, but this is not the case now. He says "that would undermine our position with world trading bodies that we are not passing on dollars."

The Wheat Board is trying to manage the assaults coming from the international trading stage, but it is very aware that the fatal blow may come from Canada itself. The Wheat Board is going through the most beleaguered period in its history. Western farmers are deeply divided over whether the board should retain its monopoly. Discontent has been building since the 1980s, when U.S. export enhancement programs drove down world grain prices, including the Wheat Board's pool price. Farmers were tormented with the artificially inflated prices they saw being offered south of the border. Some Canadian producers thumbed their noses at the Wheat Board and trucked their grain south, to American elevators.

The value of the Wheat Board is a question that stirs emotions; it is at the heart of the debate about how Western farming will survive. On one side is an ethic that has been passed down from one generation to the next, a conviction that farmers have to stick together if they hope to have the muscle to fight grain companies and railways. Some supporters say the same conditions that first convinced farmers to demand a wheat board are now returning. Producers like Ken Larsen say the Wheat Board provides price stability and its monopoly returns more money to prairie producers. It also offers farmers power they would not have on their own. A few years ago, for example, the CWB took the railways to task for poor performance in delivering grain, something individual farmers would not have the resources to do. Larsen feels so strongly about the merits of the CWB that he decided to put his opinions to the test in the fall of 2000, running as a candidate for the CWB advisory board's elections. (He lost to incumbent Jim Chatenay, an outspoken supporter of a dual marketing system.)

Warren Jolly of Mossbank, Saskatchewan, stands on the other side of the debate. From his perspective, the board stifles initiative. He farms within trucking distance of American elevators, and he has to cope with the frustration of seeing the U.S. spot price—a daily price that goes up and down—rise above the Wheat Board's price. According to the terms of the Wheat Board's monopoly, he is not allowed to take advantage of the higher price.

It is easy to argue in this world of free trade and global communications that the Wheat Board's limitations on entrepreneurship are grossly out of step. Jolly is sure he could do just as well as the Wheat Board in selling his own durum wheat. "I am convinced that I could make more money outside of the cwb." From his perspective the only answer is demanding the Wheat Board compete in a dual marketing system.

A 1996 study by economists Hartley Furtan, Daryl Kraft and Ed Tyrchniewicz, generally considered the most thorough and balanced report on the subject, found that the Wheat Board monopoly did in fact extract higher prices for farmers, adding an average of $13.35 per tonne of wheat sold. For a farmer seeding a thousand acres, that adds up to $15,000 to $20,000 more each year.

The polls nevertheless show a divided community. One-third of farmers support the Wheat Board, one-third oppose it and one-third want dual marketing. The Wheat Board has tried to adjust to the mood for change. In 1998 it introduced an elected board of directors to replace ten government appointees. In 2000, of a slate of five new directors, three were single-desk supporters; two were dual marketers.

The cwb is aware of how the political winds are blowing in these early years of the twenty-first-century. The Ontario Wheat Producers' Marketing Board recently approved a controversial exemption to satisfy farmers who want out of that pooling system. And the Australian Wheat Board recently lost its monopoly on domestic wheat sales. In this context, Brian White expresses some wonderment at the support the federal Liberals have given the Wheat Board. "It's been surprising that the Liberals have stuck with the cwb. This minister and this government have shown surprising support." He adds with a note of amazement, "It is possible they are acting out of belief."

The government's backing of the Wheat Board manifested itself during the 2000 reform of the grain-handling system. Although it was opposed by grain companies, railways and a coalition of conservative farm groups, Ottawa decided to leave the Wheat Board in the middle of the transportation action. The grain companies will negotiate with the railways for rail cars, but the Wheat Board will still have the power to allocate cars to specific grain collection points if it feels this is necessary. The critics say this leaves too much power in the Wheat Board's hands and blurs accountability if there are system problems. But the government steadfastly refused to back down. It is a position that may bode well for the future of the Canadian Wheat Board.

Governmental support for the Wheat Board in a domestic wrangle over transportation reform will not necessarily translate into success at the international trading table. Canada may want to defend the Canadian Wheat Board and its supply management systems, but that might not be enough in the face of global pressures. Some critics note that the government does not have much negotiating leverage left when it tries to make deals on agriculture. What can it put on the table to protect supply management or the CWB when it has already given away the Crow benefit and just about any other subsidy it once offered to farmers?

Barry Wilson of the *Western Producer* has watched the trade negotiations for years. He is an able observer of Ottawa machinations, and an author. He thinks Canada may not have much of a bargaining hand left. "When it comes to hard bargaining, Canada may find it already has given away most of its chips," he wrote in a column in August 1999.

Canadian agriculture cannot afford to lose any more of its supports. Farmers producing for an open, international market have already been hit with the loss of critical subsidies and support programs at a time when commodity prices have fallen to record low levels. Farmers have complained bitterly about the deregulation they have been confronted with. But the interest of most Canadians has been focused elsewhere, leaving the government free to kick the legs out from under the agricultural community with few repercussions. The challenge for farmers now is to determine how they can wield political influence in the unfamiliar corridors of power.

*Ten*

# The Missing Political Card

*September 13, 2000*

It was an early harvest—in theory. The weather co-operated long enough to let the Wielers get their wheat combined and into the bins. But the crop looked defeated by blight and moisture, kernel heads hanging in shame.

Towards the end of August, Gary began combining the field of peas. He tried to ignore the spatters of rain that obscured the combine windscreen. Then the spatters became more insistent, morphing into a deluge that forced him to give up the job in frustration. "And there was just an acre to go," he says in aggrieved recollection.

The rain did not stop. In fact, it rained for two weeks, drenching the ripened crops with moisture they did not need. It paused only long enough to raise futile hopes. Throughout the landscape of rural southern Manitoba, combines and swathers stood idle in waterlogged fields scarred with ruts where the equipment faltered before it gave up. Some farmers

187

*were even hoping for a frost, thinking it might harden their fields enough for them to fire up the equipment.*

*The Wielers' canola has been confused by the fickle weather. The seed pods lying cut in the swaths burst and were beaten into the ground by the rain. Then they sprouted and flowered, casting the field in a blush of July yellow—in September.*

*Somehow, Lorna manages to shake off the bad news about what was supposed to be a wonder crop, laughing in the manner of someone who knows there is no other choice. I sense she has had lots of practice at this sardonic brand of consolation. "Ours is not the only one." Even before the weather bewildered the canola, the family had decided not to give the Roundup Ready bioengineered canola another chance on the farm. Applying a very practical judgment, the Wielers say they do not like how consumers are reacting to genetically engineered crops. "We want to be able to sell what we grow," says Lorna.*

*Gary reports in that droll, matter-of-fact way of his that it has rained forty centimetres from April 1 to September 1. That is higher than any year he can remember except for 1992. Gary offers up the weather facts in a controlled voice, but the rain-enforced inactivity is fraying nerves—even the carefully guarded nerves on the Wieler farm.*

*It is not just the weather, it is the reality of modern farming that tests the patience even of people born to this way of life. The Wielers sold the peas they managed to harvest because they had to get some cash to pay bills. It was a terrible time for a sale. A few years ago field peas were selling for $5.20 a bushel; when the Wielers took their peas in to Carman a few weeks ago, they received only $3.10 a bushel. That was barely enough to make it all worthwhile.*

*It stopped raining a few days ago, the sky lifting some of the dampness from the ground. The sun appeared, offering September warmth. A steady but not too fierce wind stroked the earth, evaporating the water from the ruts and potholes in the fields. On noon-hour radio they called this "good combining weather." And sure enough, combines are everywhere on the horizon, clouds of grain dust marking their paths. Gary fired up his combine too after its two-week mid-harvest break and tack-led that one wayward acre of peas.*

It was dry enough for a neighbour north of them to light a match to his stubble. That is the old technique for getting rid of the stubby stalks left standing after a field is combined, and with them, some of the disease harboured in those stalks. The Wielers do not burn their stubble. Instead, they go over the field with a harrow — like a giant rake — and then culti-vate the straw into the soil, as a green manure. It is a natural, organic fertilizer, and it slows down soil erosion. "We don't want our field to blow," says Lorna, who is on harrowing and cultivating detail now that Philip is back at school. She ends up circling the field three or four times. This is gardening on a grand scale.

The Wielers had planned to bale the straw from this field to provide bedding for their cattle through the winter, but the neighbour's fire snaked across into their field, into their straw. Gary rushed for the tractor, scrambling to build a makeshift fireguard. Lorna vaulted onto the culti-vator, smothering the burning stubble into the ground. She remembers her feet were wet with the moisture that had accumulated over the weeks, even as the hairs on her legs were singed off with the heat. It took a frantic hour for Gary and Lorna in their duelling tractors to subdue the runaway fire. It was precious time better spent elsewhere. It is hard to imagine from him, but Lorna says Gary was "really mad."

The frustrations do not stop there. Gary spent this morning fixing the tractor. He took it all apart and worked his farmer-mechanic magic. Once it was back together and healthy again, he sent it out with Lorna and the cultivator to the canola field. He finished combining it late last night. Her assignment now is to chop the straw into the ground. It is a task that will add not a penny to this year's earnings. Instead, it is an optimist's preparation for the next year. Cultivate. Harrow. Harrow. Round and round.

The question the Wielers now have to ask themselves is, can they afford to apply anhydrous ammonia fertilizer to their fields? It is the cheapest way to get extra nitrogen into the soil, which has probably been

189

*exhausted from the effort of growing a crop. Farmers apply the liquid gas in the fall and it lies dormant all winter until the spring warmth triggers its action. But the price of anhydrous ammonia is up 40 percent — 22.4 cents a pound of nitrogen compared with 16 cents a pound last year. The Wielers have skipped applications in the past. It may be that kind of year again.*

 

It is raining and nine degrees above zero . . . in February. Ottawa is a long way from the Canadian Prairies, but even here black umbrellas are not a standard accessory for what should be a parka winter. Sheltered from the unseasonable weather, Agriculture and Agri-Food minister Lyle Vanclief is, appropriately enough, speaking to reporters about his plans to study climate change's effect on agriculture. On the outskirts of the downtown, a ragtag group of farmers from the Prairies is hunkered down at the Doral Inn, exhausted from a day of trying to convince harried parliamentarians that farming really does matter. And at the somewhat more sumptuous Château Laurier the country's biggest farm lobby, the Canadian Federation of Agriculture, is holding its annual general meeting.

In an announcement apparently timed to coincide with events agricultural, the federal government has declared it will provide a disaster support lifeline worth $400 million (just $240 million of it in federal funds) to Saskatchewan and Manitoba farmers. "Farmers are members of the Canadian family and family members stand together in times of trouble," Prime Minister Jean Chrétien tells reporters, as he is flanked by the beaming premiers of Saskatchewan and Manitoba. The announcement comes just four days before Finance Minister Paul Martin will make known that Ottawa has squirrelled away the biggest budget surplus in federal history. At the CFA meeting the farm leaders from Ontario and Quebec and Atlantic Canada ask why they have not received a handout. And at the Doral Inn the Prairie farm families will disappoint the government too. Instead of thanks, they angrily offer up the essential question: "Is this it? Is this the government's agricultural policy?"

The answer to that question is, yes, probably. One-time, patchwork emergency funds seem to be how Ottawa has chosen to deal with this farm crisis. Canada's 277,000 farmers must flounder without a clear statement as to what value the country places on the family farm. In the view of desperate farmers, the federal government sheds crocodile tears over family farms while advancing their demise through the withdrawal of supports like the Crow benefit. The continuing emphasis on the global agenda and the agribusiness industry over the farm sector suggests that the occasional disaster support package is all farmers can expect. So even when $400-million gifts arrive, they are not accepted graciously. CFA president Bob Friesen, a man well versed in government relations, is not about to make waves unnecessarily. He tells his farm audience that he is regularly asked: "Do we have an agricultural policy?" He answers curtly: "It quickly becomes apparent that government doesn't have a policy."

Agricultural policy in Canada has always been a confusion of regional and sectoral differences. Although the primary responsibility for agriculture has fallen to the federal government throughout Canada's history, agriculture is technically a shared responsibility between the provinces and the federal government. But provinces like Saskatchewan simply do not have the tax base to finance a failing agricultural sector. Agriculture also tends to be regionally concentrated: horticulture in British Columbia, grains and oilseeds on the Prairies, dairy and poultry industries in central Canada, potatoes in New Brunswick and Prince Edward Island. There is constant tension amongst the regions and the sectors. The federal government's challenge is to orchestrate trade-offs and compromises to create a united direction for farmers and farming.

Despite the formidable challenges, for most of its history Canada's national agricultural policy has had farmers' interests at its core. The federal government aimed to provide farmers with a fair and stable income while at the same time reducing economic disparities within agriculture. With these principles in mind, Canada developed the Crow's Nest Pass

Agreement, the Canadian Wheat Board and supply management systems. In response to a concerned and vocal electorate, the federal government appointed no fewer than six Royal Commissions on agriculture between 1899 and 1936.

That focus on the producer began to wane in the mid-1980s. A new enthusiasm for "competitiveness" put a heightened interest on exports, the free market and deregulation of support programs. The sea change was reflected in June 1993, when Agriculture Canada, a department that was originally designed to serve producers, became Agriculture and Agri-Food Canada. The government of the day insisted the name change simply reflected a decision to put government services related to "agri-food," formerly shared by Industry, Science and Technology, Consumer and Corporate Affairs, and Agriculture Canada, under one roof. "This realignment does not mean a change in philosophy for the Department," said then minister Charles Mayer. Perhaps it was just a coincidence, but that was the time when a subtle but significant shift began, from servicing farmers to servicing agribusiness. Grants to agri-food companies were made available through various program envelopes; for example, the Western Economic Diversification fund gave Hoechst, then Europe's largest chemical firm, $1.6 million to set up its North American headquarters in Regina. At the same time there was a change in policy on research funding, as money to universities became contingent on researchers finding matching funds from the private sector. University of Manitoba plant scientist Rene Van Acker says 80 percent of his research is now cost-shared between public and private sources. Genetic engineering research is so widespread because vital private funds are available for it.

The federal government has been loath to admit publicly any official change in policy. However, the term "agribusiness" peppers ministers' speeches much more than any references to the "family farm." But for practical political considerations the federal government has not been eager to challenge sacred cows openly. So it is left with a hodgepodge of programs and initiatives that say very different things about its philosophy. On the one hand Canada has the highly regulated supply management systems and the monopoly of the Canadian Wheat Board. On the other the government is opting for deregulation, eliminating the Crow benefit under the Western Grain Transportation Agreement.

It has begun to look like an agricultural game show as farmers and political leaders try to figure out what the government's agricultural policy is. At a House of Commons Agriculture Committee hearing in the fall of 1999, University of Saskatchewan agricultural economist Hartley Furtan urged the government to define its goals for the sector. He said the EU, Japan and the U.S. all have legislated bills that list goals and give farmers an understanding of the support they can expect.

In March 2000 a group representing farm women from across the country left a meeting with Lyle Vanclief in confusion. "We are very encouraged that opposition parties are thinking about the development of agricultural policy that could sustain and support farm communities. We cannot see any evidence that the current government even has an agricultural policy," said their rather blunt press release.

Even the Western Canadian Wheat Growers Association, a group that promotes the principles of businesslike entrepreneurship while denying the need for supports, criticizes the Chrétien administration for its lack of policies. "Contrary to popular belief, there is no cheap food policy in Canada," notes a report entitled *The Business of Farming*. "There simply is no coherent policy at all as the mish-mash of farm aid programs clearly shows."

At February's CFA meeting, Vanclief is asked directly and publicly to explain his government's agricultural policy. He sidesteps the issue, opting to quote Yogi Berra: "Predictions are very difficult, especially when you are talking about the future." He goes on to say: "We have to work with the hand we are dealt. We have to influence the hand as best as we can." It is a confusing bit of political speaking, but then he notes in what might be the central theme of his thinking, "You must not lose sight of the big picture and that is to get on with the business of farming."

Watching how Vanclief and Jean Chrétien's Liberal government have dealt with the crisis that is destroying a way of life on the farm has been a lesson in practical politics. After months of lobbying as Canadian farmers suffered through an unprecedented drop in commodity prices, Vanclief finally announced a government aid program in December 1998. The Agricultural Income Disaster Assistance program was supposed to be a two-year, $1.5-billion program to be cost-shared with the provinces. There had been so much intergovernmental squabbling that only five provinces signed up: Saskatchewan, Manitoba, Nova Scotia, Newfoundland and later New Brunswick. The other provinces decided to take the money and administer their own programs.

The federal government's AIDA was immediately condemned, by the people it was supposed to serve, as poorly designed and excessively complicated. The eligibility guidelines in the ten-page form were so intricate that farmers had to call in accountants to unscramble them. And even after paying the bills for an accountant's review, many farmers found they could not tap into the program. The theory in the countryside was that the program was designed not for the desperate grain farmers of Saskatchewan but to help out the doctors, lawyers and dentists who had invested money in the new mega-hog barns. There was also speculation that the program was intended to have money left over at the end of it— money that would never get to the farmers who needed it.

Under the terms of AIDA, farmers were eligible only if their gross margin—income minus expenses—in the claim year fell below 70 percent of the average of their three previous years. "Negative margins," or losses, were not allowed. That meant farmers had to suffer an appreciable and sudden drop in income—but not too much. The inadmissibility of negative margins became a key sticking point for the CFA. The farm lobby group claimed another ten thousand producers would get aid if the government altered its onerous eligibility requirements.

Vanclief offered no apologies. He said it was necessary to weed out the poor farmers, the ones who could not cut it in the business. AIDA was supposed to go only to "farmers who need it." And he said the government had to be frugal. (At the same time Ottawa was showing little restraint in its spending through the Human Resources Development Corporation and was considering giving millions to the National Hockey League.)

To the surprise of no one in the farm community, the take-up on AIDA was excessively slow, even in Saskatchewan, where producers had been sharply hit by the dismal economy. By late May 1999—five months after support had been announced and well into the year's seeding season— only 1,500 applications had been received, and only 16 percent of those had been approved. In Manitoba and Saskatchewan that added up to $500,000 in support. Just to rub salt in the wound, prairie farmers learned that the Ontario program was working much more efficiently. In the same period about $18 million in support went out the door under the Ontario Ministry of Agriculture, Food and Rural Affairs' Whole Farm Relief Program.

The federal government responded to the farm revolt that was brewing on the Prairies with more than three hundred information sessions, not just for farmers but also for accountants. Through an access to information request the Canadian Taxpayers Federation found out it cost about $320,000 to inform ten thousand farmers. The federal government also laid on an advertising campaign: "It is not helpful to farmers to have misinformation floating around about things like eligibility, delays and complicated forms," said one ad billed as a message to farmers from Vanclief. The ad claimed most applicants could fill out the forms in a few hours. That advertising campaign cost $1.9 million.

And then weather clouded the picture. Literally. It rained without fail for weeks in southwestern Manitoba and southeastern Saskatchewan, right during seeding time. By June 1999 nearly two million acres were swamped by a lake of water. It was a case of flooding from the sky. That the situation was a disaster was clear to the five thousand people directly affected and the thousands who depended on their success.

The government, however, refused to call it a "disaster," which would thereby have triggered the money that normally goes hand in glove with a catastrophe. Instead, Vanclief conducted a site survey by flying overhead and stopping down briefly for meetings with hand-picked farmers in Car-lyle, Saskatchewan, and Souris, Manitoba. He talked with no provincial officials, but checked in on one defeated Liberal MLA.

Vanclief downplayed the idea of a crisis and dismissed the possibility of additional money. He suggested farmers use their Net Income Stabi-lization Accounts (NISA), savings accounts to which farmers make pay-ments in good years, prompting an equal contribution from the government. Obviously, younger farmers would be at a disadvantage because they typically have little money in their accounts, which accumu-late like an RRSP. And in any case, farmers had already drawn down on their accounts to survive over a number of lean years. At the end of 2000 the average NISA held $21,516.

Vanclief also promised to release advance payments under the AIDA program. Vanclief's answer to the deluged farmers was immediately denounced. Melita farmer Alan Clark exploded after he heard Vanclief's proposals. "I don't know what this is!" Clark was not eligible for AIDA in 1998 because he had had a few low-income years in a row. In 1999, with 1,700 acres left unseeded, he expected to receive only $20,000 from AIDA, or about $12 an acre. It would cost him at least four times that much just to maintain the land so it could be seeded in the subsequent year.

AIDA was roundly reviled, so Vanclief's promise of early access to this program would was not much help. In an effort to plead the case for Prairie farmers, Saskatchewan's premier Roy Romanow and Gary Doer of Manitoba led a lobbying trip to Ottawa in October 1999. They were looking for $1.3 billion in farm aid, not adjustments to AIDA and NISA. Romanow, who had been one of Jean Chrétien's closest allies on the national unity file, was clearly unprepared for the reception he and Doer got when they made their pitch to the prime minister. But he might have guessed what Chrétien's reaction would be. After all, the prime minister is not a frequent visitor to Saskatchewan. Chrétien may have been to North-ern Ireland, South Africa and Central America, but he is less likely to spring for a ticket west. (Perhaps he has sour memories of the 1997 Red River flood that swamped much of southern Manitoba. Chrétien called an election in the middle of the flood even though Manitobans begged him not to. When he stopped by for an election visit, he was ridiculed for throwing a single sandbag during what was meant to be a good photo opportunity. )

In this October meeting in well-fed Ottawa, Chrétien infuriated Romanow and Doer by giving them a lecture on how the farm crisis in their provinces was not nearly as bad as they maintained. He rejected out of hand their request for $1.3 billion. What they got one month later was a basic sweetening of the AIDA pot by $170 million, to $1.7 billion, with the inclusion of negative margins. Vanclief said it was all he could wrest from cabinet. "AIDA does not work," Romanow sputtered in indignation. "It didn't work before this announcement and it is not working now."

The AIDA program stopped accepting applications on September 29, 2000. The statistics certainly make Romanow's complaints seem justified. The Canadian Taxpayers Federation found that the costs for administration were hefty—$21.5 million for the period from December 1, 1998, to June 30, 2000. Among the largest expenses were salaries and benefits accounting for $14.3 million, professional services and consulting at $3.8 million, and materials and office supplies at $2.8 million. Brandon Conservative MP Rick Borotsik told the House of Commons, "There is something seriously wrong with a program that costs this much. This is money that could far better be used helping farmers get a crop in."

According to AIDA spokesperson Ellen Funk, the federal government hired 550 people to administer the program in Winnipeg and Regina at salaries between $30,000 and $40,000 a year. In contrast, the average payout to a farmer who had succeeded in jumping through the AIDA hoops was $16,000. By October 2000 the AIDA workers had dealt with just 12,248 applications from the five provinces under their administration, approving 7,937. By the end of 2000, farmers from across Canada had received $705 million, or 41 percent of the $1.7 billion that had been promised them. Apparently, another 30,000 applications remained to be dealt with.

Funk said the bureaucracy set up to process AIDA would, hopefully, be able to follow up on the next disaster support plan. Federal and provincial governments had resolved in the summer of 2000 to set up another assistance fund that would be part of the reworking of existing safety net programs. The new Canadian Farm Income Program was trumpeted as a $5.5-billion, three-year commitment. But this initiative, like AIDA before it, seemed more style than substance. Most of the much-touted $5.5 billion was already being paid under long-standing programs like crop insurance and NISA. In fact, the new disaster assistance portion had an annual cost-shared budget of just $725 million. And by the end of 2000 no details had been announced on how those program funds were to be dispersed.

The Canadian Federation of Agriculture's Bob Friesen, who had chaired a safety net advisory committee for the federal government, was taken by surprise. After three years of co-operative planning, consulting and reviewing with producers, ministers had come up with a "scaled-back package filled with confusing calculations and contradictions leaving farmers with a less credible program." He noted the new plan offered less coverage and fewer benefits than AIDA had. "There is no doubt this is a rollback from what we have," said Friesen. "We are thankful they kept some of the key changes to AIDA 1999, but there has been some slippage. We think AIDA '99 was the minimum base we should have." Vanclief's amendments to AIDA in 1999 had allowed farmers to apply for support even if they had spent more than they had earned. Although support for this move came from all corners, the new Canadian Farm Income Program eliminated these so-called negative margins.

Friesen was also taken aback at the proposed link between the CFIP and NISA. Under the proposals, when a farmer was approved for a disaster payment, Ottawa planned to deduct from the cheque the contributions it had made to the farmer's NISA account. Vanclief said the move was designed to ensure that farmers understood and appreciated the government's contributions to NISA. Farm leaders, on the other hand, saw it as a way of penalizing farmers who took the time to maintain NISA accounts. "That would mean the year the farmer really needs help, he would receive far less than the program is supposed to offer. We find that absurd," said Friesen. "The NISA link has been developed without any input from the farming community. It is complex and it will be a challenge to communicate the new procedures to farmers."

The federal government made it clear once again that although it would offer some basic security to farmers, that support would be limited. At the beginning of the twenty-first century the continued existence of family farmers, supported by government dollars, was not to be a priority.

In the world of Ottawa politics the agriculture portfolio is generally not seen to be in the senior ranks of cabinet. Most federal agriculture ministers do not get much attention from media, Parliament or the prime minister. The one exception in recent times was Eugene Whelan, Pierre Trudeau's long-serving minister, who demanded attention with his green Stetson hat, his very rural outfits and his provocative style. He put agriculture on the national agenda, introducing such initiatives as supply management. But those were different times.

Lyle Vanclief probably serves these times well, reflecting the Liberal government's no-policy policies. There is no doubt that he has a difficult job. The question is whether to support farmers or food processing, whether to encourage production or trade. The challenge is how to support all of them in a time of restricted spending.

Vanclief is condemned in Western Canada for what is viewed as his bloodless lack of concern. It is particularly curious, because he should understand first-hand what farmers are going through. Vanclief ran a diversified 1,650-acre fruit, vegetable, grain and oilseeds operation in Prince Edward County, Ontario, until 1988, when it fell into financial difficulties. Then he sold it to his son, Kurt, and began a life in politics. Vanclief talked openly about what he went through, apparently to demonstrate that there is life after farming. The experience gave him a "tough love" philosophy, with no particular sympathy or sentimentality towards other farmers in trouble.

What is chilling is the realization that Vanclief did not succeed as a farmer even though he followed the very advice he now gives other farmers.

He and his wife, Sharon, apparently tried to expand too much, too quickly, borrowing money at 19 percent interest. They chose to grow crops that needed more intensive management. The Vancliefs lost two $50,000 tomato crops back to back, once because the weather made it impossible to harvest and once because the crop ripened too quickly for the processing plant to accommodate it. He practised what he preaches today, and still he was vulnerable. Somehow that lesson is lost on him. "When the margins are incredibly small, all too often sometimes in any business, whether it is agriculture or otherwise, volume is very, very meaningful," he told the CBC.

Vanclief's perspective continues to be that of a free enterpriser. He told the *Western Producer* for its special report on the farm crisis in November 1999: "I think any business person, whether they're a farmer, or whether they're in any other type of business, must be very cautious if they are looking down the road and anticipating that government is going to give them any more support than they are at the present time. That is not, in my view, a way of making a sound management or business decision."

Farmers have let their governments get away with this logic and these hands-off approaches partly because they are so busy arguing amongst themselves. Farmers from the early twentieth century would be shocked to see how divisive agriculture has become a hundred years later. There are not many farmers left in the country, but they are divided by provincial boundaries, commodity groups and political differences.

Farmers may do the same job, but they do not necessarily see things the same way. Agriculture is a landscape in which the writing on your ball cap tells the world how to label you. A Saskatchewan Wheat Pool cap says one thing, a Pioneer cap something very different. The Western Canadian Wheat Growers believe in an open-market philosophy while the National Farmers Union thinks government should regulate the system. There is no way you could put representatives from the two organizations in a room and expect them to find any points of agreement.

The interprovincial variations in producer and governmental goals, along with the multiplicity of producer organizations with diverse and often contradictory perspectives, make national decision making difficult. The Canadian Federation of Agriculture is an umbrella group that struggles to present a united voice on behalf of farmers. It likes to talk about its "Team Canada" approach in its relations with government. There are no peaked caps in the Château Laurier ballroom, with its salmon-coloured drapes and gold gilt, for the CFA's February annual meeting. The delegates here are well suited; they have polished their presentation through practice. Only one tiny sign in the window discreetly says Canadian Federation of Agriculture. Otherwise, this session could be taken as a sales meeting for office supplies or a government policy session. The rough edges only become apparent during breaks. The farmers here rush for the foyer, smoking with abandon. Urban niceties have told them not to smoke in the meeting, but enough is enough.

CFA president Bob Friesen has worked hard to fit into the Ottawa environment. He is contained in a stiffly starched white shirt and tailored suit. He congratulates the farm audience for its willingness to work together. "Solidarity is good. When we go to the minister, let's make sure he knows that means solidarity."

But the chasms in the solidarity crack open after the prime minister announces the $400 million special aid for Manitoba and Saskatchewan. There is a gallop for the microphones when Lyle Vanclief agrees to take questions. Quebec farm leader Laurent Pellerin tells the minister, "Your government has invested many dollars to convince us we live in a beautiful big country." He predicts the unfair distribution of funds will mean "this beautiful country will be in pieces." Neil Wagstaff, president of Alberta's Wild Rose Agricultural Producers, tells Vanclief an aid package that stops at the Alberta/Saskatchewan border "is as inequitable as you can get." Peter Hill from the Nova Scotia Federation of Farmers reminds Vanclief that Annapolis producers have suffered through three years of drought and are victims of their own disaster.

The discordant voices at the microphone aptly reflect the reality of farming today in the broad stretches of this country. It has been said that getting farmers to agree on anything is like herding cats. It is a political truth the government clearly understands.

Philosophical differences never became an issue when it was time to save Canada's east coast fishermen from the impact of declining cod stocks. Universal support along with government assistance ensured that the tiny outport towns of the fishing economy were not allowed to die. Although the fishing industry, like the farming business, was devastated, support from the federal government was generous.

Fishing defined the identity, both economically and culturally, of New-foundland and Labrador for more than five hundred years. When John Cabot returned to England from Newfoundland in 1497, his crew gushed about the huge schools of fish that were swarming in the ocean off Canada's Atlantic coast. Throughout the subsequent centuries the ocean's bounty attracted fishing fleets from Portugal, France, Spain and England. The world assumed the cod stocks were boundless. In 1885 the Canadian minister of agriculture expressed the thinking of the times: "Unless the order of nature is overthrown, for centuries to come our fisheries will continue to be fertile."

However, the "order of nature" was overthrown in less than a century. European fishing intensified in the 1950s with high-powered, all-year factory trawlers that located fish on their spawning grounds with sonar equipment and pulled them off the seabed with huge dragnets. The fish were then filleted and frozen right on board the floating processing plants. The technology massively increased the harvest. Under the old, rudimentary system of the first half of the twentieth century, the annual catch logged in at around 500,000 tonnes. With the massive factory trawlers plying the waters, annual catches tripled, to about 1,475,000 tonnes. The end of one of the richest fisheries in the world loomed.

In the 1970s Canadian scientists warned about the frailty of the fish stocks, yet the government ignored their advice. In 1970 a federal cabinet memorandum estimated Canada's commercial catch could be harvested by 60 percent fewer boats, half as much gear and half the number of fishermen. Canada's reaction was to limit the number of foreign ships that came within a two-hundred-mile limit. But then it encouraged Canadian boats to take their place. One biologist described the gold rush mentality: "The streets were paved with fish and now that the Europeans were gone, it would come to the Canadians." Of course there were plenty of signs of trouble to come, but government programs, like the offer of low-interest loans, simply encouraged overfishing.

Unemployment insurance had supported generations of Atlantic fishermen and processors. The program became progressively more generous over the years, essentially evolving from an insurance program into a permanent income program. In 1971, with six weeks of employment, workers qualified for five weeks of benefits. In 1976, eight weeks of work resulted in twenty-seven weeks of pogey. By 1990 ten weeks of work added up to benefits for the rest of the year. In 1992 the average UI benefit for fishing families was $12,219. The UI generosity encouraged more people to fish, even for a short time, to get onto the pogey cycle.

By 1992 it was impossible to ignore the reality of declining cod stocks. Michael Harris's 1999 book *Lament for an Ocean*, probably the most damning assessment of the cod collapse, laid the blame for the failure at the federal government's feet. "Ottawa's whistling past the graveyard was getting loud enough to wake the dead." The federal government had no choice but to impose a moratorium on cod fishing in the North Atlantic. It recognized the shutdown meant the end of a tradition—a way of life—for thousands of Newfoundlanders and Labradorians. The fisheries' closure threw forty thousand fishermen and fish processors out of work. About 1,300 tiny communities, with their own little fish packing plants, depended almost entirely on the fishery. Earle McCurdy, then president of the Fish, Food, and Allied Workers Union, spoke in a tone that would be familiar to Western farmers when he said: "What we have is not an adjustment problem, but the most wrenching societal upheaval since the Great Depression. Our communities are in crisis. The people of the fishery are in turmoil."

To compensate fishermen and workers in the fish processing industry the government offered an interim aid program, with support up to $406 a week. Then in May 1994 came the $1.9-billion TAGS, the Atlantic Ground-fish Strategy. It was supposed to be a transitional program to help people find new opportunities outside of fishing. Under the program, displaced fishermen and plant workers got income support, employment coun-selling and assistance to help them develop new skills and jobs outside the industry. But critics say it simply bankrolled fishermen and communities rather than encouraging them to exit the industry. A total of about twenty-five thousand people were still drawing benefits in August 1998, when TAGS was due to expire. With the end of the so-called interim pro-gram looming, Ottawa responded with a promise that TAGS beneficiaries would receive employment insurance benefits once the program expired. Then, rather than let the program terminate, the government announced more help in June 1998, worth $730 million. TAGS did not wean; instead, it made continued attachment to the fishery profitable, even six years after the industry shut down.

The east coast fisheries industry received lots of subsidies, even when there were loud warnings about impending doom. Some people say it is unfair to compare agriculture with the fishery; after all, the land will not disappear. But land, like fish, is a finite resource. It has to be tended care-fully if it is to thrive and produce. Unfortunately, the people who know how to tend the land are disappearing, and it seems there is little effort being made to stop the bleeding.

You do not have to be a cynic, just a political pragmatist, to come up with a plausible explanation of why one part of the country gets support and the other does not. Atlantic Canada is considered vital to Liberal fortunes; the West is not. In the 2000 election the hope was to regain the seats in the

Atlantic provinces that had been lost in 1997, when it seemed voters punished the Liberals for cuts to social programs like employment insurance. The Liberals had won thirty-one of thirty-two seats in Atlantic Canada in the 1993 election, and then dropped twenty of them in 1997. The measure of the Liberal resolve to win back those seats came when Jean Chrétien unveiled a new economic development strategy for the region, reversed himself on reforms to employment insurance and brought Brian Tobin back in to the federal fold. Tobin had been a long-standing favourite of Jean Chrétien, a federal industry minister and fisheries minister, and then Newfoundland's premier.

Liberal prospects in the West were much grimmer. Of eighty-eight seats, only seventeen were Liberal before the 2000 election—and not a single one of them was in a rural riding. Most constituencies were held by the Reform Party, the precursor to the Canadian Alliance. And the Liberals seemed prepared to write off most of those seats, focusing instead simply on re-electing Justice Minister Anne McLellan in Edmonton, Environment Minister David Anderson in Victoria and Ralph Goodale in Saskatoon. Saskatoon-Rosetown-Biggar Liberal candidate Alice Farness expressed Liberal thoughts out loud when she told farmers protesting in Regina during the campaign that they should not expect to be acknowledged in Ottawa unless they voted Liberal.

The friction between the Liberals and the West dates back to Pierre Trudeau's days. His energy policies enraged the region, particularly Alberta. In 1982, while vacationing out West, the prime minister's train was pelted with tomatoes and eggs. The distaste seemed to be mutual. Trudeau raised his finger—the middle one—in a dismissive and rude salute to protestors in Salmon Arm. On another occasion he bluntly asked farmers, "Why should I sell your wheat?"

Jean Chrétien seems to have continued the attitudes of his mentor. During the thirty-six days of the 2000 election campaign, he made one visit to Saskatchewan. It was a quick whistle stop in Regina, his first visit to the province in about eighteen months. He was able to say he had dealt with the farm lobby after he met privately with six hand-picked farmers.

He managed to duck the ordinary voters. About thirty farmers organized by the Pro-West lobby group tried, unsuccessfully, to buttonhole him. Rather than speak to them, he simply slipped away. Chrétien later told reporters, "In agriculture, it's never fixed. There is always some problem, and I am listening to them." On another occasion he furthered the snub: "I like to do politics with people from the East."

With less than 3 percent of the population, the farm vote does not matter much in today's political context. We are worlds away from the 1920s, when farmers were able to dominate federal politics by virtue of their numbers. Today there are not even enough farmers to sway the outcome of elections in Saskatchewan.

Agriculture is no longer an important election issue. The word "farm" was not central to any of the campaigns. In fact, it warranted just a few lines in the Liberal campaign's "red book." Agriculture was not mentioned in either of the two televised leaders' debates. The CFA made it its business to count the references throughout the campaign. Midway through, it applauded Conservative leader Joe Clark for actually mentioning agriculture three times on the hustings. Even though the Canadian Alliance was likely to win most of the seats in the West, leader Stockwell Day never mentioned agriculture. Nor did he explain a fundamental flaw in Alliance logic: the party talked about getting rid of the Canadian Wheat Board's monopoly even while it declared support for supply management. It too had apparently discovered political pragmatism.

Frustration drove farmers to call attention to themselves. They held protest meetings from the back of a half-ton truck in Biggar and Dafoe, Saskatchewan. They jammed train traffic. And finally they set up a blockade on the Trans-Canada Highway with trucks and tractors, slowing down traffic in an effort to inform motorists about their plight. Television cameras captured images of grandmothers who said they could no longer manage on the farm; children who said they were worried about their daddies; and middle-aged, law-abiding men who said they were being forced into militant action. The tactics won some media attention, but their impact on the election was negligible.

On election day, November 27, 2000, Canadian electors returned Jean Chrétien's Liberals to Ottawa with a third straight majority government. The win, with 172 seats in the House of Commons, was even more definitive than it had been in 1997. The Liberals won back seven seats in Atlantic Canada. The West, however, was a disappointment: the Liberal Party lost three of its seats. And once again it was shut out of all rural Western ridings.

In the West there has long been a visceral belief that Ottawa treats it unfairly—overrepresenting Quebec and underrepresenting the Prairies. Statistics compiled by the Manitoba-based Keystone Agricultural Producers in January 2000 offered evidence that Western producers have shouldered nearly 90 percent of the federal government's cuts to agricultural support in the past decade. The statistics demonstrated that the Prairie provinces were hit by $1.7 billion worth of cuts while the Eastern provinces escaped virtually unscathed. Manitoba's share of the budget slashing exceeded the combined total of cuts experienced by Ontario, Quebec, Nova Scotia, P.E.I. and Newfoundland.

Those allegations added fuel to the sense of Western alienation that had been smouldering beneath the surface for years. In the spring of 1999 Chrétien assigned Winnipeg Liberal MP John Harvard the task of evaluating the extent of Western discontentment. Harvard's task force held a series of meetings with nearly four hundred individuals and groups in towns across the West. The final product—a sixty-two-page report—offered a pointed message to the prime minister and his Ontario-dominated government, saying that the West and its farmers were indeed getting shortchanged. "The plight of producers throughout the western provinces, particularly Saskatchewan and Manitoba, came through loud and clear," the report stated. It advised the government to pay more attention to Western issues, from the farm crisis to Aboriginal concerns, or risk having to deal with more Western alienation.

Critics dismissed the task force as an exercise designed to keep complaints away from Chrétien. And sure enough, nothing much had changed by the time the prime minister called the election in October 2000. The results on election day left the country deeply divided along East-West lines. Western Canada, particularly west of Manitoba, was a Canadian Alliance stronghold. Within a few weeks of the election Stéphane Dion, the intergovernmental affairs minister, was given the task of repairing the damage. At Chrétien's request, the minister, a francophone Quebecer who had been credited with revitalizing federalism in his native province, said he planned to launch a high-profile campaign to quash Western alienation.

The assignment is a challenging one. Western alienation is particularly deeply felt in Alberta, where Alliance Party supporters interpreted the election results as a snub to their Western political values. The former Alberta-based Reform Party had renamed itself, acquired a new leader and developed policies it hoped would be attractive to all Canadians. Yet when the votes were counted, the party won only two seats east of the Ontario–Manitoba border.

In January 2001 the *National Post* released details of a poll that concluded almost half of Albertans favoured constitutional reform to limit the power of the federal government. Respondents from Alberta voiced a strong perception—stronger than that from Quebec—that Ottawa was dictatorial and disrespectful. A group of conservative activists, including such high-profile Albertans as former Reform MP Stephen Harper, followed up by founding the Alberta Independence Party. The new party's Alberta Agenda called on the province to take greater control of its destiny, for example, by creating an Alberta pension plan and a provincial police force.

Although it seemed as if Western alienation was concentrated in Alberta, farmers across the Prairies, led by grassroots organizations like Pro-West, shared in the frustration. At the beginning of the new millennium the threat of Quebec's separation from Canada was beginning to seem less urgent, while the West seemed intent on making it clear there were still deep divisions in the country.

• • •

Federal agriculture minister Vanclief ended the year promising farmers that the re-elected Liberal government would move quickly in 2001 to deal with farm income problems. Vanclief said the message that farmers needed more help had been received loud and clear by the government.

Nevertheless, Canada's farm leaders refused to sit back quietly. They found it galling in January when Ottawa decided to give Montreal-based Bombardier loan guarantees totalling $1.5 billion to beat off competition from a Brazilian company. Farm groups said that if the government could afford to help Bombardier fight off export subsidies, it should do the same thing for farmers. Vanclief told them the government was not playing favourites with Bombardier; rather, it was taking "specific and strategic" action to solve a problem.

The next focus for Canadian farm leaders was Ottawa itself in late January. About 150 producers from the West and Ontario gathered with their tractors and combines in front of the Parliament buildings on the day before the Throne Speech that would launch the next session of the House of Commons. Nick Parsons had again made the trip with "Prairie Belle" because, as he said, nothing had improved since he made his first odyssey to Ottawa one year earlier. "We should not have to be in a position where we always have to be begging and borrowing to farm," he said, much as he had the year before. But the demonstration was small by protest standards, and it did not garner much attention from the media or the politicians.

However, the next day's Speech from the Throne did talk vaguely about how the federal government would "help Canada's agricultural sector move beyond crisis management—leading to more genuine diversification and value-added growth, new investments and employment, better land use and high standards of environmental stewardship and food safety." There was little indication of what that meant.

In a telephone interview just days later, Vanclief said the agricultural situation demanded a "several-pronged approach." However, he did not describe what that would entail. And when asked what new agricultural policies the government would enact, Vanclief made it clear his view of an overall policy was based on handouts. "Our agriculture policy is there to the best of our ability to help those who for whatever reason have had a drastic decline in income," he said. "Agriculture is incredibly important to us as a government. When we have had the resources available, we have increased in all areas."

Vanclief insisted there was lots of support for agriculture around the cabinet table. However, he said farming now has to compete for attention with industries that simply did not exist several decades ago. The high-technology sector has developed in the last thirty years and international trade agreements like NAFTA and the WTO are also new.

Farmers hoping for some sign that Vanclief was concerned about the hemorrhaging of a way of life would have been disappointed by our conversation. There will be no Canadian version of European multifunctionality under Lyle Vanclief's watch. The minister did not single out family farmers for any special attention, and he discounted the notion of depopulation, saying the Prairies had been losing farm families for decades. He acknowledged that Western grain and oilseed producers were suffering from an income disaster much like hog producers across Canada in late 1998 and Ontario farmers in the soggy and cold summer of 2000. "I don't ever recall a time when there was not a crisis."

Sounding a bit beleaguered by the job, Vanclief noted that globalization is changing how farming works. "Unless countries are islands unto themselves, they can't avoid what's happening." Canada may once have been the grain basket of the world, but those days are gone as countries like China and India increase their growing potential in what has become a global village.

Delivering another dose of tough love, Vanclief said farmers will have to decide for themselves if they want to continue in the new global world. "There are still family farmers. I mean, how many family shoe stores are there now? How many family grocery stores are there any more? That's a reality that is happening in business today because the margin of profit on many things, whether it is agriculture or not, is increasingly challenged. Globalization brings part of that. Straight competition for many reasons brings part of that, but the family farm is here. The family farm is here to stay."

In early March Lyle Vanclief put action to his words. At the Canadian Federation of Agriculture's 2001 annual meeting he announced another "one-time emergency aid" package, this one worth $500 million. For months farmers had lobbied, protested and demanded additional support. Advance information had them counting on at least $900 million. So there was no applause when Vanclief told the CFA he had not been able to convince cabinet to authorize that much. Some farmers in the audience left the room in angry objection. The CFA's Bob Friesen tried to be gracious when he thanked the minister, but instead slid into a stiff rebuke. "I would be remiss in not saying that this more clearly is not what we thought or are convinced is the amount of money that agriculture across Canada needs to stabilize it." He chose his words carefully. "I'm going to express the great disappointment of farmers. Why does cabinet not see fit to back its farmers?"

Provincial agriculture ministers were annoyed too—annoyed that Ottawa had not consulted them and that it had pre-empted a meeting the ministers were scheduled to have in the next week.

Vanclief offered the familiar refrain to explain the curtailed support. "There is only so much money," he told the CFA. I wish it were more, but it's half a billion dollars more than we had an hour and a half ago." (On the same day, Ottawa gave $600 million to the military and in the next week it contributed $750 million to health and scientific research.)

Vanclief promised the $500 million, along with greater access to interest-free loans, would be available to farmers by seeding time. But rather than quietly planning their upcoming crop rotations, producers began arranging protest rallies to demand more government aid. The year 2001 was beginning to shape up as a season of discontent.


In the United States farmers make up only 2 percent of the population, yet they managed to extract $28 billion in farm assistance from the federal treasury in 1999. Canadian farmers are desperately trying to find their own political card, but it is not easy. Politicians pay little heed to agriculture. Nor does the media, which is often responsible for interpreting the complex world of agricultural programs, subsidies and exports to the public. Much like the industry itself, agricultural reporting has declined in importance since Cora Hind's day. The newspaper where Hind was the influential agricultural editor in the early 1900s—the *Winnipeg Free Press*—no longer has an agricultural reporter.

The irony is that the public might be much more interested in agriculture than politicians or newspaper owners imagine. Recent polls show the public is concerned about Canadian farmers. In the Angus Reid Group's survey of September 1999, 72 percent of Canadians agreed that farmers are facing severe problems. More than half of those surveyed said the government is not doing enough. This may translate into that elusive political clout farmers are looking for.

Dennis Mills may also offer a measure of the political influence farmers are seeking. Mills is a maverick on the Liberal backbenches, someone who has become the poster boy for farm issues—an MP who talks about farming. He organized the Family Farm Tribute in Toronto in January 2000 that attracted attention across the country. It was supposed to be the first step in his Harvest of Hope campaign. The next step is what he anticipates will become a "national food policy."

Mills represents Toronto-Danforth, a constituency that is physically and psychologically thousands of kilometres from the farm. Ten years ago he papered the windows of his constituency office with posters that detailed who got what share from the price of a loaf of bread. He has since managed to convince the greater Toronto caucus to show its support for farmers. Although he admits he is not exactly flooded with calls from constituents concerned about the farm, he is puzzled when you ask him why he thinks Toronto consumers should care. He says his constituents are just one generation removed from the farm. And everybody eats, he says in deadpan earnestness.

Mills was a Trudeau staffer until 1984. It was there, he says, that he learned the idea of representing those who need representation. He became an MP himself in 1988 and won his seat during the 2000 election by ten thousand votes. Mills is a political anomaly: he actually forgets to talk in the careful phraseology of today's politics. There is not one reference to agribusiness, exports or agricultural competitiveness in his rapid-fire, high-energy speech. He admits the government tends to look at agriculture on an ad hoc basis, that it needs to be much more proactive. He offers a mix of left-wing philosophy and genuine concern for the individuals involved. "But I don't believe in hug-a-farmer," he says, discounting any suggestion that he is an old-fashioned romantic.

Mills challenges the system that would relegate backbenchers like him to the role of "voting machines." Notorious for floating wacky schemes and weird concepts, his outspoken manner has some dismissing him as a loose cannon. *NOW* magazine twice voted Mills the best MP in Toronto, but it recently labelled him a "flake" with big ideas and no one to hear them. He does seem to have many issues that capture his imagination, like the fate of Canadian sports franchises or Internet gambling. He was going to be toasted at the Canadian Federation of Agriculture annual meeting for his work in organizing the Family Farm Tribute concert, but he begged off, feeling he was not really welcome. In the same way that a guy driving a combine across the West does not quite fit in, neither does a Liberal loose cannon, someone who is not playing by the rules.

But the rules are flawed. The rules say that any group in society should let its political and organizational representatives speak for it. However, despite their increased economic output, there are fewer and fewer farmers in Canada. Their concerns rarely get on the national agenda. Either farmers and their issues will quietly disappear or they will find a way to be heard—through the likes of urban maverick Dennis Mills, or by militant action designed to capture the attention of TV cameras, or by building bridges with the public that now only rarely thinks about where its food comes from.

*Eleven*

# Pick Pork: A Case Study

October 17, 2000

*It is cool—definitely sweater weather—on one of those short prairie autumn days. In Manitoba, by this time of year, snow would not be out of the question. But as the miles slip away on the route from city to country, the clouds that might have harboured unwelcome flurries begin to evaporate. A low, blinding sun pushes its way through the puffy vestiges of the clouds. It becomes warm.*

*The harvest is long in the bins, but Gary Wieler is working the fields with summer-like intensity. With defiant optimism he says the challenge now is getting ready for the next season. Although this year's crop suffered from loss of quality, it did produce an average yield—enough that the plants sucked the essential nitrogen content out of the soil. Gary and Lorna had the Agricore soil specialists come round and draw soil samples from all of their fields. After an analysis at a laboratory the verdict was definitive: if the Wielers hope to have a crop next year, they have to*

214

*fertilize. But the prices for chemical fertilizer are staggering. Anhydrous ammonia has gone up 40 percent. When all the bills come in, the fertilizer tab could top $17,000, compared with $10,000 the previous year for more acreage.*

*The need to fertilize is doubly unwelcome because anhydrous ammonia is dangerous, a pressurized gas much like propane. It is pumped into huge tanks the Wielers fill at the Agricore service centre. Then one of the tanks is hooked up to the cultivator, which is outfitted with an octopus-like network of hoses that feed the gas to the tines that slice the earth. A false move can send the ammonia gas into an unprotected face. Gary is wearing goggles and rubber gloves, but the case of the farmer down the road who lost an eye to an anhydrous accident is never far from his mind.*

*The Wielers are approaching next spring with a sense of resignation, but they are never despondent. Lorna tells me with a self-deprecating laugh (Gary surely would not be as open about it) that at the end of August both of their bank accounts were running into overdraft. They turned to the CWB and the local bank for a $20,000 advance loan on their wheat sales. Gary has been working for hire feverishly ever since, for a neighbourhood farmer who used to depend on a hired hand he brought in from Mexico. When that did not work out, Gary Wieler, family man, hard worker, community member, was the ideal replacement. "It's paying work," Gary says in matter-of-fact explanation.*

*Lorna's hopes of getting a part-time position at the new food store in Carman have been dashed. "You often don't get any kind of call these days," she says, recognizing the realities of the modern working world. So while Gary is doing his paying work, Lorna is on the tractor, cultivating the fields, turning over the stubble.*

*The canola is still in the bins, waiting for prices to improve. The other bins are crammed with wheat, waiting for the call to deliver. The elevator in Kane is stuffed, its operators waiting for a chance to shuttle the grain to the Paterson facility in Morris.*

*The Wielers have concluded there is no point buying any more land because they do not have the equipment to handle it. And they cannot afford to buy any more equipment, particularly with the paltry returns they can expect from farming this year. So, instead, the Wielers are looking to expand their small cow-calf herd. Cattle are a pretty rare sight here in the heart of industrial grain country, but the Wielers are still under a bit of a glow from the summer's 4-H Grand Championship victory. And looking back to earlier days, livestock is a sure way to diversify. Lorna says they want to expand their herd up to about forty-five cows. They are imagining getting into more breed cattle—Simmental and Red Angus.*

*Lorna leans over the gate to admire the five new Simmental heifers they just bought with some of their advance money. The cows are blond and white and remarkably friendly. They are excited to see the two dogs, nuzzling their snouts with bovine delight. One heifer sent Daphne, the corgi-cross pup, flying this morning when, in search of a scratch, she flicked her head just a little too enthusiastically.*

*Lorna looks out over the corral with characteristic hopefulness. She pictures a new squeeze chute; a new barn to replace the greying, faded structure that stands there now; extended sheds to protect the cows, heifers and calves from winter's wind. For the Wielers these are the signs of hope for another season's promise.*

❧ When Stan Yaskiw turned ten years old, his uncle gave him an unusual birthday present, but one that was in keeping with the times and the place. It was Stan's first pig, a sow. It was a gift that would set him on his future path as a hog farmer.

The birthday sow spent her first year in a little hutch in the scrub brush on the Yaskiw farm, near Birtle in western Manitoba. Stan remembers him and his sisters playing with her as only ten-year-olds can. But when she had piglets the next year, it was time to build a more serious barn. That was forty years ago. The barn for Stan's sow, her offspring and the first batch of additional feeder pigs was the foundation for a new beginning. The little clutch of pigs grew, and Stan's father became one of the biggest hog producers in western Manitoba.

Other farmers watched his success with envy and followed his example. There were seven hog producers clustered within a 16-kilometre radius of the Yaskiw operation. In honour of the new hog domination, locals began to call the road to the Yaskiw farm Pig Skin Alley.

When it was Stan's turn to take over his father's operation, he expanded the barn and built another. Over fifteen years he and his wife and two kids focused on developing a bigger, more business-minded operation. They tripled the size of their mixed grain and hog operation. In 1996 it was 2,500 acres, with two hundred sows and eight hundred feeder pigs.

In the mid-1990s, however, Stan Yaskiw's way of life began to falter in the shadow of industrial agriculture. Across North America the hog-growing business was shifting to massive confinement barns with direct links to corporate systems. In early 1996 the Manitoba government conceded to that industrialization by eliminating the provincial hog marketing board's long-standing monopoly. The new open-market system favoured larger operations, or those that were part of a corporate management team, over smaller farms like Yaskiw's. Stan Yaskiw closed one of his two barns.

And then, accelerating the pinch, in the fall of 1998 prices suddenly dropped. The producer who supplied Yaskiw with weanlings went out of business. With no easy access to baby pigs, Yaskiw felt he had no option but to close the second barn. In 1999, after twenty-seven years in the hog business, Yaskiw gave up on the way of life he first embraced when, as a boy, he wrapped his arms around the broad girth of his first sow. The other hog farmers in the neighbourhood are gone now too. Today, no one bothers to call the road to Yaskiw's farm Pig Skin Alley.

Falling commodity prices, along with government policies designed to support an industrial system, have cleared out many of the small family farms like Yaskiw's that used to run the hog industry in Manitoba. In their place is an industrial hog production practice that has brought the promise of economic benefit to the province—along with the threat of environmental damage. The rapid, very obvious industrialization of the hog sector in Manitoba is a clear case study of how agriculture generally is changing. It is a case study that may offer lessons on the implications of the sprint to a new business-oriented agriculture, lessons that apply to grain, cattle, horticulture or any other agricultural sector that is not protected by supply management. "There is a shift that is going on here and it probably is not too healthy for rural communities and rural life," says Stan Yaskiw, remembering the transformation in the pig business. "It is safe to say there was a bad taste in everybody's mouths."

In the early 1990s, when Stan Yaskiw and other family farmers ruled the hog industry in Manitoba, Canada was the second-biggest pork exporter in the world. Most of those exports went to the U.S. But as the U.S. moved to industrial farming, that changed. In 1995 Canadian exports to the U.S. dropped by 60 percent as the Americans expanded hog production, even shipping to the burgeoning Asian market. Manitoba's then agriculture minister, Harry Enns, saw the competitive gauntlet being dropped. "If we want to be part of that growing opportunity in pork exports, and not simply leave it to the Americans, then we have to have the kind of conditions that can tap into the virtually insatiable demand for pork," he said. He hoped Manitoba would not just unseat Ontario and Quebec for the title of hog capital of Canada, but would become one of the cheapest places in the world to raise hogs, thanks to plenty of land, cheap feed grain and moderate farm wages. Enns imagined the province's hog output would double by the year 2000.

Sure enough, in 2000, thanks to new factory-scale hog barns throughout the Manitoba countryside, the province hit its target. It produced 5.2 million hogs, almost all for export. After the province attracted the promise of two massive slaughterhouses, the stakes rose once again. This time the target was to increase production to 10 million hogs. The hefty pig population would change the face of the province, bringing new economic benefits but shutting down smaller operations and threatening the environment with mammoth volumes of untreated hog waste.

The first step in the transformation of Manitoba's pork industry from a way of life to a business came in 1995 when the federal government eliminated the Crow benefit. It suddenly became very expensive for Manitoba farmers to ship their grain to distant west coast ports. It made more sense to use the grain as feed for livestock at home. Manitoba could have followed the Wielers' example and stepped energetically into cattle production. Instead, it opted for hogs. At that time the global appetite for pork seemed insatiable, particularly in Asia. And a new way of growing hogs was capturing the imagination of North America's agribusiness industry. North Carolina set the standard for new industrial hog production that was viewed as efficient, productive and cost-effective.

I knew as much about North Carolina as those unfortunate Americans know about Canada when Rick Mercer of *This Hour Has 22 Minutes* turns his tongue-in-cheek interviewing style on them. I knew that Raleigh, North Carolina, was rated one of the best places to live in the U.S. because of its burgeoning biotechnology industry. I knew tobacco and cotton plantations used to dominate what I imagined was a pastoral countryside. And I knew that no frequent-flyer route connected Winnipeg to Raleigh. Nevertheless, there I was on my way to Raleigh with a CBC documentary crew in tow, to do a story on the real North Carolina.

Only a few weeks earlier I had discovered that tiny North Carolina was the second-biggest hog producer in the U.S. In 1995, the heyday of its industrial pig culture, the state had a population of 6.8 million humans and 6.6 million hogs. Almost all the swine were crowded into a strip that ran southeast of Raleigh, along the Cape Fear River, skirting the Pinehurst Golf Course, to the Atlantic beaches. Locally, it was known as Swine Alley. In one county, Duplin, there were twenty-five hogs for every person.

North Carolina's dominance in the hog business was astounding, because it has so little history in grain or livestock production. The skeletons of the old agriculture stood as greying, abandoned tobacco sheds.

Trainloads of grain and corn from the Midwest arrived each day at giant feed mills that interrupted the flat green horizon like proud statues honouring a new economy. The mills would produce the feed to fatten the machines of the new economy.

There once was a time when pigs were, well, pigs. They lived outside, rooting gleefully through harvested fields. But under the new system, refined to a science in North Carolina, thousands of hogs were confined in factory-like barns tucked from prying eyes behind a copse of trees or down a meandering gravel road. It was only from the air that the extent of the state's hog production became obvious. From the air the barns were laid out virtually cheek by jowl, like symmetrical Lego houses, each outfitted with an attached grey-coloured swimming pool. These off-colour pools were actually lagoons, brimming with gallons of hog urine and feces.

The barns were owned by farmers who had been convinced to go into long-term debt by corporations that controlled every stage of a hog's life, from conception to consumption. The "integrators," as the companies were known, were the world's largest hog producers. They owned the hogs inside the walls of these factory barns. The contract farmers were essentially employees of the integrators. Their job was to build the multi-million-dollar barns and then to fatten the hogs. In return, they were paid a wage. The integrators owned the hogs, in fact dictated everything about how they were to be grown. They earned the profits while the farmers assumed much of the risk.

Local swine folklore credits Wendell Murphy for developing the integrator system. Indeed, the patriarch of Murphy Family Farms revolutionized the way hogs are grown in North Carolina. Forty years ago he started a little feed mill. Then he convinced some of his neighbours to grow pigs for him. More importantly, in the 1980s he became a state senator and persuaded the North Carolina government to introduce laws that would benefit hog producers. That hog-friendly legislation came to be known in North Carolina as Murphy's laws. Murphy Family Farms may have started small, but by the mid-1990s it was no quaint neighbourhood hog operation; it was the nation's biggest hog grower, raising two and a half million pigs for slaughter a year.

Wendell Murphy was not one to brag about his role in the industry. In fact, he did not want to talk to our documentary crew at all. The hog industry in North Carolina was evidently a very private enterprise. The closest I got to Wendell Murphy was at the barred and brick-flanked gate to his home. There, the security cameras swivelled in curiosity as I tried to peer past the thick forest of trees that effectively blocked all inquisitive eyes.

But Murphy was not alone. Prestage Farms did not want to talk. Nor did Carroll. Nor did any of the other integrators. It may have been big, but this was an industry that liked to remain private. None of the hog companies would let us into one of the hog houses under contract to them. The argument was that we could introduce disease-carrying germs. In the new industrial system, it is the humans, not the pigs, that are considered dirty.

It took the kindness of strangers to allow us a glimpse inside the factory walls. Jay Humphrey of Burgaw was one of the few independent hog farmers still operating in North Carolina. Young and resolute, he had adopted all the techniques of the modern system but refused to sell out to the integrators. His breed was on the endangered species list as smaller, independent farmers in North Carolina disappeared in the state's rush to industrialization. In 1985 there were twenty-three thousand hog producers in the state; by 1995 there were only eight thousand farms left. In the same time, hog production tripled. Humphrey was convinced he could make it by playing the game the way the companies did. "We saw early in the 1990s, volume is the thing in North Carolina. We saw that volume is the only way you can compete," he said in a soft Southern drawl. To get into his barns we had to scrub down in the shower, use the complimentary Lady Breck shampoo and slip on the company blue overalls over nearly naked skin.

I was overwhelmed, not only by the time-honoured smell but by the incredible noise of thousands of snouts clattering on the bars of their cages. The barns were totally automated; food, water, ventilation and air conditioning were delivered by machines. When the touch of a computer poured feed pellets down glass pipes to the pens, the jangle of excitement got even more intense. The pigs lived their days on slatted concrete floors with no bedding; their waste fell through the cracks in the floor to a water-filled basement below the barn. That pit flushed to a huge pool, or lagoon, scraped out of the earth out back. Once a year that lagoon in turn was emptied by spraying the waste in a smelly jet of dung across farm fields. The production system was so streamlined that Humphrey had only one worker overseeing two thousand hogs.

Using computers, artificial insemination and special diets, the system controlled every stage of a hog's life from womb to slaughterhouse. The process began with pregnant sows, the females used for breeding. Humphrey had a thousand of them lined up in narrow cages not much bigger than the sows themselves. They had to eat, sleep, urinate and defecate all in the same spot for 112 days at a time—the duration of their pregnancy. Once their piglets were born, they suckled on their mother under the bars of the crate. They were warmed by a heat lamp rather than their mother's body. After nursing their offspring for two weeks, the sows got a one-week holiday. Then they were bred again—usually through artificial insemination—and the cycle started over. A good sow was supposed to produce about twenty-three piglets a year for three years. After her three years of service as a breeding machine, she too was slaughtered.

Weaned after two weeks, the piglets were moved across the road to Humphrey's father's nursery barns in an effort to stop the transfer of disease. When they weighed in at about twenty-three kilograms, they were moved back to Jay's for fattening. They lived out their five-month lives on the concrete floors, breathing the acrid smell of ammonia rising from the basement pit. Their only glimpse of the sun came as they were shipped from barn to barn, or when they made that final trip to the slaughterhouse, likely Carolina Food Processors, the world's largest packing plant, which killed about 160,000 pigs a week. (We weren't allowed in there either.)

The North Carolina government was an enthusiastic cheerleader for the new hog industry. It served up reams of statistics to prove pigs were good for the state. They declared pork brought $1 billion in income to North Carolina each year. Pork delivered jobs, even though most of them were low-paying positions tending or slaughtering hogs. One hog-barn builder had boasted he had eight hundred employees in 1995 compared with one hundred in 1979. Whether in construction, tending hogs or slaughtering them, the work did cause incomes to rise in what had been a depressed area. Between 1987 and 1995 per capita income in Sampson County rose from $11,258 to $17,349.

But not everyone was as keen. What the government did not account for were the environmental implications of allowing hog waste to be flushed, untreated, into the fields. A single hog factory generates more sewage than most of the towns in North Carolina. One hundred 150-pound hogs produce as much waste as 250 adult humans.

Don Webb, a former hog farmer himself (albeit in the old style), was the head of the Alliance for a Responsible Swine Industry. He was a blunt-spoken, no-holds-barred kind of guy who seemed to know every-one and every story in the backcountry of Swine Alley. With the envi-ronmentalists' theme song "Don't Hog Our Air" blaring from the tape deck, he piloted his truck past every ditch coloured green by algae bloom, every lake closed to swimming by contamination, every poor black family who suddenly saw a hog house going up next door. "You don't spray thousands of gallons of feces and urine on a field and it don't run off. And that's the fallacy. The stone-age method of spraying. It doesn't work."

Webb was a big man with a big voice—a recipe, you might think, for intimidation. But politicians and the industry had strength in numbers and the confidence in their political power simply to ignore his warnings. In years to come they may have wished they had listened.

•　•　•

Manitoba looked at North Carolina and could only smell the money. Agriculture Minister Harry Enns dreamed of starting an industry as productive as North Carolina's. There were already the seeds of that kind of business in the province. One-third of hogs were being grown in massive barns like those in North Carolina, under the auspices of a couple of Manitoba-based companies. Elite Swine and Puratone led the pack, supplying feed to the barns. They offered management to the growers but shied away from owning the hogs outright and simply contracting the services of the farmers. Because all hogs had to be marketed through the marketing board, Manitoba Pork, the hog companies had little scope or flexibility.

Enns wanted to kick-start the fledgling industry, so without any warning or discussion he announced in late 1995 that he planned to eliminate the monopoly Manitoba Pork had enjoyed for thirty-four years. Much like the Canadian Wheat Board's monopoly control over wheat and barley, all hogs in the province were sold to Manitoba Pork. It set the price for farmers and decided where the hogs would be slaughtered. All hogs of a certain quality demanded the same price, regardless of how many hogs a farmer could offer up. All producers, whether big or small, were treated equally. All that would change under the new open-market system. Much like the debate about the Canadian Wheat Board, under the new terms of business Manitoba Pork would have to sink or swim in a "dual marketing" environment.

The Conservative minister said that more competition would shake up both hog farmers and pork processors, hopefully attracting a big new packing house like the sort seen in North Carolina. "It's been a cozy arrangement for them as well. They don't have to compete for their supply of hogs. Everyone's kept on the same level field."

The NDP opposition's agriculture critic Rosann Wowchuk complained that the loss of the monopoly would spell the end of "orderly selling." "It will open the door for a vertically integrated system like the one in the United States where large farms have displaced the family farms, and producers who were once independent are now employees of large firms,"

she said. This, she warned, was not what Manitoba wanted for its producers or rural communities.

Without the protection of Manitoba Pork's monopoly, those offering
greater volumes of hogs could arrange special contracts with slaughterhouses for a higher price than smaller producers, who would find it
difficult to make such a deal. The terms of the deals would be confiden-
tial, so smaller producers would not even know the true market value of
hogs. Sure enough, within a few months the price transparency that producers used to benefit from had disappeared. Manitoba Agriculture and
the packers stopped publishing their prices, so farmers no longer knew
what they were up against.

Farmers were shaken by the abrupt changes in the industry. Karl
Kynoch ran a hog operation in southwestern Manitoba, near Baldur. It
was truly a family affair, with his wife, Christine, and their two sons providing all the labour. It was an unconventional operation by the new
industrial standards. There was a homemade barn with one lean-to added
onto another, built as money allowed. Like the Wielers, the Kynochs were
loath to get into debt. The barn was home to about two hundred pregnant
and nursing sows and the piglets they produced. The feeder pigs were
outside in a row of hoop houses, or "bio-techs," essentially tents of thin
plastic stretched over support rings. About 150 hogs were loose in each of
the bio-techs, rooting around in old-fashioned straw on the ground.
Unlike their cousins in the industrial systems, they could sniff the outdoor
air and glimpse the sky. In a Manitoba winter they would jostle together
and huddle beneath the straw to generate a collective warmth that acted
as a rudimentary heating system. "They sure seem to enjoy it out here,"
said Kynoch. "I guess you would call it more their natural environment.
A lot closer to nature."

It may have been healthier for the hogs, but it was also more cost-
effective for the Kynochs. It cost about $15,000 to put up one hoop
house—one-third the price of a modern barn for the same number of animals. Kynoch did not have to saddle himself with the huge mortgage that
would be necessary to put up climate-controlled, expensive buildings.

Twice a year the Kynochs would clean out the manure-laced straw and spread it on their fields. On the downside, the outdoor system demanded a lot more labour, even in the dead of winter when moist breath stiffens into ice crystals on a scarf in mere moments.

It was a system that worked for Kynoch. He focused on growing the hogs and left the marketing to Manitoba Pork. He was taken aback when he heard about the government's move. "We really need our marketing board because it doesn't matter how small you are, you get paid on quality and you can have equal access to the marketplace," he said in 1996. He was angry enough that he spoke out at subsequent meetings. "What would the government say if we just said 'stick it'?" he asked an audience of irate hog farmers one winter's night in southwestern Manitoba.

Farmers like Stan Yaskiw took it one step further. Producers banded together to form P-PIG—Producers Protesting Interference by Government—in an effort to block the move. "It was pushed down our throats by the government," Yaskiw remembers. "We as producers were looking after our industry very well." There were countless angry meetings where hog farmers vented their frustrations. They even consulted a lawyer about suing the government for daring to cut the monopoly. But it all added up to nothing. One by one, producers quit the business, and the energies of the opposition began to dissipate.

The new competitive environment did accomplish what Enns had hoped. Investing in hog barns became a homegrown way of contributing to Manitoba's own porcine gold rush. Doctors, lawyers, dentists, often far away from the countryside, invested in the huge capital start-up costs of the industrial barns. They became Manitoba's new hog farmers. But as distant owners they had to hire people to tend the hogs. They often turned to the very folks who had been independent hog farmers, who knew how to handle pigs. So the hog farmers of old became employees in a corporate system.

•　•　•

Then prices took a dramatic downturn that lasted a year. It was a global slump caused by the loss of markets in the Far East. Neither the Manitoba government nor efficient hog companies could do anything about it. Prices bottomed out in December 1998 at 60 cents a kilogram; in the previous year hogs had sold for more than $1.80 a kilogram. No one could make any money, not even the investors who thought they had sniffed out a good deal. There were horrible stories of family farmers who could barely afford to feed themselves, never mind their hogs.

This was the all-too-familiar account. One Manitoba producer lost $40,000 in the last quarter of 1998. That added up to $500 a day. The losses were so steep that he could not continue, so he gave up the way of life he had enjoyed for thirty years. His equity was wiped out in the process. Today he lends his labour and expertise to a massive new hog barn owned by someone else.

The only ones who flourished under the collapsed price structure were the packing plants. Maple Leaf Foods, the largest food processing company in Canada and a Canadian transnational with operations in Canada, the U.S., Europe and Asia, was eager to build a super-slaughterhouse.

In 1996, Harry Enns had said the biggest impediment to growth was lack of a world-class-sized processing facility. In Canada, hogs were slaughtered at small provincial plants where line speeds allowed only hundreds of hogs to be killed each day. It was an infuriatingly slow rate compared, for example, with Smithfield's Carolina Food Processors plant in North Carolina.

Maple Leaf Foods, a wholly owned subsidiary of McCain Foods, announced it would build a $112-million operation on the outskirts of Brandon. It was going to be the world-class facility Enns had dreamed of. It would kill 90,000 hogs a week, or 18,000 hogs a day. To do so, it said it would hire a small army of 2,000 white-suited, chain-mail-aproned employees at about $16 an hour. Not surprisingly, this was seen as a huge boon for Brandon, population forty thousand, and the surrounding communities.

To bring Maple Leaf to Brandon the government had to sweeten the deal, with a pledge of $11 million in support. The City of Brandon promised to contribute $8.5 million towards water and waste facilities. And then the province agreed to forgo the annoyance of a Clean Environment Commission hearing to assess the possible impact of a plant on the edge of the Assiniboine River. It did this even though the federal government had expressed concerns about the potential pollution of the waterway. So the plant was constructed without an environmental impact assessment, over the protests of environmentalists and residents concerned about discharges into the river. The slaughterhouse was up and running by September 1999.

J.M. Schneider, owned by Smithfield Foods, watched the government support for Maple Leaf with dismay. Schneider had a long-standing competition with Maple Leaf that dated back to Maple Leaf's attempt to buy Schneider in the mid-1990s, before Schneider sold to Smithfield. Smithfield Foods may have been the largest hog producer in the world, but it complained that it deserved the same support Maple Leaf got so it could expand the plant Schneider had built for $50 million in Winnipeg just a few years earlier. Schneider wanted to transform that plant, to the tune of $125 million, into a super-slaughterhouse. It said its expansion would create up to 1,200 new jobs, with another 5,500 spinoff jobs. After five years, like Maple Leaf, it too would be killing ninety thousand hogs a week.

Government had just begun its negotiations with Schneider when an irritant of political life interfered: an election. The Tories lost power in September 1999 to the New Democratic Party. Hogs were not a big campaign issue, but the NDP had positioned itself for years against the planned expansion in the hog industry. It had complained about big hog barn construction, the plant in Brandon, the unannounced stripping of the monopoly and government grants to corporations. This was a party with a reputation for shaking fists at the establishment, one that pledged to "Save the Family Farm." Gary Doer, the man who would become premier, told an audience of young entrepreneurs in Brandon before he was elected that the NDP would stand up to the hog industry in order to protect the environment.

The seeds for a major expansion in the province's hog industry had been sown by the Conservative government, but now it would be up to the NDP to steer the province through the shoals of supporters and critics, to determine whether industrial hog farming would indeed be allowed to transform the province.

Hog expansion in Manitoba presented a challenge for the fledgling NDP government. Critics of the NDP's social democratic philosophy claimed the party had a poor track record on fiscal matters and found it difficult to work with business to create jobs. A well-managed development in the hog industry could go a long way towards overcoming that image. Premier Gary Doer vowed he would govern for everyone and would not bow down to extremists. As part of the new balancing act the word "hog" disappeared from the political lexicon as soon as the NDP was elected. If family farmers had expected the new government to turn back the clock, they would be disappointed.

A direct challenge to the party's new non-confrontational approach came at the NDP's convention in March 2000, the first since taking power. A resolution from one of the delegates called on the convention to address immediately the issues raised by the changes in the hog industry. The resolution said expansion would threaten the rural environment and encourage corporate and factory farming to the detriment of family farming. At first the show of hands from the floor passed the resolution. Then another delegate challenged the outcome, asking for a recount. The second time around, the voting New Democrats clearly decided it was best not to rock the boat.

Although it tried to walk the line between the proponents and the opponents of expansion, when it came to the J.M. Schneider plant expansion the NDP government had to take sides. Doer was caught between the fairness argument—what is given to one company should be offered to another—and the no-corporate-handouts position the NDP had always endorsed.

In its final analysis the government opted for the former. Even before it passed its first budget, it announced a multimillion-dollar handout for the transnational pork processor. Along with the City of Winnipeg, the Manitoba government agreed to give Schneider $9 million, plus a possible $4.6 million more in sewer upgrades. Janet Brady, a member of Hog Watch, a group opposed to hog expansion, and a twenty-year New Democrat, expressed the widespread distaste with the NDP's new political pragmatism. "Since when is the NDP believing in corporate welfare?"

The Manitoba government could not close its eyes and ears to people like Brady, who had counted on an NDP administration to take action against hog expansion. So it employed the classic diversionary tactic: it launched a series of studies and reviews. The most comprehensive review, complete with opportunities for the public to vent their feelings, was the Livestock Stewardship 2000 initiative. "We recognize that the industry is growing and we want to give the public an opportunity to bring forward their recommendations," Rosann Wowchuk, now the agriculture minister, said in classic non-commitment as she announced the initiative in June 2000. The review would give the NDP almost another year's grace before it was compelled to take a position.


Once they were both up and running at full capacity, the Schneider and Maple Leaf plants would kill 10 million hogs a year. Production would have to double from 1999 to 2004 if the industry was to work efficiently. If this goal were met, Manitoba pigs would produce as much fecal waste as the entire human population of Canada. Environmentalists said the province's water, land and air could not sustain the proposed jump in the industry and the waste it would generate. The massive growth, they said, would turn parts of Manitoba into a vast, unflushed toilet.

The voracious appetite for pork stepped up hog barn construction. And that, in turn, not only promoted disputes between environmentalists and industry proponents but cut deep divisions within many communities. Although some people felt hogs would bring economic well-being to depressed rural areas, others believed the introduction of an industrial system upset the environmental and social order of the countryside. The arrival of thousands of pigs in a confinement factory was much different from a farmer like Stan Yaskiw or Karl Kynoch setting up a small family hog-farm operation. Often farmers found they could not stomach the pungent smells emanating from the modern hog barns. Worse still was when the huge open pits or lagoons that fill up with hog waste were sprayed or spread over farmers' fields. A barbecue, hanging the wash out-side, even opening a window, became verboten.

Local government, which had control over the siting and zoning of the barns, became the battleground for the opposing philosophies. Local councillors, often focused on expanding the tax base in their municipali-ties, repeatedly found themselves face to face with angry residents at meetings. When the scenic, rolling Souris River valley was targeted for expansion because it was within easy driving distance of the Maple Leaf plant in Brandon, residents simply rebelled. In the rural municipality of Glenwood they even filed a court action to try to have proposed 2,000-head nursery and 4,000-head feeder barns stopped. They claimed council-lors had met privately with hog barn proponents just days before issuing a conditional use permit.

Although the smell of hog money was an aggravation, more serious were concerns about what this form of industrial agriculture meant for the environment. According to *Winnipeg Free Press* columnist Gerald Flood's rough, tongue-in-cheek calculations, by 2004, hogs in Manitoba would produce enough waste to fill about 314,000 backyard swimming pools each year.

Hog manure may be a great natural fertilizer, but over-application can cause excessive buildup of nitrates and phosphates that may then leach downwards into aquifers. And a breach of a lagoon can cause a messy, smelly and fatal spill of dangerous bacteria like E. coli and coliform into natural streams. In North Carolina a lagoon broke its bank in 1996, spilling 25 million gallons of waste—twice as much as the *Exxon Valdez* spill. Much of what was later called the state's largest environmental acci-dent tumbled into the Neuse River, killing fish and polluting water-ways. Over the next two years several hurricanes swept through the state, swamping sewage lagoons. The massive Carolina Food Processors plant, owned by Smithfield Foods—the same company that owns Schneider— was cited forty times for polluting the Cape Fear River. Adding it all up, it was impossible to say the industry was mistake-proof. The unpleasant implications of massive hog farming were no longer possible to ignore, just as Don Webb had said back in 1995. The North Carolina government had little choice but to apply a no-expansion order on hog operations, essentially shutting down further development.

However, in Manitoba, the government and the industry insisted it was not appropriate to compare the records of other jurisdictions, like North Carolina, with Manitoba. They said the province was in the process of doing its own research. "We're not going down that road, thank you very much," Ted Muir, general manager of the Manitoba Pork Council, told the Livestock Stewardship 2000 hearings. "We know you have to be careful and that is backed up by our regulations."

The regulations say a hog operation needs a permit from Manitoba Environment to build a manure lagoon—a permit that demands an on-site inspection. Large producers have to submit yearly manure management plans, including soil test results for the land where the manure will be spread. Manitoba's regulations are designed to ensure that nitrogen does not build up in the soil. Garry Stott, the director of Maple Leaf's Western livestock procurement, says supportively, "We have the toughest, most substantial environmental rules and regulations."

The province also says Manitoba has a generous land base to support hog production. For example, Manitoba has 13.3 million acres of cropland plus 4 million acres of forage to absorb the nutrient-rich manure. Ten million hogs would have the equivalent of 1.73 acres apiece. In comparison, Holland's farm base is so small, it has eight pigs per acre, while Denmark has two.

However, most environmentalists in Manitoba are not consoled by talk of broad spaces or tough rules and regulations. The province may have voluntary guidelines, they concede, but it does not have the staff to check who is following those guidelines. Additionally, environmentalists say it is absurd to claim that the experience of other jurisdictions does not apply. Bill Paton of Brandon University says it is ridiculous to suggest Manitoba has to reinvent the wheel. He says there is lots of scientific experience from other jurisdictions like Europe and North Carolina, or even Quebec, that Manitoba could draw on. The biologist says his experience, based on a review of those areas along with a close look at operations in Manitoba, shows intensive industrial operations are most often responsible for problems.

By 2000 there had been no major accidents that could be irrefutably tied to the hog industry. Instead, opponents resorted to trucking out anecdotes and stories that they claimed were the product of prodigious amounts of hog dung. They had photographs of algae-clogged streams, blooms in Lake Winnipeg, well-water tests that showed evidence of nitrogen pollution.

Scientists with academic credentials, like Eva Pip, a toxicologist with the University of Winnipeg, began to get involved. Pip produced a detailed research paper for the Livestock Stewardship 2000 panel after travelling thousands of kilometres throughout the province and visiting more than eighty farms. "Not one of them didn't smell or didn't create some kind of other problems." She told the panel the existing guidelines were set up for a relatively minor industry that was made up of small family farms scattered throughout the province. She said the current expansion was happening in often unsuitable districts, where underlying substrates are extremely porous, where the water table is at or near the surface, or where recreation and tourism struggle to remain viable. Pip scoffed at the government's suggestion that the experience of other jurisdictions should not be applied to Manitoba. She offered a blunt denunciation: "Greed is the foundation on which the activities and the values of our society are based. In the rush to the pig trough, there is liable to be some trampling and short-changing of hapless victims."

The industry is not inclined to accept the criticism of environmentalists even if they do have doctoral initials behind their names. It insists it can manage the expansion of the hog industry without damaging the environment. The environmentalists, for their part, say the seductive promise of windfall profits threatens to blind provincial and local politicians who would better serve the public by putting the brakes on the hog boom.

In addition to the environmental worries, concerns are being expressed about the conditions under which pigs are raised. There is no evidence that the hogs in the modern pork factories are mistreated. The Winnipeg Humane Society nevertheless continues to urge Manitobans to press for a moratorium on the industry "until we can be sure the animals are not being cruelly confined in these unnatural, confined conditions."

Of greatest concern to animal welfare and rights groups is the sow crate, which limits a sow's most basic movement all her life. The sow crate was originally introduced in the 1960s for legitimate animal husbandry reasons. When housed and fed as a herd, sows have a tendency to fight to establish hierarchies, with the more aggressive animals "hogging" the food. Stalls allow for individualized feeding, which improves overall productivity and makes looking after the sows less labour-intensive. When sow crates were introduced, there was also a belief that moving sows from straw to concrete would lower disease rates. What was not anticipated were the other impacts on the sows' health. The lack of movement leads to loss in bone mass and muscle tone, which may in turn lead to increased incidence of leg problems, long labour and high cull rates.

There are options. Two Hutterite colonies in Manitoba have developed group housing systems for their sow herds by maintaining a separate area that the sows enter only for feeding. And in Europe, where the animal welfare and animal rights movement is well entrenched, sow crates are losing popularity. The United Kingdom, the Netherlands and Sweden are leading Europe with a wholesale ban on the pens. In the U.S., the Humane Farming Association, the campaign against factory farming, is actively using lawsuits and the media to make its point about the industrial hog farms. Actor and activist James Cromwell, the kindly farmer in the movie *Babe*, lent his name to the protests.

In Canada, meanwhile, animal welfare interests have to struggle for notice. The Winnipeg Humane Society tried to register the idea that it was possible to raise pigs in straw, in groups, with room to move around. It argued this would be a more humane way of treating social, intelligent animals. The society was convinced consumers would be prepared to pay more for pork that was raised humanely. But in the early years of the new millennium it seems as if the humane treatment of hogs is not a sufficiently compelling reason to stop the pork expansion juggernaut.

The possible impacts of the industrial hog system on animal welfare and the environment have to be weighed against what is presented as the irrefutable economic benefits swine production could bring to a have-not province. Like so much in life, it is essential to weigh the risks and benefits.

Past experience in the U.S. suggests that the benefits of hog expansion to a struggling rural economy could be significantly less than hoped. American studies of the mega-ventures shows that, although their projects initially created employment, local businesses usually missed out on benefits because they were not geared to supplying large operations. Meat packing plants experienced more than 100 percent turnover in the first year of operation, so economic stability is not a side effect of a new slaughterhouse.

When the province refused to hold Clean Environment Commission hearings on the Maple Leaf proposal, a citizens' commission organized by environmental groups held its own public session in Brandon in the fall of 1999. The product of those hearings, a thirty-two-page report, looked at the experience of slaughterhouses in the U.S. in the past twenty years. It said: "Large-scale corporate hog production is one of the most contentious issues to confront rural North America in recent history. The social fabric of many communities has been ripped apart by controversy between opposing views about these large-scale corporate hog operations." The report concluded that the construction phase of such a plant had the biggest impact on the local community, lowering the unemployment rate, increasing commercial activity, and encouraging the real estate market, particularly that for lower-priced homes. Once a plant was in operation, demand for consumer goods and entertainment, particularly in the lower price ranges, increased, as did the demand for low-cost rental housing.

However, in the longer term, benefits become more ephemeral. The majority of the jobs at a slaughterhouse, the commission report noted, are relatively low-paid, difficult and dangerous. The workforce for these jobs tends to be highly mobile, young, often immigrants or visible minorities, with little stake in the community. At the Carolina Food Processors plant in Tar Heel, North Carolina, half of the employees were immigrants from Latin America. There, the plant helped to fill out the workforce complement by bussing in inmates from the county jail. Past experience has shown that a mega-slaughterhouse also brings increased costs for handling social problems like marital disputes, child abuse and language services. And there are law enforcement challenges, particularly those associated with a young, male and mobile workforce.

A packing plant uses huge amounts of water. If a plant has been excused from full service costs, other taxpayers have to carry a larger share. The report noted that a slaughterhouse also discharges liquid wastes containing coliform bacteria, disease organisms and plant nutrients. And once up and running, processing plants depress the price of hogs by dominating the market and buying from independent producers only by contract.

According to the report of the citizens' commission, it may be that the benefits of a packing plant like Maple Leaf Foods in Brandon are illusory. As the income levels of family farmers shrink and local communities continue to erode, economic costs, not benefits, may be the depressing reality.

•　　•　　•

Pick Pork: A Case Study

Since it costs between $1 million and $5 million to build a modern industrial hog facility, no one can afford to put up a pig barn on their own. In Manitoba that fact has led to surprising alliances between producers, investors, grain companies and other corporations. For example, United Grain Growers and the Ensis Growth fund teamed up to put $10 million into the Puratone Corporation. Puratone, which owns both the barns and the hogs in them, produces between 400,000 and 500,000 hogs a year.

The grain company N.M. Paterson & Sons teamed up with the co-operative that grew out of the vestiges of the former monopoly holder, Manitoba Pork, to form Dynamic Pork. The Manitoba-based Crocus Investment Fund sweetened the deal by putting $800,000 into the new company. Dynamic Pork develops and manages contract hog farming networks that are independently owned and operated by farmers and investors. The network idea, modelled on similar operations in the U.S., is supposed to be an antidote to big integrated operations. In North Carolina such networks give the few independent producers like Jay Humphrey some clout in the marketplace.

By the late 1990s there were increasing signs of corporate vertical integration in Manitoba's hog sector. In a deal that was called one of the biggest developments in the Canadian pork industry in thirty years, Maple Leaf Foods announced in September 1999 the $150-million takeover of The Landmark Group. Landmark was a Manitoba-based company with holdings that included Western Canada's largest animal feed manufacturer, Landmark Feeds, and the West's largest swine production company, Elite Swine. The move would allow Maple Leaf to control every step in the hog production process, short of actually owning the hogs itself. McCain Foods president Michael McCain told the *Brandon Sun* it had acquired Elite Swine because "it had the best vertical co-ordinating system in North America." Garry Stott of Maple Leaf insisted that the company operates differently from U.S. operations because it will not actually own the hogs that contract producers grow. He said, "Maple Leaf feels the best people for raising hogs are farmers. We want independent producers owning their own farms."

Despite the consoling words, the merger of the major hog players shook the industry. "Nobody has done anything like this that I know of before in Canada," Larry Martin, chief executive officer of the George Morris Centre, the Guelph-based agricultural think-tank, told the *Winnipeg Free Press*. He predicted the takeover would lead other major players in the pork supply chain to make alliances with one another. The corporate players involved in the deal insisted Elite Swine's customers will still have the option of selling their hogs to other processors. However, it was generally assumed that Maple Leaf and Elite would soon come up with some sort of price mechanism that would guarantee producers a more stable price for their hogs in exchange for selling to Elite.

The Schneider operation too has considerable clout in the marketplace. Its parent company, Smithfield Foods, is the largest vertically integrated producer and marketer of fresh pork and processed meats in the U.S. It has an extensive network of contract farms, owning six out of ten pigs going through its slaughterhouses. And it has a voracious corporate appetite: in 1998 and 1999, Smithfield gobbled up ten major pork corporations like J.M. Schneider around the world. Sadly, the company has a spotty record on the environmental front. It was fined $12.6 million in 1997 for dumping slaughterhouse waste into Virginia's Pagan River. The plant manager at the time spent eighteen months in federal prison for destroying records.

Corporate concentration and vertical integration were clearly the watchwords of Manitoba's new, improved hog industry. By the end of the first year of the new millennium the province was the setting for a competitive struggle between two multinational titans—both supported by millions from the provincial treasury.

There was no indication of what was to come.


At the end of 2000 Manitoba's expanded hog industry was still a work in progress. Barns were going up across the province, often igniting local brushfires as they went. They were given consumer-friendly names like

Pro-Gilt Farms or Play Green Farms. The beautiful valleys south of Brandon, within easy trucking distance of the Maple Leaf plant, were being transformed into a hog alley. Stories about protests had become so commonplace that they had slipped off the front page. The NDP government was still claiming indecision; the Livestock Stewardship 2000 initiative would not be reporting until 2001.

Maple Leaf had not yet come anywhere close to employing two shifts of workers at its massive metal-clad plant on the outskirts of Brandon. In fact, it took nine months after killing its first hog for the plant to reach its target line speeds. It operated four days a week for most of the spring and summer of 2000. Employees were paid much less than had been expected: line workers started at $8.25 an hour, which was less than pork cutters were paid at the J.M. Schneider plant in Winnipeg. Nor did the operation produce the kind of stable workforce Brandon might have hoped for. The routine environment, repetitive work and high line speeds prompted high staff turnover. In November, in an effort to stem the tide of workers leaving the plant, Maple Leaf announced it would reopen the collective agreement and offer a wage bonus to workers who stayed with the firm.

The hopeful anticipation Brandon had felt before Maple Leaf came to town had shifted to mild disapproval. The *Brandon Sun* ran a story about how crime in Brandon was up by 14 percent in 1999 after dropping steadily from 1996 to 1998. Although he was reluctant to single out Maple Leaf, a sergeant noted that it did seem as if police had been involved frequently with slaughterhouse employees. The victims of the city's only murder and traffic fatality were both Maple Leaf employees.

In Winnipeg there was little news from the Schneider plant. Schneider workers were on a four-day workweek too. There was no word on the expansion, either from the company or from government officials. From the processing industry's point of view, hog prices were just too high. The super-slaughterhouses need a large, steady and cheap supply of pigs to be profitable.

Both the Manitoba government and the industry claimed they had no statistics or impressions as to how the industry had changed since Manitoba

Pork's monopoly was stripped four years earlier. Even Manitoba's agriculture department could only guess what had happened to family farms and corporate farms. Manitoba Agriculture market analyst Janet Honey said the proportion of the industry controlled by Hutterite Brethren colonies seemed to have fallen; independent farms now controlled about 20 percent of production; and Elite and Puratone accounted for 40 to 50 percent of the hog business. One thing, though, could not be denied. While production continues to increase, the number of farms shrinks. Between 1990 and 2000 the number of hog farms in Manitoba declined by more than 50 percent—from 3,150 to 1,450. At the same time the number of pigs per farm tripled, to nearly 1,300 head.

Karl Kynoch has adjusted to the new world order. He serves as a delegate to Manitoba Pork, trying to work within the system. Kynoch has accepted the loss of the monopoly and the loss of his influence in an increasingly industrial sector. There is little resentment when he says, "We were never told why we got rid of single-desk selling. The government had an agenda. It was to do with getting investment into the province."

Although he still has his hogs in outdoor bio-techs, Kynoch has adopted a thoroughly modern approach to marketing, selling on the futures exchange through a Data Transmission Network. Because his eye is on the global situation, he bought his entire supply of feed corn for fifteen months. "You cannot sit on a tractor all day long anymore. You have to do your own marketing." Surprising words from a man who once said all he wanted to do was grow hogs. But despite his efforts and a farm that, with 4,000 hogs, is hardly tiny, he acknowledges that it is getting harder and harder to stay independent. There is increasing pressure on producers like him to sign a contract with a packing house. He says the processing industry likes contracts because it guarantees a steady supply of pigs, something that is crucial if you run a slaughterhouse that can kill 90,000 hogs a week.

He and his wife are handling the farm all alone now. Their sons have moved on to different careers, so it is not a case of building up the farm to pass on to the next generation. Karl says they are working far too hard, but profit margins are too small to employ someone. Soon they hope to downsize, to sell all of their two hundred sows and keep only the feeder pigs.

Stan Yaskiw bailed out of the hog business before industrial agriculture made its final assault. "Our parents had helped build up the industry. And it seemed we had very little say in the change in the industry. It was pushed down our throat by the government." Today, Yaskiw is living the life of a grain farmer. About 2,500 acres of bargain-basement-priced wheat, barley, peas, oats and lentils give him a good sense of the ups and downs of that business. The old hog houses are empty now, worth nothing and not easily adapted for anything else.

Yaskiw is a delegate of Agricore. With a sense of foreboding he says it looks as if grain is going down the same integrated, industrial route that hog production took. "We will be on the same treadmill very quickly. It can't go on too long before you say you can't do it any longer."

In January 2001 came news that would shake the foundations of Sam Yaskiw's and Karl Kynoch's world still further—and catch the government and industry observers by surprise. Maple Leaf announced it was buying J.M. Schneider's two Winnipeg plants—closing one and nixing plans for the massive $125-million expansion of the other. Schneider company representatives simply said they wanted to refocus their efforts elsewhere. Corporate consolidation was ending dreams for a super-slaughterhouse in Winnipeg, and with it, probably dreams for a massive hog industry that would redefine Manitoba. The province's exploding pig business had just come back down to earth.

The Conservative opposition blamed the NDP government for chasing Schneider from the province. The Tories said hog barns were not going up quickly enough to support two world-class processing plants. And the slowdown in expansion was happening because investors were waiting for the government's Livestock Stewardship Initiative to report.

Coincidentally, the stewardship panel handed its report to government ministers just hours after the Maple Leaf announcement. As expected, it walked a careful line between the desire for economic development and concerns about the environment. However, it did recommend the government should improve its research and study of the hog business, mapping the locations of the province's barns, studying water quality around hog operations and hiring more staff for enforcement. It urged that future barns should get approval not just from the local municipality but from the provincial government—a move designed to take environmental decisions out of the hands of municipal councillors. And as a tribute to family farms the panel recommended slacker rules for smaller producers and tougher regulations and more stringent enforcement for large, intensive barns.

The NDP administration did not immediately respond to the report. However, it was already clear that whatever it chose to do, the government would have less impact on the industry than the corporations that dominated it. The harsh reality of the global, industrial system the previous government had promoted was that giant companies might come and go, build plants and close them, all according to business strategies based on international costs, prices and demand. The Manitoba and City of Winnipeg governments' offer of $9 million—so hard-won—was ultimately meaningless. Consolidation had come to Manitoba's hog industry regardless of what the government might say.

And hog farmers were suddenly left with one less market option for their product. Competition had virtually disappeared. Their frustration echoed on the airwaves when a call-in radio show invited comment. "In just four years we've gone from single-desk selling to single-desk buying," said one farmer, describing the change that had buffeted the industry. The "adapt or die" philosophy had already forced many thousands of hog farmers out of the business. In the next stage of Manitoba's hog industry it seemed government and business too had to adjust to the new corporate, industrial reality.

*Twelve*

# *Back to the Future*

*Winter 2000*

*The first snow arrives like a coyote stealing into a chicken coop under the shadow of night. Before lights out it was raining a cold, dreary November rain. In the morning, when I pull the curtains aside, the landscape is painted in white. Winter has come, silently, swiftly. As usual, no one is quite ready.*

*By latching onto the coattails of the cold rain, the snow has turned the roads of southern Manitoba into long, snaking hockey rinks. Ice knocked out the hydro service, felled branches off the shelter-belt trees. School is out for two days, much to the delight of the Wieler boys. But Lorna uses the opportunity to put them to work. The patio in front of the Wielers' house is an unappetizing layer cake of ice and snow — about eight centimetres of ice frosted by thirteen centimetres of snow. "The boys and I tried to get the ice off the patio and steps. It was unbelievable. It took forever," Lorna says with frustration. They chip away enough to* secure some footing, but the rest of the yard is a treacherous skating rink blanketed under a cloak of snow.

The cattle, annoyed at the sudden loss of their green pasture, sullenly shuffle about their enclosure, their heavy weight turning ice and snow into a soup of mud. The impressions where their feet sink into the ground freeze every night into a pockmarked moonscape perilous for both bovines and humans. "It's just horrible doing chores. I just wish it would get colder to freeze things up and clean it up. Maybe minus ten," says Lorna.

Lorna's wish is granted. It does get colder. By the first week in December southern Manitoba has tripped into a cold snap that contradicts all the talk about global warming. The night of December 6 the thermostat falls to minus 27 degrees. With the wind chill it feels like minus 45; exposed skin will freeze in a minute. And still the snow falls. Enough snow has fallen to top every grain bin on the Wieler farm with a perfect mushroom cap of white.

The weather makes me contemplate hibernation, but in the country, life continues as usual, with just a little more challenge. At the end of November, Gary was still, unbelievably, working the fields. He was combining sunflowers on a for-hire basis for another farmer; working until 3:30 a.m. under a moonless sky slicing the big-headed plants as they stood covered to their shoulders in the white snow. It is apparently not unusual to let sunflowers freeze on the stalk and combine them in the snow.

There are demands at home too. Once the Kane elevator has space, Gary wants to be able to ship the wheat that is now clogging his bins. But first he has to fix the grain truck. It is out of commission just like almost every other piece of equipment on the farm. The combine needs work, the old half-ton is in the shop, and the tractor needs a new radiator. Gary says he is tempted to put off that last expense until next season.

The cold does not let up. In mid-December, as I drive out for my last visit of the year, ice crystals hang in the air, painting sky and land with a monotone wash of grey. Inside the warmth of the Wieler home the neatly *ordered kitchen has been transformed into a would-be commercial bakery. The counters, the table and even the floor are covered with baking pans filled with chocolate ripple butterscotch bars and cookie sheets of shortbread trimmed with maraschino cherries. Lorna has decided to do Christmas baking for all those families who want the taste of home baking but do not have the time to do it themselves. "It costs 49 cents to make a dozen sugar cookies. And I sell them for $1.50 a dozen," she explains. She has accounted for the cost of her labour, but perhaps not for the size of the market she has tapped into. Lorna is usually calm and cheerful, but now even she is rattled. She stops answering the phone; but then the orders come by e-mail. When the boys arrive home from school, they are lucky to get a paying customer's leftovers. Gary is commissioned as the delivery boy for this fledgling enterprise, trucking bags of cookies to doors across a 50-kilometre radius.*

*What had been Lorna's spring cleaning service has morphed into a pre-Christmas service as people try to get their homes looking their best for the holidays. Cleaning, baking—those were once the routine tasks of every household. Now country folks count themselves lucky if they can find someone like Lorna Wieler to do the work for them. Lorna, in turn, counts herself lucky because she can earn the extra money the family desperately needs and still be at home when the school bus deposits the boys at the top of the driveway.*

*The money is critical, because it has not been a good year on the farm. The room where the bills are collected is a cold, unadorned space, out of keeping with the rest of the house, which has been brightened by Lorna's craftwork. It is almost as if the office was designed to be the repository of bad news. It takes no encouragement to persuade Gary to bring the files out to the kitchen table, where the smell and clatter of Lorna's baking offers the promise of good things to come. "I know exactly how things stand," he says as he spreads the invoices and receipts on the table. "It is just too depressing to deal with sometimes."*

*The 2000 season was the worst ever for the Wielers—worse even than the previous year, when half of their crops were flooded out. This year's* *yields were average or above average, but prices are still abysmally low and input costs shockingly high. Gary's field efforts at "diversification" have not paid off. With the rain-induced weed pressure, neither the peas nor the canola brought home more than a few thousand dollars. Even though disease and weather downgraded the Wielers' wheat to #2 grade, it was the four hundred acres of wheat that have been most profitable for the Wielers. They expect they will have a take-home price of $4.40 a bushel after freight and handling. The variable input costs—seed, fertilizer and herbicide spraying—will cost about $105 an acre; their average fixed costs—hydro, telephone, depreciation, land rent or mortgage—add up to another $55 an acre. So it costs $160 to grow an acre of wheat; with yields of about 44 bushels an acre, they earn about $33 an acre. It adds up to a grand total of $13,200—and that does not take into account one hour of Gary, Lorna or the boys' labour.*

*"What is keeping us going is the cattle," says Gary. In the typical teeter-totter of agriculture, when grain prices are low, cattle prices tend to be high. And this year the high price of beef comes in at about $1.30 a pound, or about $800 for each of the calves sold. After the cost of upkeep Gary figures they earned a net income of about $8,800. Of course most of that went right back into buying more heifers. Add to the cattle earnings Gary's custom combining, for-hire haying and other field work, and Lorna's cleaning and baking skills, and you have a living wage. It is not a wage that many Canadians would be satisfied with; in fact, it puts the Wielers under what is generally viewed as the poverty line.*

*But the Wielers do not feel poor. They have a warm, modern house, their freezer is filled with their own beef and garden-grown vegetables, and they are dressed in the fashionable casual clothes that would take them to the trend-conscious city. The second-hand Ski-Doo that Philip bought himself is poised for takeoff from a snowbank near the front door. None of this indicates deprivation. But the Wielers think twice about every expenditure they make. It also helps that they have few debts; much of the equipment is still, technically, owned by Gary's father. However, they fear one day the aging equipment will defy all of*

Gary's ministrations with duct tape and pliers. "You can work in the red for a couple of years. But that is it," concludes Gary.

The future looms unpromisingly, yet the Wielers resist the temptation to complain. It is almost impossible to get them to grumble. How do they feel about rising input costs? A shrug of the shoulders. Do they think the government should do more? "Those subsidy cheques were sure nice." Are they upset that they lost the freight rate benefit? "When did that happen again?" But they do hesitantly note, with just a touch of nostalgia, that things have somehow got worse over the years. "In my father's day, every farm was small. With livestock and grain. There was none of this specialization. And there were lots of farms," says Gary.

The Wielers have managed to survive in the dismal farm economy with a single-minded focus on maintaining a way of life that offers independence, clean air and the values they hold dear. That translates into hard work and an entrepreneurial spirit. All their work is warranted, they say, if they can carry on. At supper—french fries, corn and beef hash, washed down by milk—they all offer an animated defence of country living. "I would never go back to the city," says Lorna, who is after all a recent country convert. "I like everything about farm life . . . except for those crows. They are so obnoxious." Philip gallops to the defence of the much-maligned crows. "They sound nice," he offers in his father's unembellished style. He wrote an essay for 4-H last summer celebrating the beauty of the Prairies, squawking crows and all. And of the three boys, he is most interested in taking over the farm one day.

Whether that will ever be possible is too much for Gary and Lorna to consider at this time. They admit they have not been able to put away a single dollar for their sons' future education or their own retirement. These days life on the Wieler farm is all about finding enough cash to pay the next bill. Regardless, Gary notes, Philip would probably have to have a full-time job to keep the farm going.

The older boys thank their mother for dinner, excuse themselves to do their homework and promise to come back afterwards to do the dishes. Daphne the dog lies in the corner of the room, her bushy tail sweeping *the air with delight at every movement, but never venturing from her bed to mooch or otherwise ingratiate herself. In this household, rules, courtesy and hard work reign supreme. Leavened by positive thinking, the Wielers have—so far—found a way to survive in a world of agriculture plagued by devastating global competition, rising costs and an unsupportive government.*

*They say their Mennonite faith has given them the ability to be content with what they have. "You sometimes have breakdowns and it's a bad day," says Gary in explanation. "I just say to myself, tomorrow will be better." The practice of positive thinking is something they have honed with training. Lorna says, "You always keep hoping." "I've done that for years," Gary agrees. When the Wielers sit down in a few weeks around the little artificial tree that has replaced a big natural one ("It's a cost we could avoid"), they will be grateful for what they have. "Next year will be different," says a hopeful Gary Wieler. "We're going to make money."*

*It is after 7 p.m. when I leave the Wielers'. White, glistening snow is falling against the backdrop of an inky black sky. Gary is dressed in full winter gear against the bitter cold. He has to check on the cattle. It is a task he does without any grumbling. For a moment I envy him his chores that take him into the silent, black night, illuminated by the Christmas-card beauty of the flashing snow. As he disappears into the cow paddock, the crunch of his boots on the fresh snow fades into the still night.*

*In my car, on the way back to my city life, the snow changes character. The increasing wind turns it into blinding streaks of white in the headlights, eliminating all traces of the road. As trucks approach and pass me, they kick up a blinding cloud of snow. How, I wonder, can anyone find his way in this beautiful yet sometimes brutal countryside? As I wrestle to keep the car on the road, I wonder how long the hard-working, uncomplaining Wielers will be able to navigate their way in this corner of the world that has been forgotten by much of Canada.*

•   •   •

&. John Ikerd has the ideal credentials to be a disciple of today's modern industrial agriculture: a doctoral degree in agricultural economics from the University of Missouri. He was once what he calls an "ordained economist." But Ikerd has turned his back on his old religion of industrial agriculture. Instead, he has become a naysayer, someone who argues that industrialization has ruined farming. "Don't believe the economists. Yes, I was one of them. Economists don't deal with the environment and social issues. Economics is all about how to use up the resources."

Small, wiry, a knot of nervous energy, Ikerd now travels the continent speaking and writing on the need for a new kind of agriculture. "The failure of farming is not a matter of bad management, it's not a matter of a reluctance to change. It's a consequence of the kind of agriculture that we've been developing," he told the 250 people at a conference in Brandon, Manitoba, in October.

Ikerd has spent his life in agriculture. He grew up on a small dairy farm in the backwoods of Missouri. Going to school in Columbia, Missouri, and pursuing his degrees in agricultural economics seemed the next logical step. His early years in academia brought him to work as a university livestock marketing and extension specialist. He served at North Carolina State University at a time when the state was just beginning to develop its large-scale factory hog production. Ikerd was a promoter of the new industrial livestock systems; he saw them as an ideal option for tobacco farmers who were squeezed by declining markets. "I was very much a part of the conventional mainstream of the industrial model of agriculture," says Ikerd.

In the 1980s, as a financial crisis swept across the American farm belt, Ikerd found himself face to face with farmers grappling with monetary ruin. He saw that they were not inefficient or lazy; often they were the very opposite—competent and capable. "I saw that the people who had the biggest problems at the time had done all the things that we economists were telling them to do." Those who were in real trouble in the 1980s were those who had borrowed money to buy land and equipment in an effort to rise to the challenges of increased globalization. They were the specialists, the people who embraced new technology and mechanization. Ironically, Ikerd saw that those who survived the crisis of the 1980s were those who had flouted the trend to grow and specialize.

Those years proved to be a revelation for Ikerd. He realized that much of what he had accepted as gospel—the push for an industrial model— was actually part of the problem. Trying to develop an agricultural system that mimicked industry had put the focus on economic efficiency at the expense of almost everything else. In retrospect Ikerd now realizes he and other economists promoted a structure that called for fewer farmers to run a more efficient system, the ultimate goal of which was to keep down the price of food.

His brush with personal misfortune led him to rethink his approach. He became convinced that economists had to do more than simply assess costs; they had to assess values. So he quit a comfortable university job in the early 1990s to come home to Missouri to join what was emerging as a new sustainable agriculture movement. He was employed at the University of Missouri under a co-operative agreement with the Department of Agriculture to provide leadership for research programs related to sustainable agriculture. He had found his calling, but his views left him ostracized by his colleagues.

When he retired from the university in early 2000, he finally had the time to devote himself to becoming an outspoken and credible critic of industrial agriculture. These days, he says, crisis has become a chronic symptom of an agriculture gone wrong. The promise of profit from high yields has disappeared. Many farmers believe the only way to survive in the current climate is for someone else to make room. "Someone has to fail so someone else can succeed," he says.

To really thrive in today's agriculture, Ikerd says, farmers have to consider new ways of farming that involve more than just the short-term pursuit of money. Farmers should strive for what Ikerd calls "a higher quality of life" built on the ideal of co-operation, not competition, that adds value to the rural community and the environment. The successful farmers of tomorrow will not be those who want to get bigger to extract more from the land, but those who hope to earn more with less land, less machinery, less capital and less investment.

The current industrial model of agriculture, designed for a global export market and dominated by transnational corporations, does not serve most Canadians well. Under that system, farmers like the Wielers are becoming an endangered species, hovering on the brink of extinction. Consumers may have cheap food, but it is mass-produced and homogenized, and its price bears little connection to the real cost of farm produce. And would-be Canadian processors cannot compete with the multinationals that control global agribusiness.

Our market-driven economy is so widespread and deeply entrenched that it is hard to conceive of things being otherwise. We assume that the value of the GDP is the ultimate measure of worth. The language of "profit," "efficiency" and "competition" has leached through the media and distorted our vocabulary to the point where manure becomes bio-solids, pig barns become livestock units and farming becomes agribusiness.

A public accounting of the real costs of the current industrial model of agriculture is needed before anyone can conclude that big truly is better. An initial comparison suggests that sustainable, small-scale family farms are on a much more favourable footing. For example, we know there are growing agronomic challenges facing industrial agriculture. Nature is fighting back. Diseases such as fusarium head blight are becoming endemic, threatening Canada's reputation as a supplier of quality malting and milling grains.

Weeds are increasingly resistant to commonly used herbicides. To date, 235 species of weed in forty-five countries have developed resistance to modern agriculture's chemical arsenal. Thirty-two of them are in Canada, including wild mustard, hemp nettle, chickweed, wild oats, cleavers and green foxtail. What is doubly concerning is that weed species are beginning to show signs of multiple resistance, to a number of different herbicides. In 1997 Manitoba reported that 27 percent of fields infected with wild mustard were showing signs of multiple resistance. And genetic engineering is only compounding the problem. Manipulating the very DNA of crops to make them herbicide-resistant is leading to new weed varieties that are resistant to broad-spectrum herbicides like Roundup. Herbicides are no longer the magic bullet they once were.

Industrial agriculture is slipping into its old age, stumbling through its fading years. It can no longer claim the productivity yields that defined its youth in the decades after World War II. Grain production rose 40 percent per person between 1950 and 1984. But from then until 1995 it fell about 15 percent. In the last twenty-five years neither the output nor the number of people fed by an acre of land have risen as quickly as they did before. The soil is no longer responding as it once did to the application of chemical fertilizers. Industrial agriculture simply does not work on a whole range of fronts.

In 1987 the UN Commission on Environment and Development produced what is commonly called the Brundtland Report, which first popularized the idea of "sustainable development." It called for "development which meets the needs of the present without compromising the ability of future generations to meet their own needs." The concept was warmly received and quickly entered the mainstream by embracing the idea of growth as well as acknowledging the need to deal with global poverty. "Sustainable development" was on everyone's lips—but no one knew exactly what the phrase meant. There were estimated to be about eighty different interpretations of sustainable development, according to different values, priorities and goals.

The same confusion exists today when it comes to agriculture. Everyone thinks sustainable agriculture is a laudable goal, but exactly what it means is a subject of dispute. For some it implies a system that continues for a long time; for others it means not damaging natural resources. However, our current industrial system cannot honestly be described as sustainable under any definition. How can it be sustainable if farmers of today are going broke and there is no opportunity for a future generation? How can it be sustainable if it relies on non-renewable resources, plunders the environment, erodes the soil and pollutes our waterways? How can it be sustainable if it ignores social responsibility in favour of economic indicators? Agriculture is efficient today only according to corporate bookkeeping. When you calculate energy depletion, land degradation, water pollution, loss of genetic resources and destruction of rural communities, you have to wonder how anyone can conclude the system works.

For my purposes, sustainable agriculture is one that is environmentally, socially and financially sustainable. That means farmers must be able to afford to live on the land; they must use practices that do not damage the environment, pollute waterways or erode the soil; and they must have a sense of social responsibility, to their community and the people they produce food for.

To be successful on these terms, the farming of the future must look to the past, not with nostalgia but by borrowing the best in an effort to build a less damaging, more sustainable system of agriculture. The hoop houses that Karl Kynoch uses for his feeder pigs may have been a low-cost option for him, but they are now the rave in Iowa, the number-one pork processing state in the U.S. Organic production harnesses nature rather than fights it. By dispensing with the costly chemical requirements of modern agriculture, it offers an alternative for cash-strapped farmers while benefiting the environment. Saskatchewan is fast becoming a world leader in large-scale organic cereal and grain production. In 2001 there are expected to be about 700,000 acres of organic crops in the province, compared with just 24,000 in 1996. It seems more and more farmers are beginning to recognize that the past offers old-fashioned and low-cost options for the future.

Rene Van Acker's roots are on a tobacco farm in southern Ontario. He remembers that his father always resisted the temptation to grow too much. While other tobacco farms got bigger, reduced markets and swelling costs often caused them to fail. Meanwhile, the Van Acker farm survived. The lesson that there may be merit in staying small and sustainable, taught to him by his father, is not lost on the grown-up Rene Van Acker—assistant professor in the plant sciences department of the faculty of agriculture at the University of Manitoba.

Van Acker's official specialty is weed science, but his unofficial focus is the state of agriculture today. He is young and looks even younger than his years. He has the energy of someone just beginning his fights. He does not bother to pull any punches, instead talking non-stop, with a vigour borne of his convictions. His students call him "the clipster" for his skill at creating a memorable quote. His language is peppered with phrases like "land husbandry," "old-time farming is precision farming" and "industrial agriculture is simple agriculture." Indeed, Van Acker has theories on all facets of modern agriculture, but he sees himself first and foremost as a champion of farmers.

Unlike some of his counterparts in the agricultural economics department, he is not prepared to dismiss producers as mere statistics in a sector undergoing structural change. "We can't show our faces to farmers if we don't take a broader perspective," he says. Like John Ikerd, he feels our system of industrial agriculture has let farmers down. "The pressure to get bigger and bigger, to maximize yields, to go for more acreage, is just pushing farmers out on the risk balance. That is how they fall hard," he says.

When farmers fall, says the talkative Van Acker, everyone loses. The loss of thousands of producers across the Canadian Prairies cannot be written off as an unimportant side effect of inevitable change. By limiting the size of their holdings to something manageable, farmers can really understand their land and the agronomic conditions that affect it. They can do something worthwhile for society, something a large corporation cannot do. They produce good, nutritious food, build an economy in rural Canada and act as careful stewards of the environment.

Van Acker is offended that the current system is trying to strip the creativity out of farming by making farmers into assembly-line workers. He says the corporate incursion into agriculture through producer contracts is just a way to make farmers slaves on their own land. "Vertical integration works if you dumb down the farmer and see him as a factory worker." He says the environment will suffer if farming becomes a brainless activity, requiring less thought, less wisdom, less ingenuity. If farmers and farming are to survive, we must "replace intensive agriculture with intimate agriculture."

Van Acker laments the government's chosen role in agriculture. Its focus on international subsidies is nothing but a "smokescreen, built on the myth that yield equals profit." With a regretful shake of his head Van Acker says it almost seems as if the government is trying to make Canadian food, produced by Canadian farmers, the cheapest in the world. "We've been hoodwinked into thinking the global corporate way," says Van Acker. But although those multinational corporations, usually American, may be good for the U.S., they offer little benefit to Canada. Instead, he says, Canada would be much better off if we did more processing here rather than shipping bulk commodities out of the country. He says the federal government should recognize that its transfer payments would be reduced if there was viable economic development in the West.

He says the government could go a long way to fixing agriculture if it simply put producers first, recognizing the value they offer. It is a perspective that many in the department of plant sciences share. They are doing their part by developing research projects that will give producers agronomic, low-cost information to help them survive the current crisis.

Van Acker's colleague Martin Entz has run a cropping systems study for more than eight years, time for the plots to go through two four-year rotation cycles. Rather than use expensive fertilizer, herbicide and pesticide inputs, Entz and the researchers are exploring more natural, perhaps more old-fashioned techniques, such as assessing what impact soil-building crops like alfalfa and sweet clover have when they are part of a four-year rotation.

It is a warm, sunny August day when Van Acker drives me out to the department's test plots, down the highway at Glenlea, in a university-issue truck, clean like it never would be on the farm. Van Acker is in a buttoned-down shirt, neat jeans and runners with laces that continually come undone. He has a straw hat ready. We are definitely visitors to the gritty world of agriculture. There have been other urban visitors here—government officials like Manitoba agriculture minister Rosann Wowchuk. But mostly the plots have offered an alternative to the chemical-company tours that are so popular with farmers during the prairie summer.

The harvest began here, in the Red River valley, a few weeks ago. But the ground at the Glenlea Research Station is so soggy, researchers dare not bring out the baby combine and chaff collector the university uses. We abandon the truck on the unbroken rise that serves as the access road and walk in, risking dirt on clean sneakers.

The plots show very visible alternatives to conventional, industrial agriculture. The experiment explores what might happen if a farmer decides to quit using either pesticides or herbicides, or both. And it reviews what impact crop rotations might have on profitability. In one plot, only annual crops, like wheat and flax, are grown. In another, one year of four is planted with sweet clover; in yet another, two years of alfalfa. The sweet clover and alfalfa are good forage crops—useful for livestock but not for the annual commodities market. They both naturally boost the nutrients in the soil.

The mini-fields abut each other like the squares on a checkerboard. The profusion and variety of weeds draw the lines between the squares. The field in the annual crop rotation that has been allowed to run wild without any inputs is a tangle of weeds. Van Acker has to search before he finds a single frond of wheat. It seems that if a farmer insists on repeatedly growing annual crops, he must spend the money on the fertilizers and pesticides of industrial agriculture. In fact, the plots show that if farmers grow two years' worth of alfalfa every four years, they will earn significantly more over the four years than they would if they tried to pull in a crop every year. It is a decidedly low-tech solution, but effective nevertheless.

The organic system—no fertilizers and no pesticides—had the lowest cost of production and the highest net returns over the term of the eight-year study. To their surprise, in analyzing the 1999 flax crop, researchers found planting organic flax after a year of alfalfa produced exactly the same yields as spending money on full inputs in a conventional system. Van Acker says the research simply shows in a very tangible way that there are options, perhaps organic farming, to the high-cost input model farmers have accepted as conventional wisdom.

Van Acker wants to deliver that message of hope to other farmers. In his campaign to convince producers there are options, he is trying to organize a conference in late fall that will attract not academics and government officials, but real farmers. Reflecting his confidence in the future, it is optimistically called Recapturing Wealth on the Canadian Prairies.

Despite the evidence growing at the Glenlea Research Station, many farmers still believe the secret to success in agriculture is increasing yields. As far as they are concerned, the problem is low commodity prices. They are disillusioned with the global free trade market that does not offer them a living wage. In the last year or so several farm groups and people involved with agriculture have floated a variety of ideas designed to limit grain supplies and, they hope, force up prices.

The most popular is the set-aside concept, where government would pay producers *not* to grow grain. The National Farmers Union has proposed that major grain-producing countries set aside 3 percent of their land each year, shrinking the world supply until grain prices double. Under the plan Ottawa would pay farmers $40 an acre to leave fields fallow. Two Saskatchewan economists, Gary Storey and Ken Rosaasen, pitched a similar idea that would pay farmers to convert land from annual crops to forage and pasture. They say a 5 percent cut in wheat production could boost prices 4 percent above 1998 levels. At $50 per hectare, the initiative would cost about $60 million. Manitoba's Keystone Agricultural Producers proposed yet another version, but linked it more closely to environmental objectives. The farm organization said producers should be paid to convert arable land to land that could be used for conservation and environmental health. This plan would cost $500,000 to $600,000 a year, and the money would come from private organizations as well.

The set-aside idea is not new. It was used once before in Canada, in 1970. LIFT (Lower Inventories for Tomorrow) paid farmers $6 an acre to convert from wheat production to summer fallow or perennial forage. That cut the 1970 crop by 45 percent. Similar set-aside plans are now used in the U.S. and Europe to ensure the continued health of farms.

The problem is that these set-aside programs usually call for government aid. And that, in Canada at least, is hard to come by. Ken Goudy, a former Melfort, Saskatchewan, resident, has been working on a proposal that would sidestep government. In fact, Goudy says farmers have to stop lobbying government for help and start taking control of their own destiny. His set-aside program, he says, builds on the independence farmers have always had.

Goudy, fifty-five, is not a farmer himself. Instead, he has been on the periphery of agriculture for thirty years, for a time working for a chemical company, then spearheading Focus on Inputs, a group that was determined to force down the price of Roundup by raising money to produce glyphosate themselves. Goudy's current plan, Focus on Sabbatical, is now his all-consuming passion. He is travelling across the North American prairies in his white minivan trying to convince farmers to contribute $250 each to join the set-aside initiative. He is appealing to 150,000 producers, trying to persuade them to cut production of wheat, oilseeds and feed grain by 40 percent. Instead of earning income selling grain, Goudy says farmers participating in the sabbatical would make their money in the commodities market. It would be a set-aside plan with teeth that would directly confront the pricing systems.

Goudy believes, if he can unite farmers from both sides of the border, there will be enough money in the fund in 2002 to buy futures contracts and then cut production by eight million bushels in 2003, driving up prices. His challenge is to unite farmers in what is a risky plan. In spring he and his wife, Mary Lou, moved to Iowa so Goudy would be closer to potential converts in the U.S. By late 2000 he had a thousand Canadian and seventy American farmers signed up.

The wishful thinking is that either a farmer-directed or a government-supported set-aside program would force up commodity prices, in turn putting more cash in farmers' pockets. However, the grim reality is that even healthy prices will not be enough to offset the side effects of the industrialization of agriculture. Farmers will still be confronted by the rising cost of inputs. The pressure to get bigger, often at the expense of other farmers or the environment, will continue. If the aspects of farming that address environmental and social sustainability are considered to have any value, more than just prices must change.

There are farmers who are, even now, quietly, without fanfare, doing things differently. And there are research supports like the Land Institute in Kansas, which has spent years trying to develop a model for sustainable agriculture in which field crops are tailored to the natural ecosystem rather than unnatural crops being imposed on unsuitable land.

Many farmers are beginning to recognize that they cannot wait for the government to come up with solutions to their problems—in other words, more money. For several decades early in the twentieth century, much of Canadian life revolved around farming and farm communities. Moreover, the struggles of farmers figured prominently on the national political agenda. In these struggles to achieve their objectives, the unity of producers was always an essential ingredient. Today, as agriculture goes through a dramatic crisis that is pushing many farmers off the land, producers cannot seem to agree on how to tackle their problems. But at least they know they must work together and search for solutions that elude them individually.

In modern mythology "the family farm" attracts the kind of respect usually reserved for milk and apple pie. Even though urban Canadians often have little to do with rural producers, there is a longing for the farms they read and heard about when they were children. *Charlotte's Web* and Old MacDonald's farm are alive and well in the remembrance of urban Canada. However, there is a huge distance, and not just one of miles, between the urban consumer who shops at the local Loblaws and the rural farmer who toils under a hot sun to produce food for markets around the world. Many Canadians would be shocked to see that today's pigs live in factory-like barns or that pesticides rain on endless acres that stretch as far as the eye can see.

Today's consumers are very concerned about the health of the environment. For now, they view farmers as the best custodians of that environment. Lawrence Solomon, executive director of the Urban Renaissance Institute, says that could change quickly. The experience of Walkerton, Ontario, with its fatal water supply, was the first time many people understood that cattle produce an E. coli bacterium that can kill. If consumers were to turn against farming, agriculture would disintegrate.

Already, consumers are very anxious about chemical use. They are opting for organic food in dramatically increasing numbers. Although it still accounts for only a tiny percentage of production, the organic market is growing by about 20 percent a year. The public also strongly endorses the goal of reducing pesticide usage. A 1995 poll by Environics indicated that 89 percent of Canadians supported the objective of a 50 percent reduction in pesticide use within five years, even if the practice resulted in produce costing more and looking less attractive.

The World Wildlife Fund is leading the push for the 50 percent cut in agricultural chemical use. It urged Finance Minister Paul Martin before his February 2000 budget to provide a minimum of $90 million a year for ten years to assist farmers in reducing pesticide use and adopting more ecologically friendly practices. The WWF's report, *Making Pesticide Reduction a Reality in Canada*, recommended the provinces match the federal contribution, for a total expenditure of $180 million. Needless to say, there was no commitment of any money in the budget.

Although they may not think much about it, Canadians do want a country that is able to feed itself. Canada has never suffered a food shortage, not even in the Dirty Thirties. There may be 800 million people in this world who are malnourished, but Canada is enjoying unprecedented prosperity. A war that might disrupt the flow of goods into the country seems most unlikely. Even so, it is time for Canadians to ask ourselves the basic question: do we want to be totally dependent on imports for our food?

This may not come down to a question of food security, because many people just cannot believe we will ever be short of food. However, there are increasing concerns about food safety. It is impossible to know how much DDT has been sprayed on produce from distant countries. We live in a world where mad cow disease spread throughout Europe in just a few years; where turkey products in the U.S. contaminated with listeria bacteria had to be recalled just weeks before Christmas. When food is produced closer to home, there is some measure of comfort in knowing that Canadian regulations apply.

If farmers continue to leave the land, we may find ourselves in a situation where Canada no longer has the ability to feed itself. We are losing a whole generation of farmers whose skills, ingenuity and creativity may well disappear with them. Future generations will simply not know how to plant a field of wheat or run a dairy herd.

Consumer tastes are changing, too. The baby-boomer bulge in the population is growing older and is increasingly focused on nutrition and food quality. As children grow up and leave home, there is time available like never before during the parenting years. The drive to McDonald's no longer seems as crucial. Consumers are tired of spongy pork and waterlogged chicken. The mere existence of The Food Channel suggests that cooking may become popular again, along with an appetite for local, quality food. That kind of demand could spark whole new local markets for Canadian farmers.

In the future, price will no longer be the key factor for the consuming public. Canadians now benefit from the cheapest food in the industrialized world, but the current model of agribusiness is not serving consumers well. There may be lots of talk about a cheap food policy, but the price of a box of cornflakes has tripled in the past twenty years, and so has the price of a loaf of bread. About 80 percent of today's food bill goes to pay for marketing and packaging; it costs that much to convince consumers to try the latest cereal or pizza-pop.

Canadian consumers are affluent enough that they would not mind paying a little more for their food, particularly if the returns went to farmers. They may not be eager to finance a corporate culture that dominates the food system from Petri dish to plate, but they would welcome the opportunity to support the Canadian dream, a homestead built by great-grandfather's hands and continued by today's offspring.

According to a poll by the Angus Reid Group in September 1999, 72 percent of Canadians agreed farmers were facing severe problems, and 52 percent said government was not doing enough. Only one in four said "farmers are always complaining, but they are not that badly off." In another survey in early 2000, designed to plumb the depths of consumers' concerns about GMOs, researchers were surprised to find that even more respondents identified the sustainability of agriculture as their biggest concern. When asked which issues facing the agri-food industry were most important, 28 percent said the future of farming, compared with 23 percent who said genetically modified organisms.

Canadian society has to decide what value it puts on the family farm. It has to recognize that the family farm it might remember with sentiment does not exist anymore. If Canada is to have a sustainable agriculture—financially secure, ecologically sound and socially responsible—consumers will have to pay for it. And they may have to convince government that family farms, as the foundation for a sustainable agriculture, are worth supporting.

In the last week of October the Royal Oak Inn in Brandon was ringed with half-ton trucks. Several hundred farmers were inside attending the conference that Rene Van Acker, his university colleagues and representatives from a number of farm organizations had been planning for months. Van Acker was intent that farmers not only network and hear some provocative speakers, but actually work to come up with a plan on how to "recapture wealth on the Canadian Prairies."

The conference was carefully structured not to offend any particular farm group. Knowing how polarized farm politics is, Van Acker got the funding for the meeting from groups that would not inflame passions: the university, the Manitoba Rural Adaptation Council, Keystone Agricultural Producers, the *Manitoba Co-operator* newspaper and the Prairie Farm Rehabilitation Administration. The organizing committee accepted a little support from the Canadian Wheat Board and immediately found itself criticized for "ties" to that organization. It seems modern farming is all about politics.

To encourage real work beyond the standard coffee-row griping, participants were assigned tables. Farmers found themselves shuffling for elbow room with government officials and journalists. Everyone was given a fistful of play money to spend later on "ideas" they found worthwhile.

John Ikerd led the speaker roll. With coiled energy and that big American drawl, he bounced on his feet, arms flying—ever the picture of the southern Baptist preacher. He condemned the treadmill that forces farmers to get bigger to offset lower returns or to sign production contracts with big corporations. In the meantime, he said, farmers are beginning to abuse their land and forsake their families and communities in the struggle to survive. He told farmers, no matter how hard it seems, there are alternatives, whether growing organic, diversifying production or finding niche markets that consumers want.

A number of American farmers who have already begun to look back to the future were next up. Tom Franzten from Iowa said he found much of what happens in the modern hog business hard to stomach, so he turned his farm into a mixed organic operation with a special hog component. As he talked with staccato intensity, he flipped through video images of his farm that would satisfy the nostalgia requirement of most consumers—the quaint red barns, the pigs rooting outside, the nut bushes providing shade and shelter for wildlife. Franzten said he is now marketing what he grows through the Internet, making the direct connections with consumers that are denied by the anonymous, industrial agribusiness system. Although he has opted for organic production, he did not say all farmers should follow that path. However, he insisted that one basic philosophy should be the foundation for everything farmers try to do: "It's high time that we work with nature instead of fighting nature."

Karen Armstrong-Cummings works with family farms in Kentucky and sat on the USDA's advisory committee on small farms. She stressed the need to build alliances, even with groups who might not seem supportive. Acting on behalf of tobacco farmers in Kentucky, she began meeting regularly with health activists in an effort to help each understand the other's position. Now, she says, someone from the Cancer Society has been known to speak out on behalf of tobacco farmers who are squeezed by industry.

There were no federal government representatives at the conference, although several, including Dennis Mills, had been on the agenda. The upcoming federal election provided the perfect excuse to avoid the event. Manitoba's agriculture minister Rosann Wowchuk found herself in the unenviable position of being the only politician prepared to face the farmers. She offered the conference an unsatisfying speech that reviewed life and offered basic homilies. "Although these are challenging times for many farmers, there are also exciting opportunities." The exasperation from the audience at the end of the speech was palpable. Ruth Pryzner of Alexander expressed the mood when she stood up to bluntly ask the minister: "Is the strategy just to let us sink or swim?" Wowchuk replied that there are programs to help small farms, but then she acknowledged they apply to all farms, no matter what their size. Someone in the audience shouted that the government could earn more taxes from ten small farmers than one corporate farm. There were whoops and laughter in support.

There was a growing sense at this conference that the solution to agriculture's problems will not come from government. There was the standard complaining over coffee: prices too low, too many bills, government disregard. But throughout the two days of sessions, there seemed to be a developing recognition that energies should not be spent trying to get the government to change its ways. The days when Mike Pearson and John Diefenbaker squared off over the farm vote are gone. Instead, these farmers wanted to wrestle back the anonymity they now have in the grocery store aisles, to put a face on their production. They began talking about wealth not just in money terms but in the sense of people and communities. For example, Larry and Murielle Bugera from St. Pierre-Jolys have been farming for twenty-five years. The conference had them thinking they may have to do things differently. "We're producing lots but can't sell it to pay the bills."

When it came time to spend their play money, the conference participants put it down on "building stronger communities" "developing closer relationships with consumers" and "maintaining control over their farms." Perhaps not surprisingly, not one penny was spent on "more corporate involvement." After a round of horse-trading, they compromised on an overall vision calling for a "farmer-driven renewed agricultural sector which supports communities, works in close relationship with consumers and sustains a healthy environment."

It may have seemed like a giant game of agricultural Monopoly, but it did provide a rudimentary road map for survival. For a change, farmers worked together, in a spirit of co-operation rather than competition. And the conference, surprisingly, altered some attitudes. Don Dewar, the head of Keystone Agricultural Producers, Manitoba's primary umbrella farm organization, concluded the sessions by saying that "we can't follow the industrial model. It doesn't make sense to sell more when we earn less." Rene Van Acker was the last to speak. "We have to recognize that producers have to do something themselves rather than wait for the government. They may not survive until the word comes."

As the farmers filed out, relieved to be free of the confines of the hotel room, Van Acker was pleased they were leaving with some sense of hope. He knew the conference had not fixed "the farm crisis," but he believed it had given farmers some tiny measure of optimism in an economic situation heavy with gloom.

It is not a question of turning back the clock. All industries, all ways of life, go through a cycle of change. The question is more properly defined as: Do Canadians want to lose a way of life that has helped define our country? Do we want to lose our prairie schools, churches and towns? Do we want to hand over control of our food production to a few faceless corporations? The family farm is the backbone of rural Canada. Misguided government policies and unrestrained global competition have created an unfair environment, an environment where we are kicking the farmer while he is lying on the ground.

Those farmers get so little help from us—much less than they did in the past. Western Canadian agriculture, and society, was built on the backs of farmers; it was not built by international grain companies or fertilizer firms or food processors. The future of Canadian agriculture depends on our government and our society recognizing the enduring importance of the family farm.

The challenge also lies with the nation's farmers. It will be up to them to spend real money, energy and creativity to build a sense of hope out of a climate of despair. With our help and support, they may be able to look forward to another season's promise.

# *Bibliography*

❧ In no way can this be construed as a complete reading list, but it does offer some titles for those who want to explore agriculture further.

Anderson, Charles W. *Grain: The Entrepreneurs.* Winnipeg: Watson & Dwyer Publishing, 1991.

Brinkman, George. *Farm Incomes in Canada: A study prepared for the Economic Council of Canada, and the Institute for Research on Public Policy.* Ottawa: Minister of Supply and Services Canada, 1981.

Centre for Rural Studies and Enrichment. *Compare the Share.* Muenster, Saskatchewan: St. Peter's College, 2000.

Cochrane, Jean. *Down on the Farm: Childhood Memories of Farming in Canada.* Calgary: Fifth House, 1996.

Earl, Paul D. *Mac Runciman: A Life in the Grain Trade.* Winnipeg: University of Manitoba Press, 2000.

Ferguson, Ralph. *Compare the Share.* Phases 1 and 2. Ottawa: House of Commons, 1991, 1992.

Fowke, Vernon. *Canadian Agricultural Policy: The Historical Pattern*. Toronto: University of Toronto Press, 1946.

Francis, David. *Family Agriculture: Tradition and Transformation*. London: Earthscan Publications, 1994.

Friesen, Gerald. *The Canadian Prairies*. Toronto and London: University of Toronto Press, 1984.

Gray, Richard, et al., eds. *World Agriculture in a Post-GATT Environment: New Rules, New Strategies*. Saskatoon: University Extension Press, University of Saskatchewan, 1995.

Heffernan, William. *Consolidation in the Food and Agricultural System*. Report to the NFU, Columbia: University of Missouri, 1999.

Ilbery, Brian, ed. *The Geography of Rural Change*. Harlow, Essex: Addison Wesley Longman, 1998.

Jenkins, Phil. *Fields of Vision: A Journey to Canada's Family Farms*. Toronto: McClelland & Stewart, 1992.

Kneen, Brewster. *From Land to Mouth: Understanding the Food System*. 2nd ed. Toronto: NC Press Ltd., 1993.

Lacey, Richard. *Hard to Swallow: A Brief History of Food*. Cambridge: Cambridge University Press, 1994.

Levine, Allan. *The Exchange: 100 Years of Trading Grain in Winnipeg*. Winnipeg: Peguis Publishers, 1987.

MacEwan, Grant. *Between the Red and the Rockies*. Saskatoon: Western Producer Prairie Books, 1979.

———. *Illustrated History of Western Canadian Agriculture*. Saskatoon: Western Producer Prairie Books, 1980.

Mitchell, Don. *The Politics of Food*. Toronto: James Lorimer and Co., 1975.

Morgan, Dan. *Merchants of Grain: The Power and Profits of the Five Giant Companies at the Center of the World's Food Supply*. New York: Viking, 1979.

Morris, William E. *Chosen Instrument II, A History of the Canadian Wheat Board: New Horizons*. Winnipeg: The Prolific Group, 2000.

National Farmers Union. *The Farm Crisis, EU Subsidies, and Agribusiness*

*Market Power.* Paper presented to the Senate Standing Committee on Agriculture and Forestry, Saskatoon, 2000.

OECD. *The Future of Food: Long-term Prospects for the Agro-food Sector.* Paris: OECD, 1998.

Rees, Ronald. *New and Naked Land: Making the Prairies Home.* Saskatoon: Western Producer Prairie Books, 1988.

Roling, N.G. and M.A.E. Wagemakers, eds. *Facilitating Sustainable Agriculture.* Cambridge: Cambridge University Press, 1998.

Solkoff, Joel. *The Politics of Food: The Decline of Agriculture and the Rise of Agribusiness in America.* San Francisco: Sierra Club Books, 1985.

Statistics Canada, Agriculture Division. *Canadian Agriculture at a Glance.* Ottawa: Statistics Canada, 1999.

Williams, Robert C. *Fordson, Farmall, and Poppin' Johnny: A History of the Farm Tractor and Its Impact on America.* Urbana and Chicago: University of Illinois Press, 1987.

Wilson, Barry, *Farming the System; How Politicians and Producers Shape Canadian Agricultural Policy.* Saskatoon: Western Producer Prairie Books, 1990.

Wilson, C.F. *A Century of Canadian Grain: Government Policy to 1951.* Saskatoon: Western Producer Prairie Books, 1978.

Winson, Anthony. *The Intimate Commodity: Food and the Development of the Agro-Industrial Complex in Canada.* Toronto: Garamond Press, 1993.

# Index

A&P, 95

Agenda 2000, 155–157

Agricore, 37, 78, 241

Agricultural Income Disaster Assistance (AIDA), xiv, 4, 6, 48, 172, 177–178, bureaucracy, 197, changes to, 196, eligibility guidelines, 194, payments under, 197, *see emergency aid*

agricultural policy, lack of, xiv, xv, 190–193, jurisdiction 191

Agriculture and Agri-Food Canada (AAFC), 82, 100, 138, 171, 192

agriculture, beginnings, 24, contract production, 98–101, contribution to greenhouse gases, 115–116, decline in farms, 7, 9, 35, diversification, 121–126, energy use 115, genetic uniformity, 111–112, impact on economy, 5, impact on soil, 114, increasing chemical use, 113, mechanization, 46–47, 69–73, passing the farm to the next generation, 52, pressure to get big, 12, 47, public research, 82, role of women, 51, sustainability, 252–253, 262, *see industrialization*

Agrium, 92

Alberta Agenda, 208

Alberta Co-Operative Wheat Producers, 32

Alberta Wheat Pool, 37

Anderson, David, 205

anhydrous ammonia fertilizer, rising costs, 74–75

animal welfare, animal rights, 234, sow crates, 234

Archer Daniels Midland (ADM), 37, 94, 96, 141, 183

Armstrong-Cummings, Karen, 264

Assiniboia, Sask., 43

Axworthy, Lloyd, 77

banks, credit unions, 57, 93

Bennett, R.B., 35

Benson, Ezra, 106
Bestfoods, 95
Biggar, Sask., 206
Birtle, Man., 216
Bloc Quebecois, 78
Board of Grain Supervisors, 30
Borden, Robert, 32
Borotsik, Rick, 197
Bracken, John, 31
Brady, Janet, 230
branch lines, *see railways*
Brandon, Man., 262
Bugera, Larry and Murielle, 265
Buhler Industries, 93
Burlington Northern Sante Fe, *see railways*
Butala, Sharon, 47
Butz, Earl, 106

Cairns Group, 165
Canada Post, 57
Canadian Agra International, 123
Canadian Farm Income Program, 198, *see emergency aid*
Canadian Federation of Agriculture (CFA), 12, 89, 140, 173, 190, 198, 200, 211
Canadian Fertilizer, 92
Canadian National, see *railways*
Canadian Pacific, *see railways*
Canadian Taxpayers Federation, 195, 197
Canadian Transportation Agency, 76, 175
Canadian Wheat Board (CWB), 12, 128, 135–136, 171, 185, 192–193, Canadian protests against, 148, 184, development of, 35, government support for, 186, international trade, 183, trade complaints against 147, 165, *see wheat*
canary seed, 123–124
canola, 124
Cape Fear River, 232
Cargill, 78, 90–91, 94, 183
Carolina Food Processors, 222, 228, 232

Carson, Rachel, 113
Case, 93
cattle feedlots, 118–120
Centre for Agricultural Medicine, 53
Centre for Rural Studies and Enrichment, 51, 68
Chatenay, Jim, 184
chemicals, impact on wildlife, 74, increase in use, 113, effect on wildlife, 113, effect on water, 116, rising costs, 74
chickpeas, 123–124
Chretien, Jean, xii, xv, 190, 196–197, 205, 208
Clark, Alan, 196
Clark, Joe, 206
Clarke, Wendell, 48
Clean Environment Commission, 228, 235
Coalition of Americans for Anti-Trust, 101
Collenette, David, 77
Common Agricultural Policy (CAP), 154–155
ConAgra, 94, 95, 141
Congress, Sask., 108
Conservation Reserve Program, 163
Consolidated Growers and Distributors (CGP), 121–123
consumers' cost of food, 15–16, 88–89, 140, 261
Continental, 91
Cook, Lee, 163
Co-Operative movement, growth of pools, 30–31, collapse, 32, decline 36, new generation co-operatives, 127
coriander, 123
corporate consolidation, 91–97, 101–103
Council of Canadians, 142–143
Crerar, T.A., 31
Crocus Investment Fund, 237
Cromwell, James, 235
crop insurance programs, 172

# Index

Crowsnest Pass rate, development of, 76–77,
    Crow benefit, 13, 76, 121, 172, 174, 191,
    193, reduction, 174–175, Western Grain
    Transportation Act (WGTA), 76

D'Amanour-Boadu, Vincent, 128
Dafoe, Sask., 206
Dairy Farmers of Canada, 182
Daschle, Tom, 102
Dauphin, Man., 121–122
Day, Stockwell, 206
Dewar, Don, 265
Diefenbaker, John, 47, 264
diversification, growth in, 121–126
Doer, Gary, 196
Dominion Bond Rating Service, 93
Dorgon, Byron, 101–102
Douglas, Tommy, 47
Drayton Grain Producers, 129
DuPont, 92
durum wheat, 124
Dynamic Pork, 237

Earl Grey, Sask., 59–60
Earl of Selkirk, 24
east coast fishery, 202–204, development
    of, 202, decline of, 203, support
    programs, 203–204
Eckville, Alta., 176
Elite Swine, 224, 237, 240
elk, 124
emergency aid, xiv, 4, 6, 48, 172, 177–178,
    194, 196, 197, see AIDA, Canadian Farm
    Income Program
Empire-Sobeys, 95
emu, 125–126
Ensis Growth, 237
Entz, Martin, 255
Estey, Willard, 77, 175
Europe, approach to food and farming,
    152–154, decline in farms, 158,
    support for farming, 155–158
European Union, 154–155

4-H, 131-133
Family Farm Tribute, xvi, 213
family farm, 7–9, 18, 109, 262, 266,
    mythology, 259, see agriculture
Farm Assistance Act, 34
Farm Credit Corporation, 93
farm crisis, xvi, 4, 18, 53, Europe, 158
Farm Debt Mediation Service, 71
Farm Health and Safety Council, 53
farm income, xiii, 6, 140, bankruptcy, xii,
    off-farm income, 51
farm protests, xv, xvi, 206
farm stress, 52–54, 59
Farmers and Ranchers Fair Competition
    Act, 102
Farness, Alice, 205
federal election 2000, xvi, 204, 207
Feed Freight Assistance Program, 174
Feedlot Alley, 116–120
Ferguson, Ralph, 89
Fischler, Franz, 157–158, 163, 166
Fleury, Theo, 48
flour mills, 127
Focus on Sabbatical, 258
food security or sovereignty, 261
food, role in society, 88
Forbes, Gail and Murray, 48–50, 178
Fox, Terry, xi
Franzten, Tom, 263
Freedom to Farm, 162
Friesen Bob, 173, 191, 198, 200, 211
Funk, Ellen, 197
Furtan, Hartley, 148, 185, 193

Galbraith, John Kenneth, 106
Gehl, Robert, 80
General Agreement on Tariffs and Trade
    (GATT), 14, 142, 172, Article 11, 181
General Mills, 15
George Morris Centre, 128
George Weston, 90, 94
Gifford, Mike, 166
Gilbert Plains, Man., 120

Gilson, Clay, 38, 61
Ginseng, 124
Glenlea Research Station, 255–257
Glickman, Dan, 174
globalization, 142–147, impact on farm-
    ers, 146–147, Vanclief on, 210, *see trade*
Goodale, Ralph, 174, 205
Goudy, Ken, 258
grain barons, 29
grain elevators, development of, 29,
    decline of, 36, destruction of, 55–56
Grain Growers Grain Company, 29
Great Depression, 4, 32–33, 38, 87, 173,
    204, 260
Green Revolution, 47, 73, 84
Gregoire, Michelle and Roland, 125
Gross Revenue Insurance Program, 174

Harper, Stephen, 208
Harrison, Robert and Judith, 72–73
Harvard, John, 207
Hasselback, Paul, 119
Haverstock, Lynda, 53
Heffernan, William, 96
hemp, 120–123, 127
herbicide resistance, 251
Hill, Peter, 201
Hoechst, 192
Hog Watch, 230
Hogs, *see pork production*
House of Commons Agriculture
    Committee, 193
Howe, Gordie, 48
Hudson's Bay Company, 24
Humane Farming Association, 234
Humphrey, Jay, 221–222

IBP, 94
IF-New Holland, 93
Ikerd, John, 249–251
Imperial Oil, 92
industrialization 5, 9, 18, 36, 67, costs of,
    251, impact on farmers, 254

inputs, 66–68, rising cost of, 68
International Federation of
    Agriculture, 102
International Home Products, 95
International Monetary Fund (IMF), 144
Inwood, Manitoba, 58
Irish potato famine, 111

J.M. Schneider, 229, 238, 241
James Richardson International, 78
John Deere, 92
John Labatt, 94
Jolly, Warren and Paula, 106–109, 111,
    124, 129, 184
Jose Bove, 145–146

Kane, Man., 1, 42, 46, 62
Kellogg's, 15
Kerda, Belina and Rob, 51
Keystone Agricultural Producers, 207,
    257, 263
Kowalchuk, Thomas, 59
Kraft Canada, 95
Kraft, Daryl, 12, 148, 172, 185
Kurtz, Lillian, xv
Kynoch, Karl and Christine, 225,
    240–241, 253

Lacombe, Alta., 176–177
Land Act, 26
Land Institute, 259
Langdon, Bob, 59–60
Larsen, Ken, 176–177, 184
Lavoie, Gilles, 139
Leitch, Bert, 159–160
Lewis, David, 101
Little Bow River, 120
Livestock Stewardship 2000, 230, 239
Loblaws, 18, 95
Louis Dreyfus, 37
Lower Inventories for Tomorrow
    (LIFT), 258

# Index

Macdonald, John A., 26, 39, 135
Malmberg, Ed, 118–120
Malowski, Dave, 120–123
Manitoba Environment, 232
Manitoba Pork, 240, council, 232, loss of
    monopoly, 224–225
Manitoba Rural Adaptation
    Council, 263
Manitoba Securities Commission, 122
Manitoba Wheat Pool, 37
Maple Leaf Foods, 94, 227, 236–237, 239,
    241–242
Martin, Larry, 238
Martin, Paul, xiv, 173, 190
Mayer, Charles, 192
McCain Foods, 237
McCain, Michael, 237
McCarthy Milling, 94
McCurdy, Earle, 203
McDonald's, 95, 145
McLellan, Anne, 205
Metro-Richelieu, 95
Millau, France, 145–146
Mills, Dennis, 212–213, 264
Mitchell, W.O., 47
monoculture, 111-112
Monsanto, 82, 92, 103
Mossbank, Sask., 109
Muir, Ted, 232
Mull, Scotland, 159
multifunctionality, 155–157

N.M. Paterson & Sons, 237
Nabisco Holdings, 95
National Farm Products Marketing
    Act, 181
National Farmers Union (NSU), 74, 83,
    101, 130, 141, 146, 166, 173, 257, 200,
    in U.S., 96
Nazarko, Orla, 81
Nestle, 91
Net Income Stabilization Program
    (NISA), 172, 179, 196, 198

North American Free Trade Agreement
    (NAFTA), 210
North Dakota Wheat Commission,
    147, 165
North West Elevator Association, 29

Oddie, Will, 79
Ogilvie Milling, 94
Oldman River, 117–118
Olson, Bud, 181
Ontario Federation of Agriculture, 102
Ontario Ministry of Agriculture, Food
    and Rural Affairs' Whole Farm
    Relief Program, 195
Ontario Wheat Producers Marketing
    Board, 185
organic farming, 79–80, 256, growth of,
    113, in Sask., 253
Organization for Economic Co-
    Operation and Development
    (OECD), 12, 136, 164, 171
ostrich, 125
Overwaitea, 95

Parsons, Nick, xi–xiii, xv, xvii–xviii, 16
Paton, Bill, 233
Pattison, 95
Pearson, Lester B. (Mike), 264
peas, 123
Pepin, Jean-Luc, 77
Pest Management Review Agency, 113
Pesticide Free Production (PFP), 81
Petro-Canada, 92
Pettigrew, Pierre, 138, 144
Philip Morris, 91, 95
Picture Butte, Alta., 117–120
Pioneer, 92, 200
Pip, Eva, 233
political influence, decline in, 204–212
polls, on CWB, 185, on constitutional
    reform, 208, on chemical use, 113,
    260, on farming, 262, on support for
    farmers, 212

pork production, alternative systems, 225, 234–235, 240, animal welfare concerns, 234–235, collapse in prices, 12, 227, economic benefits, 235, environmental impact, 223–234, 236, factory systems, 221–222, hog manure, 231, industrialization, 218–242, Manitoba, 217–219, 223–242, North Carolina, 219–223, social impacts. 235–236, vertical integration, 237–238

Prairie Farm Rehabilitation Administration, 34, 263

Prairie Harvest Canada, 130

Prairie Pasta Producers, 129

precision farming, 78

Producers Protesting Interference by Government (P-PIG), 226

Progressive Party, 31–32

Pro-West lobby group, 206, 208

Pryzner, Ruth, 264

Puratone, 224, 240

Quaker Oats, 15

railways, 185, 93, branchlines, 36, 56, Burlington Northern Sante Fe, 93, CN 56, 93, 175, CP, 22, 27, 56, 93, 175

Readlyn, Sask., 43–46, 62

Red River Settlement, 24, 25

revenue share, 15, 87, 89–90, 103

Rick Paskal, 118–120

Romanow, Roy, xv, 196

Rosaasen, Ken, 257

Royal Commission on Corporate Consolidation, 97

Rural Advancement Foundation International (RAFI), 98

rural depopulation, vii, 7, 9, 36, 46–47, 52, 61, 67, 108–109, dairy farming in the U.S., 10

rural schools, 58

7-Eleven, 18

Safeway, 95

Saskatchewan Agriculture Development and Diversification boards, 53

Saskatchewan Co-Operative Elevator Company, 29

Saskatchewan Farm Stress Line, 54

Saskatchewan Wheat Pool, 37, 78,200

Saskatchewan, depopulation, 47, foreign ownership of land, 110, health care, 58, as inspiration, 47–48,

Saskferco, 92

Schmeiser, Percy, 99

Senate Standing Committee on Agriculture and Forestry, 91

set-aside proposals, 257–258

Shapiro, Aaron, 30

Shell Canada, 92

Sifton, Clifford, 27

Skinner, Chris and Maurie, 153

Smith, Loretta, 102–103

Smithfield Foods, 94, 230, 238

Sobeys, 95

soil, 114, conservation tillage, 115,

Solomon, Lawrence, l78–180, 260

Special Canadian Grains Program, 174

St. Jean Baptiste, Man., 125

Standing Committee on Industry, 14

Ste. Agathe, Man., 123

sterile seed technologies, 100

Storey, Gary, 257

Stott, Gary, 232, 237

subsidies, 13, European, 155–158, New Zealand elimination of, 179, reduction in Canada, 173–177, Scotland, 159, U.S., 161

Supply management, 10, 180, 192

Sustainable agriculture, 252–253, 262, *see agriculture*

Syngenta, 92, 96

Tait, Fred, 91–92, 101, 166

Tax Freedom Day, 89

# Index

Territorial Grain Growers Association, 29

The Atlantic Groundfish Strategy (TAGS) 204, *see east coast fishery*

The Landmark Group, 237

Third World Network, 143

Tobin, Brian, 205

trade, 11–14, food exports, 137, 192, food imports, 138, impact on other countries, 141, on farmers, 140–141, on CWB, 148, on corporations, 141, policy, xv, 137–140, 171, surplus, 138

Transportation Stabilization Program, 174

Tricon, 95

Trudeau, Pierre, 205

Tuelon, Manitoba, 59

Tyrchniewicz, Ed, 149, 185

Tyson Foods, 182

UN Committee on Environment and Development, 252

Unilever, 95

United Farmers of Alberta, 31

United Farmers of Man., 31

United Grain Growers (UGG), 29, 78, 94, 237

University of Manitoba research, 255

University of Nebraska, 100

Urban Renaissance Institute, 178–179, 260

value-added processing, 126–130

Van Acker, Rene, 79, 192, 253–257, 262–263

Vanclief, Lyle, 5, 166, 173, 175, 190, 193–196, 198–199, 201, 209, on emergency aid, 210, on family farms, 210, on globalization, 210, on supply management, 182

Vanderhaege, Guy, 47

Via Campesina, 146

Virginia Polytechnic Institute, 100

Wagstaff, Neil, 201

Walkerton, Ont., 117, 119

Warburtons, 128

Webb, Don, 223

Wendell, Murphy, 220–221

western alienation, 207–208

Western Canadian Wheat Growers Association, 17, 106, 193, 200

Western Economic Diversification fund, 192

Western Grain Transportation Act (WGTA), 76, 193

Westfair, 95

wheat, early development, 26, export of, 27–28, 135, exports to U.S.S.R., 137, future 136–137, King Wheat, 28, Canada's share in global markets, 136, supply during First World War, 30, *see Canadian Wheat Board*

Whelan, Eugene, 199

White, Brian, 136, 147–148, 183, 185

Wieler, Gary, Lorna, Thomas, Nicholas, and Philip, 1–3, 7, 13, 19–22, 40–42, 63–66, 85–87, 104–106, 131–134, 150–152, 168–171, 187–190, 214–216, 243–248, 263

Wilson, Barry, 186

Winnipeg Grain Exchange, 29, 31

Winnipeg Humane Society, 234–235

Wolf, Steven, 79

Wood, Henry Wise, 31

World Bank, 144

World Health Organization, 114

World Trade Organization (WTO), 11, 14, 97, 101, 138, 141–144, 165, 172, 180, 210, protests against, 143–144, 153, 157, 165

World Wildlife Fund (WWF), 74, 113, 260

Wowchuk, Rosann, 224, 256, 264

Yaskiw, Stan, 216–217, 241